VILHELM GRØNBECH

Religious Currents
in the
Nineteenth Century

by

Vilhelm Grønbech

translated from the Danish by
P. M. Mitchell and W. D. Paden

Southern Illinois University Press
Carbondale and Edwardsville

Feffer & Simons, Inc.
London and Amsterdam

Library of Congress Cataloging in Publication Data

Grønbech, Vilhelm Peter, 1873–1948.
    Religious currents in the nineteenth century.

    (Arcturus Books, AB110)
    Translation of Religiøse strømninger i det
nittende aarhundrede.
    Includes bibliographical references.
    1. Religion. 2. Religion and evolution.
3. Nineteenth century. I. Title.
[BR477.G713 1973]   201   72–11829
ISBN 0–8093–0629–8
ISBN 0–8093–0630–1 (pbk)

ARCT
URUS
BOOKS ®

Contents

Introduction

VILHELM GRØNBECH is one of the intellectual catalysts of the twentieth century. If on the one hand there is no general critical agreement regarding the nature of his work, there is on the other no disputing the impact he has had upon his readers and, while he lived, his hearers. The fascination of his theses, the force of his rhetoric, and the richness of his imagery are inescapable. The scarcity of his works on the second-hand book market, the republication of a number of his books since his death, the appearance of translations of some of his works into German, Swedish, Dutch, and Finnish, and the frequent mention of his name by Danish writers of various philosophical and political persuasions, suggest the lasting and penetrating impression which Grønbech has made upon the minds of those who have come to know him.

To state the bald fact that Vilhelm Grønbech was lecturer in the history of religion, and subsequently professor of that subject, in the University of Copenhagen from 1911 through 1943 is as misleading as it is accurate. Even if we overlook the fact that, in the years before 1911, he was trained as a philologist and was in the course of a few years a schoolteacher, librarian, organist, and lecturer in English literature, the scope of his work and his concept of religion make him an anomaly and are enough to set him apart from other historians of religion.

To simplify and to generalize, one might say that Grønbech is to twentieth-century Denmark what Kierkegaard was to nineteenth-century Denmark. A comparison and contrast with Kierkegaard is illuminating, distasteful as it would have been to Grønbech himself. While there is a unilateral intellectual relationship between the two Danish thinkers, who died nearly a century apart, it is not a friendly one and is not one of spiritual kinship.

Kierkegaard, who followed no calling during his short life, was trained as a theologian. He was an eccentric who lived mostly in isolation and retirement, although before his death he roused a storm of ecclesiastical controversy when he broke openly with the state church. Kierkegaard's production was enormous, but it exemplifies the new philosophical principle which he proclaimed: repetition. In many dif-

1

ferent ways, and in both imaginative and reflective genres, Kierkegaard belabored the same ideas. He was always concerned with the individual, not primarily in regard to his relationship to his fellow man, but in regard to the salvation of his own soul. Because of his highly individual and pessimistic religious thought, he is looked upon as the philosophical forerunner of modern Existentialism. Although nominally Kierkegaard's work was rounded out at his early death, he left a mountain of papers which subsequently have been published.

Grønbech's career in the decade after he completed his formal academic training was highly varied. His doctoral dissertation had treated of Turkish phonetics; his next publication was an anonymous volume of poems. For several years he read much but published nothing. But his many interests and several callings prior to his appointment to a lectureship in English at the university in 1908 all have some bearing on his attempt to embrace culture as an entity and to penetrate to an independent understanding of the socio-psychology of man. While lecturer in English he wrote his most widely known work, a study in four volumes of the philosophical and religious principles upon which life among the older Germanic peoples was based: *Vor Folkeæt i Oldtiden* (1909-12) or *The Culture of the Teutons,* as it is entitled in the English translation which appeared in 1931. After having refused a call to the University of Leipzig evoked by this incisive and original discussion of the Germanic mind as revealed principally in Old Norse literature, Grønbech—who by now had exchanged the lectureship in English for one in the history of religion—was at last appointed to a chair in the latter subject.

After having assumed the position which he was to hold for thirty years, Grønbech's production gradually increased, and at the time of his death in 1948, he had published some thirty-eight volumes and a large number of scholarly and semi-popular articles. In addition to *The Culture of the Teutons,* Grønbech's principal works were an essay on primitive religion (1915); *Religiøse Strømninger i det nittende Aarhundrede* ("Religious Currents in the Nineteenth Century," 1922); a four-volume series on "mystics of Europe and India" (1925-34), which included studies of Buddha, Heraclitus, Meister Eckhart, Ruysbroek, St. Theresa, Donne, Wordsworth, and Herder; in conjunction with this series separate volumes on William Blake (1933) and the

2

young Friedrich Schlegel (1935); a two-volume interpretation of
Goethe (1935-39); two volumes on Hellenism (1940); four volumes on
the culture and religion of ancient Hellas (1942-45, with a supplemental
fifth volume appearing posthumously); two collections of incisive essays; and a volume retelling the myths and tales of Germanic antiquity.
He also published several volumes of imaginative literature, both prose
and poetry, and a popular study of language. From 1946 until his death
in 1948 he edited a journal devoted to cultural matters, and to which
he himself was the major contributor.

In his early years as a teacher, Grønbech had few students, and it
was not until the last half-dozen years of his academic career that he
attracted larger audiences both within and without the university. Toward the end of his life the influence of Grønbech on his contemporaries, and especially among younger writers, increased considerably.
He was much sought as a speaker. Although for all intents and purposes he left no unfinished works or papers at his death, two series of
public lectures were published posthumously from stenographic tran-
scriptions. While Grønbech's books were more often than not a source
of irritation to many theologians because of their original and essentially non-historiographic approach, there was no clash between Grønbech and the church, and a significant group of his readers comprised
clergymen.

It might now seem that a comparison with Kierkegaard is uncalled
for; but the fact remains that Grønbech was well-read in Kierkegaard
early in his life and that he reacted strongly against Kierkegaard. Like
Kierkegaard, Grønbech was, in the last analysis, concerned only with
a single subject. His subject, which one may label existential, was of
more importance to him than the person or historical phenomenon
about which he was writing. To use his own term, which he never
defined, Grønbech's subject was the soul. If one tries to define what
Grønbech meant by the soul, one finds it to be the very non-Kierke-
gaardian concept that the soul is the conglomerate of subconscious
metaphysical assumptions which in the first instance the individual
shares with the society of which he is a part, and which in the second
instance make the human being, either as a member or a non-member
of a community, act as he does. Incidentally, Grønbech also shares with
Kierkegaard a non-traditional method of communication. Both tend to

3

convince their readers indirectly by a narrative process rather than by syllogistic argumentation. Kierkegaard's device is the extended parable; Grønbech's, the subjective paraphrase.

The similarities are far outweighed by the differences between the two countrymen. Grønbech rejected and refuted Kierkegaard: for Grønbech, Kierkegaard's egoism and Kierkegaard's fear and trembling were perverse and were contrary to the essence of religion. The egoist in an age of fear and trembling is without religion; and there have been, Grønbech believed, only two such ages in the history of Western culture: the post-classical era of Hellenism and our own time. Then, as now, religion degenerated into sensationalism. Mere personal religiosity replaced religion, and, as a consequence, man's orientation was thoroughly profane. Grønbech counted Kierkegaard among the religious sensationalists because Kierkegaard hewed to the paradox. For Grønbech life was not a paradox; nor was Jesus a paradox. The understanding of life, and the understanding of the message of the Man of Nazareth both depend on the existence of faith and on the non-rational and unthinking acceptance of the position of a co-religionist.

Grønbech was not advocating some arbitrary set of principles or trying to superimpose upon others some pattern of his own device. He was never a proselytizing reformer. To be sure, he was motivated by the conviction that our own time must reachieve unity, but in his works he was only reviewing what had been done and said in the past and explaining to the inquisitive mind historical phenomena as he understood them. First and foremost it was necessary merely to understand, for understanding was the prerequisite to the great unity which is the goal of all scientific endeavor.

Grønbech was more sympathetically disposed toward the other great figure from the Danish cultural scene of the nineteenth century, N. F. S. Grundtvig, theologian, poet, and politician—a riddle of a man with many facets, who is best known for his conception of the folk high school and his early advocacy of adult education. Grønbech could admire Grundtvig, whom he called "the greatest man in Danish intellectual life," because Grundtvig stressed the importance of the individual only as a member of the community. Grundtvig's function has been similar to Grønbech's: to inspire to new ideas and new works. Grundtvig could attract Grønbech not only out of intellectual sympathy, but because Grønbech was drawn to men who had strong convictions which were not simply the result of empirical observation and rationalistic conclusion.

Grønbech's spiritual mentor and forerunner was, however, not Grundtvig any more than Kierkegaard but, rather, the eighteenth-century German thinker, theologian, visionary, and poet, Johann Gottfried Herder. The reader will need no particular faculty of perception to observe that Herder, although he stood only at the threshold of the nineteenth century, occupies a central position in *Religious Currents*. Grønbech shared Herder's breadth of interest and prophetic insight. Like Herder, he was a non-systematic philosopher and synthesist, whose ultimate goal was the achievement of a new harmony. Like Herder, Grønbech did not separate literature from philosophy, science, and religion, which for him were not individual disciplines but the varying expressions of the same fundamental ideas. "Religion" was for Grønbech an all-embracing term. In his eulogy on Harald Høffding in 1931 he defined it as "the interest of the human being in the world drama in which he is both actor and spectator." The unity which Grønbech foresaw will mean the reëstablishment of harmony; and Grønbech encouraged his readers to have faith in the future existence of this harmony. Consequently, there may be said to be no contradiction among the several guises which Grønbech seems at first glance to have assumed—philologist, philosopher, theologian, historian, critic, and poet. Whatever his ostensible function, he remained himself and played a single role. He was not a universal genius like Goethe, engaged with an endless number of disciplines—although we have the testimony of his students and hearers that he could expatiate intelligently and easily on many subjects not mentioned in his written works, including Einstein's theory of relativity (which he viewed with great optimism), and Freudian psychology (which he repudiated).

While parallels, contrasts, and comparisons are useful in placing a figure in focus historically, they are neither precise nor definitive. Vilhelm Grønbech's importance and influence does not stem from the fact that he is a twentieth-century disciple of Herder or that he represents a reaction against the egoistic theology of Kierkegaard, but rather that he was an original and synthetic thinker who possessed the power of expression that a demagogue might begrudge him, the zeal and conviction befitting an evangelist, and the independence of judgment desired by an iconoclast.

The question of the independent origins of Grønbech's thought may remain moot for the present. Certain it is that he possessed an unexampled familiarity with source materials. His reading was vast, and his knowledge of sources so profound that it seems idle to speculate about his immediate sources of inspiration or about works that could particularly have influenced his thinking. There is no doubt of the importance that his teacher Vilhelm Thomsen had for him, but Thomsen's own scholarly work does not resemble Grønbech's canon. Grønbech frequently refers to certain books by other scholars, but the books in question provide a background but no key to Grønbech's production.

In retrospect, the original and peculiar nature of Grønbech's work can be observed in his first magnum opus, *Vor Folkeæt i Oldtiden—The Culture of the Teutons*. It was published at a time when historians of religion and students of mythology were still explaining religions as the misinterpretation of natural phenomena. Grønbech gave no credence to this sort of speculation nor to the traditional criticism of Germanic antiquity, which, especially in Germany, had been rooted in an exegesis—which Grønbech found grotesque—of the *Germania* of Tacitus. *The Culture of the Teutons* is a monumental effort to describe in breadth as well as in depth the significance of relatively few basic concepts which motivated not merely the religious and philosophical attitude toward life but life itself for our Germanic ancestors: peace, honor, luck, holiness, knavishness. Grønbech here demonstrated for the first time his ability to penetrate into the minds of earlier thinkers and poets, and on the basis of their words as still preserved, to extract and define the essential and fundamental ideas which were the *sine qua non* of their lives. Few early readers of *The Culture of the Teutons* can have understood in which direction Grønbech was moving, and they judged him somewhat querulously. A spate of noteworthy reviews nevertheless indicated that Grønbech's book had made a mark.

While opinions about the accuracy and validity of Grønbech's presentation varied sharply, there was agreement that it was both remarkable and stimulating, despite the fact that it seemed to be highly intuitive and somewhat eclectic.

Here and in many subsequent studies, Grønbech was explaining sympathetically the "myth" of an earlier age, the reality which gave to that age a unity of existence and which made the members of a society into such a community of believers Grønbech identified as a necessary goal of human existence. He was dealing with the assumption of daily life both when societies were able to function as an organism, as in the case of Germanic antiquity or of Hellas, and when they failed to do so, as in the case of the era of Roman Hellenism or of the nineteenth and twentieth centuries. He depicted the essence of a system of philosophical belief through an exhaustive enquiry into the meaning, interrelationship, and metaphysical connotations of basic assumptions incorporated in certain words and concepts. Combining bits of evidence with considerable intuition, he divined a pattern. In brushing off historical patina, he disregarded the evidence of archeology, for he was convinced that the written monument represents the only living evidence which is open to certain and authoritative interpretation. He posited the scientific understanding of spiritual phenomena as resting upon the comprehension of a whole, of which those phenomena are only a part. Working with this conviction, he was able to make general statements of unusual perceptivity and possessing enough validity to lend an aura of brilliance to his entire work. If his interpretations are imperfect, they are not necessarily wrong. They may be said rather to possess a subjective reality; and this was in fact the only reality for Grønbech.

It is of signal importance for a reader of Grønbech to understand that Grønbech did not assume that there exists a single truth or a single reality. Quite to the contrary—and startling enough for him who never has considered the possibility before—Grønbech believed in what may be termed multiple truth and multiple reality. He accepted the truth and reality of any subconscious, naïve, and sincere metaphysical system which controlled a society and bore up an entire world. For him both truth and reality were relative.

An objection to this principle might well be that if Grønbech were so tolerant and objective that he admitted the validity of other philosophical systems, or, more precisely, that other religious systems were true and real, then he must be without faith. Be that as it may, Grønbech's intent was not to be tolerant and objective. Like no other thinker

7

before him, he accepted subjectively the existence of several realities, but not because he assumed a disinterested and objective attitude. By penetration into a system of thought through the medium of the printed word, Grønbech could identify himself with it and interpret it as part of himself. Thus the reality of the convinced Buddhist was for him quite as actual as the reality of the convinced Christian or the convinced Jew. There was a certain physical actuality which all accepted unthinking and without dispute. That is, to apply the English terminology employed in the present translation, actuality made up a part of several realities. The interpretation of actuality was reality. There was not only more than a single reality; reality itself could change.

The fact bears repeating that Grønbech accepted and believed in the principle of multiple reality. The man who accepts only a single reality, his own, is to Grønbech not merely ignorant or intolerant; he simply fails to comprehend the possibilities of the human soul, the configurations of which constitute several realities simultaneously in various societies of believers. Grønbech was not attempting to describe sociologically and anthropologically but to analyze his subjects, to determine to what extent they understood their own souls. Grønbech explained the religious experience of others not as a believer or a psychologist but as a person who had himself undergone enough of a religious experience to be able to admit the existence of religious as distinct from other experience, and one which should be accepted as an independent phenomenon. As a consequence, he was able to exhibit remarkable empathy for mystics and poets whose verbal outpourings went beyond the rationally explicable.

In Grønbech's own opinion, harmony was the ideal and harmony could be achieved as long as the components of a society worked in concert. There could even be harmony of the individual outside of society, as in the case of those mystics who created a world within themselves or who, like Herder, saw into the future and perceived a development that would bring about a society in which the harmony of individuals would emerge into harmony for mankind.

While the soul of the individual who had succeeded in constructing for himself his own metaphysical world—that is, the mystic—interested Grønbech to the extent that he wrote several studies about mystics, the individual as a member of a community of believers was always more important to Grønbech than the individual *per se*, since the single person who was not a part of the community did not share what Grønbech termed the common soul and therefore did not properly function as a human being: only through ideas common to a group can the individual communicate and do more than talk to himself.

The problem of the individual and society occupied Grønbech again and again. He wrote most incisively on it in an essay entitled "The Individual and Society" in 1932, in which his own theoretical anti-individualism (which must not be confused with sociability) was most clearly formulated. In contradistinction to earlier times, states Grønbech, our time has elevated religion to be an enigma, although modern Christianity and modern Judaism do preserve a shadow of the old unity or common soul, for certain images have much the same force in the minds of all believers and these images regularly evoke certain thoughts. There is, however, only a shadow. Our time needs a new soul, a new unity, a new myth: that is Grønbech's didactic message.

In his later works, including the many studies of literary figures, Grønbech was ever concerned with the metaphysical assumptions which are the requisites of a harmonious society and which mould the life of the individual in his relation to society. Despite the poetic qualities of his own language and his own propensity for metaphor, Grønbech did not treat of the formal aspects of poetry or even the poetic use of language. He subscribed to no poetics, but examined his literary subjects only in order to define their souls. In truth, therefore, he may be said to have written the religious history of the men and societies that were his subjects. The reader of Grønbech's literary studies must simply assume that formal aspects of a work of the imagination are a necessary consequence of the functioning of the creative mind. Grønbech's philological background is visible insofar as he is concerned with the connotations of the individual word, on which one may make lengthy and stimulating perorations. It is perhaps not too far from the mark to say that he was championing a theological philology, in educing from words the religious substance of a life or a social order, although the originality of Grønbech's presentation suggests why he was the despair both of orthodox theologians and analytical historians.

His interpretation of the nineteenth century in Western culture is a projection of the convictions which dominate his earlier works, but at the same time it contains the embryo of the ideas which were to exfoliate in the later works. He attempted neither new documentation nor historical analysis but interpreted synthetically those decades of greatest change between an older world order and a new. What hitherto had seemed to be radical and even independent movements he depicted as variations on a general theme, and at bottom an effort to achieve a lost harmony and metaphysical unity.

For Grønbech, the eighteenth century is the great turning point in European history: modern times begin not with the era of the Reformation but with the end of the eighteenth century. While the Reformation ultimately may have been the prerequisite of the age of rationalism, it was the victory of rationalism itself that did away with religion as earlier times knew it. This, and not merely some alterations in liturgy and dogma or even the concomitant social upheavals of the sixteenth century, marks the great, modern historical change. Grønbech recognized that it was not until the end of the eighteenth century that man in Western Europe realized there could be another quite acceptable way of thinking, not only a different religion, than his own. This discovery brought with it both distress and relief. To give up the belief in the absolute meant for most a greater dependence on the rational faculty, but only within the traditional limitations of Renaissance thought. There arose a longing for the lost harmony and the lost God. In Herder the belief in the absolute was also abandoned, but he accepted the existence of plural reality and pointed the way to a new myth and a new unity. He, and not Goethe therefore, was in Grønbech's opinion the prophet of a new society during the era of change around 1770. Grønbech admits that Goethe, like a religious mystic, achieved his own harmony, but he pointed out that Goethe looked back to a superseded ideal of duty and labor, and to the solace of art, and that the neo-classical Goethe was really able to satisfy all of his needs in Hellas. Consequently, Goethe could not be accepted as a model for the future, the less so since he did not fulfill Grønbech's insistent demand that the individual be a part of a community of believers. The fact that Herder and Goethe, friends but very different from one another, could achieve equilibrium as they each did, suggested that the generations which followed them were forever divorced from the past. The cleavage might be overlooked, but the experience which had brought it about could not be forgotten. The subsequent general positivistic tendency to underestimate the significance of psychic phenomena and emotional life was to have far-reaching consequences.

In the past religion had been dependent upon the role that psychic phenomena and the emotions play in human life. Now religion is dissipated as the great force in life. While a new faith grows up in the nineteenth century, it is the faith of poets and natural scientists, and no longer of organized religion. A new reality comes into being, although it is in many ways the transformation of an older reality. While rejecting the tenets of medieval and Renaissance religion, it accepts older doctrines in a new dress. The gradual growth of the belief in the theory of evolution and the acceptance of a grand pattern in the physical world was a variation of the older belief in the divine pattern of the universe.

It is Grønbech's thesis in *Religious Currents* that during the Renaissance the soul had acquired harmony by a process of delimitation, and that in the late eighteenth century men broke with the limitations of the Renaissance without understanding the need for religion or the role which the emotions, as opposed to reason, played in human existence. Certain individuals now achieved harmony through retrospective contemplation, as notably in the case of Goethe, or by introspection, as in the case of the mystical thinkers, including William Blake. Herder perceived a future harmony won through the acceptance of plural reality. The need for a myth comparable to the religion of the Renaissance remained, and found some satisfaction in the new faith born of the scientific hypotheses of the nineteenth century, which, with its optimistic explanation of the organization and, especially, the evolution of the world, gradually led to as rigid a dogma as the old. The struggle between churchmen and evolutionists in the nineteenth century was in Grønbech's opinion fraternal and to a certain extent internecine. The doctrine of evolution reëstablished the older metaphysical system sans deity, and the several dogmas were renamed, but the possibilities of an explanation of actuality in terms other than those known to Western Europe were left unconsidered. The evolutionists forced on the world a fixed mechanical system of which Herder, the foremost of those visionaries who conceived a different world order at the beginning of the century, never dreamed. Herder had spoken of a God who worked from within; the evolutionists spoke of laws that worked from without.

Herder and the few other prophets of a new era—in particular Blake and Friedrich Schlegel—have Grønbech's sympathy, for they carried their fate within them, as it were, and were harbingers of an unrealized future harmony. In *Religious Currents* Grønbech gave them a preliminary review. Thereafter he published separate studies of them and of the retrospective but inwardly harmonious Goethe as well. Grønbech calls these men mystics because they could conjure not only a world and a new reality but a new metaphysical harmony within themselves. Herder, Goethe, Friedrich Schlegel, Wordsworth, and Shelley represented for Grønbech a revolt against Protestantism and its culture and an effort to achieve a human existence of greater breadth and depth. As social revolutionaries they presaged a new order where life would not be regulated only by material and economic interests but would be a spiritual brotherhood. Grønbech's great sympathy for those writers who, for better or for worse, are usually identified as Romantics, derives from the fact that they searched history for examples of peoples who, better than the man of modern culture, were able to satisfy the poetic and religious needs of the human mind.

It was Grønbech's conviction that all the answers to life's greatest questions have a poetic nature. Many blunders of the nineteenth century, he believed, can be explained by the fact that specialists, judging on the basis of their limited knowledge, decreed a solution to some of the most general problems of existence, as for example the psychologist who might be led to declare that the life of the soul was merely a material function and naïvely to believe that he had solved for all time the question of the spiritual life of man.

Religious Currents of the Nineteenth Century is at the fulcrum of Grønbech's production. It is chronologically the central work, and, more important, it is programmatic of much of his later writing. It contains the seed of many of the later books—on Schlegel, Goethe, Herder, Blake. The interrelationship of *Religious Currents* with the later works extends even to the recurrence of the same quotations; this is particularly noticeable in Grønbech's treatment of Herder and Goethe. There are even intimations of ideas which were to be developed in *Jesus* and *Paulus,* while Hellenism, the subject of one of the late longer works, is mentioned in chapter XV as the background for Pauline thought.

Although the *Religious Currents* may serve as a good introduction to Grønbech's world, it is not the book that Grønbech originally intended it to be. It was to have treated of all Europe, and must be considered fragmentary in its present form. Grønbech declared that he had cashiered a large part of his manuscript as a result of the publisher's demand that the book, which was a volume in a series, not exceed a certain length. If the part of the manuscript treating Romance literature did indeed ever reach a stage where it might have been presented to a publisher, it no longer is preserved. Probably this part of the manuscript never was completed. Otherwise Grønbech would have made use of it in later life, when he published material that he had written at an earlier date. As it is, there are but faint allusions to the subject matter of what must have been the missing parts of the manuscript in articles which appeared in Grønbech's periodical *Frie Ord* after World War II. Although Grønbech declared himself to be dissatisfied with the book, it has been one of the most accessible and popular of his works.

The lack of careful documentation in *Religious Currents* was a permanent idiosyncrasy. Prior to writing on any subjcet, Grønbech first thoroughly familiarized himself with the printed sources in the original language and then grappled for the elements of the subject which are not essentially affected by the details and niceties of historiography. Grønbech disdained what he felt to be pedantry and depended on his own astounding mnemonic ability. He did not feel the need to bolster his arguments with footnotes and page references. As a matter of fact, his writings do not lend themselves to such documentation because of their synthetic nature and because of the highly metaphorical quality of his speech. When he wrote, as when he spoke, his arguments had a flowing, organic quality which forbade footnotes and references. Indeed, he wrote as if he were speaking with great intensity and conviction, and were exhorting his reader. The system of references in two of the later works, *Hellenism* and *Hellas,* is the contribution of co-workers and secretaries. Since Grønbech rewrote his manuscript several times without referring to the source material he was using, quotations tended to be rewritten and altered along with his own words. In this English version of *Religious Currents,* the translators have tried to locate all quotations, and to cite them in the original language, if other than English, in the notes. The few serious discrepancies between Grønbech's rendering of a quotation and the actual quotation are also recorded in the notes.

Evident in *Religious Currents* as well as in all other works by Grønbech are, first, his sympathetic paraphrasing of the words of his immediate subject, and, second, a style which is marked by the constant use of imagery rather than logical argumentation. The paraphrasing, both conscious and unconscious, indicates the intimacy in which Grønbech lived with the thinkers and poets about whom he wrote. His syntheses of the ideas of others represent the product of abstract mental processes and not the systematic use of a card file, a fact which accounts for the freedom which he often took with the material he quoted. Generally speaking, it is impossible to determine whether Grønbech agrees or disagrees with his subject, for—to use Grønbech's term—he has expanded his soul to include it. As a consequence, the reader cannot disengage Grønbech's own thought and words from those of the person about whom he is speaking. This is not accidental; Grønbech was trying to be an intellectual intermediary rather than a critic. When one reads Grønbech's study of Meister Eckhart, for example, one concludes that Grønbech must also have been a mystic of the same persuasion as Eckhart, since he speaks at great length for Eckhart, without posing skeptical queries and without exhibiting the objectivity of the disinterested scholar. It would, however, be incorrect to conclude that Grønbech was personally in sympathy with Eckhart.

Because of his style and mode of expression, Grønbech resembles an imaginative or creative writer. Many of his metaphors have the peculiar quality of positing a fact from which an argument can proceed. He then frequently makes the assumption that one part of his metaphor is factual and extends his argument from it, even compounding it into still another metaphor. When one is trying to read closely for meaning, this idiosyncratic manner of writing can at times be exasperating. One may incline to the opinion that Grønbech's imagery constitutes a weakness and wonder why he has not spoken more directly. To explain this one would need to explain why the poet and the artist express themselves in images. Is it because images can communicate what factual statements cannot and achieve an effect greater than that of expository language? If imagery leads to a lack of lucidity, one must seek solace in the thought that inspiration does not derive from exposition. Perfect lucidity would probably cost many striking observations and many stimuli. Grønbech is not trying to convince but to arouse and to stimulate to revaluation. He is fulfilling the duty of the historian of religion as he saw it and as he defined it the year *Religious Currents* was published, 1922: "To show how vast the human being is, and how awesome in his vastness, and thus spur on his contemporaries to search deeper within themselves for unity."

As far as religion itself is concerned, Grønbech said a few years later in an interview, "If religion were something factual, we should not have to discuss what it is and should not need sensational experiences to be convinced of its power."

—P. M. M.

Chapter I

The Age of Harmony

WE, THE CHILDREN of the nineteenth century, are a generation without a religion and therefore we have but a single thought: how can we find a god and a devil, a heaven and a hell—all those things which made earlier times great? We know that the old god is dead and gone, and that no attempt at resuscitation can give him back the power and the glory. We can date his departure around the year 1770. He died when men found it necessary to prove his existence; he was buried when they discovered that there was nothing by which his existence was disproved. A god who does not make himself noticed lies dead in his grave; and gods never rise again after the reins of the world have once slipped from their hands.

All our life is a continuous search for a new god. The men who grew tired and sat down by the wayside, who preferred rather to close their eyes than to look out into infinite distance; the men who proclaimed the bankruptcy of science and permitted themselves to be taken into the church in order to find peace—they have their consolation, but they have had nothing to offer the world. They have inspired no dreams, no thoughts, no hope, in other men. No new religion will come to us before our society has found itself anew in an experience of the world so young and strong that a nascent god arises. In the experience of tired men there is no inception of a new day. The future must be sought where eternity, arcane and pure, wells upward like a novel and immediate reality, bringing forth a god who is felt and experienced as divine.

All our thoughts have their roots in the Renaissance—not in the Italian Renaissance, except indirectly, but in the rebirth which was the Reformation, in Elizabethan literature, in the piety of the Puritans—in a new life which was moulded to perfection in the first half of the eighteenth century, that epoch which to the great detriment of history we all too frequently underestimate and give curious names like the Era of Rationalism, the Age of Reason, and the like. Men of the latter half of the eighteenth century, who lived on the threshold of the next era, were too much concerned with their struggle for independence to

16

be just to the ideals of the Renaissance. They saw it as that portion of the past which most oppressed their youthful efforts, and they vindicated themselves by attacking it with hatred and ridicule. Now that we are farther away and need not stand in awe of the discipline of our forefathers, we can observe and admire their nobility. We need not compensate our close relationship by hurling derogatory names in their direction.

In the Renaissance the world had its fixed center in man, who enjoyed the peace and beauty of self-control. The men of the Renaissance never lived haphazardly; they were able, as perhaps only the Greeks before them had been able, to create a life in which everything moved in well-balanced rhythms. The Renaissance man organized his soul around the will, which he saw as an autocrat which reviews everything that comes to it from without and makes sure that everything takes its proper place and is at once assigned a function. This mighty will rules austerely, and takes care that nothing is accepted as a component of the soul which cannot enter into its harmony and contribute to its growth toward perfection. The will ruthlessly excludes barren experiences which, although they may please, do not aid a man to enrich and ennoble the wondrous creation which is his soul. By daily and hourly self-examination man reviews the contents of his soul, and musters thought after thought in order to insure that his day has not been wasted; he speaks sternly to his soul when the day's harvest does not seem a proper return for its labor, and he exercises a more stringent discipline on the morrow.

Consequently, man fears all that is not clear or that will obscure the prospect of the soul. He fears strong emotions which, if they do not threaten the absolute rule of the will, hinder the clear judgment of a moment and of the consequences of that moment. The passions should be accepted as driving forces, but they must recognize that, as servants, they must be restricted to the depths.

The harmony of the soul pervades all human actions. Nothing is done by chance; nothing depends on fortune or misfortune. The Renaissance man never lives for the moment; he is always on watch against being taken unaware by the moment. In the last analysis he always determines whether an experience is worth acceptance as a part of his soul. What purpose can it serve? he asks, and he puts the same

17

penetrating question to the impulses which try to force their way into the life of action: can they bring prosperity to me and to those whose welfare is my charge? Before he acts he always demands a clear estimate of the consequences, good and bad; he knows how much depends on the individual's being honest with himself, even in the smallest matter.

And therefore there is always an intermediary between a man and his experience, such as prosperity, or virtue, or human progress. He does not attend to himself, but to an ideal, and he rejoices or grieves as he perceives the ideal to be strong or weak. He does not find an absolute reality in pain; when his progress is stopped by adversity, he seeks to use his discomfiture in a way to gain virtue. He never acts without judging his action to be bad or good.

Thus the world is divided into two parts; on the one side are men, on the other side are the virtues—Goodness, Justice, and Truth. The mighty beings have an existence independent of mankind; indeed in their simplicity they seem to be sturdier than the complex human being; for men change and pass but the virtues endure. It is they who create history and sit in judgment on men as the materials with which they work. Evil and Good are never an aspect of an action, or a tendency, or a result of conditions, or an infection from the sickness of the soul: they are eternal entities, born of nature's womb. Above mankind the ideal shines with a steady radiance; succeeding generations look up to it and by it measure their significance. An action falls on either side of a line which extends through the whole world. Perhaps at most there is a neutral strip in daily life, but for the best men it is so narrow as to be negligible.

On all sides the man of the Renaissance sees the fixed and the typical, not only in the realm of the ideal but in the world of man. Actually the Renaissance man is not a particular human being; he is general humanity exemplified in an individual. He finds himself throughout the world wherever he may look; no slanting eyes and felt shoes, no togas, can hide from him the fact that human feelings and virtues are the same everywhere. And so he observes when he looks back into history; and the artist interrupts to add that taste is the same at all times and everywhere in the world, since reason is rooted in the inmost being of things: there is, therefore, but one art and one beauty.

18

The Renaissance seeks the most important experiences within everyday life. The soul of man constitutes such an overwhelming part of the world that most people need little more to fill their lives than the experience they obtain in intercourse with their fellow men. The soul is nevertheless not alone in the universe; about it lies nature, like a delightful garden which gives pleasure to the eye and the ear and, what is more important, riches to the soul. There man can go and be sure of finding himself; by communion with nature he can discover more profound expressions of his love for goodness and beauty. The hours during which he sits in meditation by a sprawling and babbling brook are so rich that he returns home strengthened in his desire to be more noble, and equipped with new resources for the service of the ideal.

Nature, however, has no life of its own, though it is easy to describe the progress of the soul in spatial terms such as the valley of doubt or the mountains of tribulation, or (in reverse) to describe nature in spiritual terms, for nature observed has its counterpart in the inner man. The world exists as a human life of vast dimensions, and all the expressions which are used to describe it are reflections of human feelings: nature is great, elevated, thoughtful, friendly; birds sing the praise of the Maker; and the brooks murmur mysteriously.

The beauty of life forces men to tune their harps and sing the praise of the soul. Poetry celebrates the joy of the human race at the divine strength of the will, and its desire to keep the sacred tasks of virtue in mind. The protagonists of literature are the great Virtues, which are easily recognizable, for they are capitalized. But in addition to serving the splendor of the soul, poetry also brings joy to the children of men. It draws them into a pleasant place, too beautiful to have any connection with actuality, into an Arcady of shepherds and shepherdesses whose feelings have been perfected to an almost superhuman delicacy. Poetry keeps to such a rarified atmosphere that when men leave the world in order to enjoy the splendor of Art they clearly feel the transition.

Harmony penetrates nature like a powerful rhythm, and bears witness to the permanence of universal order. Virtue is linked to beauty and fortune, as vice is fettered to suffering. Every creature obtains its reward, not because of the interference of an arbitrary deity, but through the law of nature. Everything that happens serves a useful purpose, in the long run. Suffering in itself is evil, but suffering serves virtue as much as any blessing, because it purifies man and leads him towards a higher state. Indeed the harmony of the world is so powerful that no man can destroy it; at most, defying the law of nature, he may confound it within his own life. Even a selfish man contributes to the well-being of others, though he may not be aware of it. For example, how could anyone work out a system which arranges for a city's milk supply better than nature does? Nature forces the farmer for the sake of profit to set out early in the morning in his wagon and trundle to town with the milk cans; and if a neighbor tries to cut in on his business, the farmer lowers his prices in order to oust his competitor; and his egoism is therefore a blessing, since through it children get cheaper milk.

Harmony gives a man security, for he knows that he has only to allow wise nature to have its way with man and society; he need only give the individual freedom to participate in the struggle—and society will be well served. Correctly understood, all virtues are compounded of pure, noble egoism. Do unto others as you would have others do unto you—that is the pivot of all noble ethics.

Therefore man hates all laws which limit the activities of the individual, as foolish interventions in the wise order of nature; to be sure, though these may cause momentary confusion and even crisis, they can never deflect nature's omniscient course. The demand which man makes for personal freedom is based on the concept of self-discipline; the law lies within his conscience. He knows that if he merely adapts himself to the great rhythm of nature it will lead him onward towards nobility and fortune. But he also knows that he must expend constant conscious effort to retain his identity. And he does not spare himself in daily discipline. Harmony is based upon faith; it is an experience. Man himself contributes to harmony by being a faithful husbandman who rewards the diligence of his subordinates, who keeps them at work and protects their welfare.

The religion of the Renaissance is complementary to daily life. Its practice constitutes true and healthy human life, the endeavor of the soul to prove itself worthy of the ideal man who exists in the conscience. Its theology consists of the correct interpretation of the soul and the surrounding world, with insight into the order and beauty of the universe and an understanding of its laws and demands. This religion has a god, who is a logical consequence of harmony. One recognizes him in nature because of its order, which suggests an omniscient and almighty being as its creator and governor. In history and in nature alike this god reveals himself clearly to everyone who has eyes. Indeed, the surrounding world gives such an insight into the divine being that man can learn not only to admire him but also to understand his thoughts. Perhaps a bit unnecessarily, the god has provided an abundant commentary, in Holy Writ. The only difference between the true sons of the church and more philosophical men is, that the first group puts greater stress on revelation.

It is a consolation to live in this beautiful world, for it is well balanced and perfected. There are no casual lines running beyond the periphery of harmony and calling for an explanation of what lies in the distance. There is no heaven—except that which is a consequence of the fact that as a unity life must receive its reward; and no hell—except perhaps some not too severe institution which is a counterpart to heaven. On these points opinions may differ widely; but a hell to the depths of which suffering and passion lead, and a heaven which towers in the opposite direction, have no place in the world of harmony.

In the Renaissance the daemons that exist within man were driven into the depths of the soul and there tied firmly to a treadmill, so that they had no spare time in which to grumble. And every new ethical act of the soul bore down upon them. But if one pushes daemons down too hard, their heads pop up in sheer reaction.

The revolt against the harmonious ideal man came from below, from the common people. Wesley's biography as a preacher reveals that the common people felt a need for intense experience. Wherever he appeared his audiences consisted of shouting, crying, howling, stamping human beings. They fell to the floor and lay with thrashing limbs, they rose up with cries of ecstasy; they fought with Satan at the portals of hell, and after their victory, they saw heaven open before their eyes. Wesley did not arrange these Dionysian storms—he was at first as surprised as anyone else at the reaction—but his words released forces which were at the bursting point. Here and there in England there arose dancing and trembling congregations whose demand for ecstasy created a divine service of the most baroque kind. Now God is in truth among us, they said when the spirit moved their bodies and forced them to jump over tables and benches; and in their words there lay a good deal of self-knowledge. It was the repressed desire for violent experience which finally burst forth; contradictions within the soul asserted themselves against all harmony. Culture created an ideal of man by disciplining the will and suppressing whatever was rebellious; it made all "evil" wrong by demonstrating that it was harmful and stupid, and thus it emasculated vice. But here among the common people sin broke its bonds and wrestled with the soul; man writhed in voluptuous fear of the dæmonic in the depths of his heart and let himself be carried up to the pinnacles of experience in a gigantic struggle between Satan and God. It is significant that Wesley, demagogue and revivalist, was unable to accompany his audience. He stood before them restraining, and admonishing, and often anathematizing the enthusiasm of the people. He was himself a man of harmony who felt an inward need for order, for common sense, and above all for salutary dogma. He did not understand the simple enthusiasts who broke the bonds he set in his wisdom, who demanded first a rebirth and then the newly-born's right to live in disregard of teaching and dogma. Many times he had to give up to Satan as "mystics and enthusiasts" those very men whose conversion had been to him the harbinger of a divine spring, and to close the doors of his congregation against them.

The common folk in its benightedness proclaimed a truth which was hidden from the sensible men of culture: that there are daemons in the human heart and that these daemons demand their due. Harmony had made them ridiculous and had subjugated them; these restless spirits in the human soul became devils when they were denied, when goodness, truth, justice, and all the virtues were chosen as angels and given a monopoly of the soul, and all else was disowned and cast out into darkness. But one must either recognize the majesty of the daemon and formally declare war upon him, or give him a part of the world.

Ecstasy did not lead to a breach of harmony; Wesley's spirit was victorious. There was rebellion enough in revivalism, but neither spirit nor thought. The movement was enveloped by a traditional theology and the only result was that Satan was assigned a larger part of the world to govern. Harmony was saved by making the boundaries of its

22

world narrower, so that everything which suggested emotion, all art and all play, was ascribed to the powers of evil. The demarcation was undertaken in the spirit of harmony, and whether a thing should belong to God or to Satan was decided on the basis of its utility. Thus work, business, family life, and self-discipline belong to the Kingdom of God, and men who formerly had experienced a Dionysian frenzy were transformed to the most bourgeois of the bourgeois in an industrious, frugal society. Evangelical circles still bear the marks of their origin; theirs is a religious proletarian culture created by men who had no other spiritual substance than that which they had received second-hand from their superiors in society, and who on that basis constructed a divinity that permitted noble feelings only if they were also simple and narrow. The fear of the soul's mysterious depths becomes continually stronger, and can be checked only by a constant deadening of the spirit. The security given by the feeling of salvation disappears if it is not constantly reënforced by the conviction that something is being done, that some sacrifice is being made for the sake of God—at the least, one keeps His day holy with a mixture of churchgoing and idleness.

In this way harmony was reëstablished within religious circles. It was the last time that there was an opportunity for the church or the chapel to lead in spiritual development; but there was no leadership among the pious; and thereupon the reins fell forever out of ecclesiastical hands. Since then the poets and thinkers have been the champions in the search for God. Men like Shelley and Wordsworth, Goethe and Herder and the German Romantics, Browning and Dostoyevsky whisper the eternal word into the ear of man.

Methodism nevertheless brought one thing into the world: a terrified respect for the formidable strength and savagery of the human soul. The men and women, the boys and girls, who rolled on the ground and shrieked with fear were a living sermon about something called sin. They made the rational moralist a laughing stock, with his zeal to show people the impudence of seeking happiness on bypaths instead of going down the paved way of virtue. And what happened to the severest critics of society, who flailed their contemporaries with the scourge of indignant wit because of their lack of charity, self-sacrifice, and pity, and who with veracious art drew the vain woman of the world and her voluptuous cavalier so that the reader shuddered at their inanity? The critic and the criticized descended alike to the level of comedy, as figures whose weakness lay not in their lack of virtue, but in their inability to sin.

The innocent knew that life is not as simple as their superiors had believed; without knowing it and without willing it, the poor enthusiasts reasserted the old adage that man cannot do without that unrest in the depth of his heart which has forced the soul toward the pinnacles of history. At the same time that the sin and suffering and death which harmony had hidden appeared in naked strength, Jesus, after long having been only a good and clever teacher who emphasized the strict but mild laws of nature in all their purity, was transformed into a living man. The strong, impoverished souls demanded in God the flesh of their flesh and the suffering of their suffering, and they found what they sought in the man of sorrow from Galilee and Golgotha. In the course of the nineteenth century the Nazarene became a stronger and stronger force in spiritual life, perhaps stronger than ever before. All the efforts of official religion to enswathe him in traditional divinity have been in vain. Inexorably, the people tear from him the accretions which for earlier times were the valued symbols of divine power in order more clearly to see into that face, filled with joy and pain. And here the poor in spirit were pioneers. However, they did not announce that they had put Jesus the Man on the throne of God, for they lacked the ability to explain their own experience and saw that task taken out of their hands by the prophets. The religious experience of the unlearned was, in actuality, incongruous with traditional religion. It could not regenerate the life of the church, for that had been smothered in theology. But the seed which germinated in enthusiasts was planted outside the church and there bore manifold fruits. The gospel of suffering which coal-miners had proclaimed with tears and convulsions, other men were to preach with clear and distinct utterance in the market places of the world.

Compared with this rebellion the spiritual movements in Germany and in France were tame. In Germany the demand of the common people for experiences which went beyond those offered by official religion found satisfaction in little circles whose members, enjoying a quiet and inward brotherly association, were cognizant of rebirth through God's wondrous grace. Apparently, the experiences that moved the spirit in the gatherings of the Moravian Brethren were not overwhelming; but behind much sensitive discussion of the wounds of Jesus and the love of the Lamb one glimpses souls who in quiet dignity experienced something of the paradox within the world of the heart. Most significantly, it was in pietistical homes that several prophets of the new age had implanted in them a spiritual unrest which made them go forth and find their own souls anew.

Chapter II

The Struggle for a New Soul

THE MEN OF THE NEW AGE were confronted by a difficult task: to find themselves anew. They were to rediscover the soul as if it were a new land, and to set its boundaries. They were to venture out into all those dark and stormy regions of the soul which men of an earlier and more harmonious time had proscribed as evil or dangerous. There they were to reëstablish the boundary between good and evil; none of them knew as yet how far out into chaos that boundary could be moved. Perhaps no boundary could be set up between good and evil. Perhaps the enmity between God and Devil was no more than a paralyzing discord within the soul. Beyond the violent emotions there were the vast dreams which earlier times had feared because they dulled the will. It was a dangerous land, for the further one explored it, the fewer signs there were which gave clear directions: the signs were replaced by vague feelings; it was a doubly dangerous land because the path led away from action, and out into regions where one could not see the difference between the real and the unreal; it was most dangerous because there one saw no goal but felt only something incomprehensible, and could not know whether its tempting power came from its very nullity. But no fear could deter the new men, for that which drove them forward was their need for being. The fear of becoming lost, which had often discouraged men from hazardous expeditions into the unknown, had no power over the men of the new generation. To them, the old self which could be lost was nothing, and what might be won was everything.

It is no wonder that when their hunger for experience had overcome resistance, they tried to satisfy it in strange places and strange ways. They often groped about blindly and tried to take life by force, and they got themselves into predicaments which to members of an older generation seemed piteous or reprehensible. The men of the German *Sturm und Drang* suddenly moved the center of the soul out into the wildest regions of passion. Only in moments of exaltation do they really live to the fullest; and as their ecstasy augments, their morale rises. The more blindly a man lets himself be driven by the intoxication of the senses, the more inconsiderately and selfishly he indulges in life's pleasures, the nobler and more honest he is. They recognize only moments of culmination as true existence, and they demand that life consists of nothing but apices. When they sing their hymns to the flesh and arrogantly praise a brutal sensuality, they exhibit the rebel's defense against the philistinism that oppresses him on all sides—and, to be sure, also something of a defense against his inner self; for the rebel must outrage nice people in order to prove to himself that he has the right to rebel. The rebel's hymns signify, however, much more than indecency. The rebel lacks, and seeks, and has a presentiment of, a beauty different from the orthodox; and in order to find that which he has never seen, he penetrates into regions in which the existence of beauty previously has been denied. When others have spoken of the soul so much that the word has become meaningless, a desperate man will speak of flesh, in pure zeal to demonstrate the actuality of the soul. He makes body into soul and evil into good because he seeks a new good, and knows not where it is to be found, but only that it is not where all the world says it should be sought.

Those men—Lenz, Klinger, Heinse—assume the role of titans who turn the world upside down and arrange life according to their own solipsistic wills; but in actuality they are human beings groping after deeper truth, and concealing their insecurity by brutal gestures in order to save their souls in a self-satisfied bourgeois society. In the same way, Byron gropes for beauty and truth when he rewrites the old story and defiantly makes Cain a hero and Satan a spirit of wisdom and truth. The Jehovah who demands unqualified obedience and his well-behaved children—Adam, Eve, and Abel—who kiss God's punitive hand, are representatives, observed from without, of a religion antagonistic to life. But *Cain* signifies much more than a skeptic's revolt against traditional truths. The good god is a mere spirit of limitation and the good people are poor souls who shiver by a flickering flame of life. Satan is the great human soul which loathes conventional suffering and conventional solace and is driven out to a point where life unfolds in eternal dimensions. The universe, where worlds are born and destroyed, which rolls through eternity, is like a leaf floating on the rivers of paradise. In the universe Cain has his world, and his kin are the demons who dwell in the halls of death; they do not need to beg for

27

life, for they are filled with their own energy; they are fallen angels who, having tasted the joys which a limited Jehovah can give, despised them. In these lost spirits Cain sees an image of his own soul. These spirits are beautiful with a beauty that is not of the world; they need not beg life of anyone; they are not afraid to accept life with its abundance of suffering; when the outside world fails them, they create without hope or fear a world in their own breast. Byron's disgust with the simple goodness of the men of harmony takes form in the mighty Lucifer, clad like the night in darkness, decorated with stars, a Lucifer who stares into the depths of sin seeking the strong defiance which his soul requires. Byron is forced to write his way through the turmoil of sin, sin which puts man far from society—incest, fratricide, the inability to bow before God's law; so far must he go in order completely to feel that he is himself.

The hunger for life which took form in the grand gestures of the titans of pain also played in Sterne's sentimental humor. Where is the charm of life without these flickering feelings, that come and go like shadows?—That is the question implicit in Sterne. The sight of a woman's ankle causes a quickened pulse, which occasions a flattering witticism. Or compassion for a little girl sitting and freezing by the side of the road causes a warm feeling to go through the body for a moment, and is gratified in the sparkling eyes brightened by a kindly shilling—and then dissolves with this little pleasure. The charm of a day is made up of such trivia and is ethically quite valueless; what can it possibly mean to a serious man who desiderates something lasting and edifying? Sterne pretends that he is only an innocent child who interrupts the conversation of adults; but one need only observe how significant Sterne was to Goethe and the next generation to understand that his wantonness concealed one of the most dangerous attacks upon the old harmony of the soul.

These adventurous outriders loom large in the eyes of later generations; but after them came bands who cautiously pulled up boundary markers to advance them. Frequently enough they did not know what they were doing—and had they known, they would hastily have moved the markers back again; but they were driven by the desire to experience that which earlier times had thought not worth experiencing. The bands include Schiller-like iconoclasts, sensation-seeking egoists like

28

Chateaubriand, timid poets like Gray, and prelates like Percy, the decorous champion of ballads. Between the older and the younger representatives of this group there lay a half century, but they all shared a yearning to look more deeply into the eyes of life. Sorrow and suffering were for them a new-found treasure. There had been sorrow in the world before, but then it existed for the edification of man. Though it was primarily intended to teach evil men the basic laws of life, it also befell good men and was useful if reasonably applied insofar as it served to educate and strengthen the good men's characters. Of a melancholy mood, Johnson had said, in his deep bass, "If it softens the mind so as to prepare it for the reception of salutary feelings, it may be good; but inasmuch as it is melancholy *per se* it is bad."[1] Now came men who wanted to experience sorrow for its own sake. They threw themselves into it eagerly and when they had been rewarded with a little unhappy love, they made the most of it, so that it would last as long as possible. If Providence refused them true suffering, they invented it for themselves and wallowed in it voluptuously. With diligence they fell in love with girls who already were engaged—and were virtuous, too—in order really to despair. If the youth had the soul of a Chateaubriand he could not be satisfied by mere betrothal and virtue. He needed a girl who requited his love with all her heart but was bound to chastity by a promise to her dying mother. From the rhythm of these hearts arose a pain so great that the primeval forests of America had to be swept by thunder and lightning in order to become a fitting background. Let the girl take slow poison and lie at the verge of death at the moment when the priest proclaims that she can be released from her promise; then Chateaubriand really feels that he is experiencing life. The abundance of pain delights him, for, unlike pleasure, pain is inexhaustible. But, alas, he discovers that man cannot continue indefinitely to draw on this inexhaustible source, and then he understands that "one of our greatest misfortunes is that we are not even in a position to be unhappy for long."[2]

Young arose at night in order to sing about death and the transience of life, and others sang with him about more death and more transience until they wept from emotion over their own emotion. They went out and sat on graves and fingered the bones of the dead in order really to enjoy the horror of death; but the most youthful, like Schiller, were not satisfied with mere bones. Transience received its true, full flavor only when they buried themselves and their beloved, poetically, and heard the thump on the coffin and the falling sod. Schiller entertained his beloved and himself by envisaging a whole world that was a sea of death, where men and women, animals and flowers withered, the one faster than the other, and regerminated in each other's rotting corpses.

It is a shock to hear the ruminating song broken off by Johnson's dictum, "Like melancholy itself, melancholy moods are bad." Now and then in the course of time there come moments when history creates something grandiosely comical merely by placing two persons side by side and lets them reflect each other so that the spectator cannot decide which of the two has the more pronounced comic air. These moments of humor occur where two cultures or two eras meet and measure one another in all seriousness according to totally dissimilar ideals. We are today in a position to poke fun at the troubadours of the coffin who night after night wandered into the graveyard, and could scarcely pass a gravestone without pausing to try their harps. But there is gratitude in our laughter, just as there should be in the smile when a rich youth remembers the forefathers whose bequests he has received. We must not forget that some experiences which are to be counted among our necessities were gained for us by these morbid singers, and that the acquisition cost them both tears and blood.

Behind pain lay yearning; yearning, the flight of the soul from the body, toward a goal which the body projected before it in its own heavy atmosphere; yearning that only existed when one did not think of yearning—and which, once achieved, became an enduring acquisition. And behold, yearning added a whole new world to the known; one might say that it forced man to seek a richer world where a flower was a bud and thoughts were dreams. Previously, assiduity had been necessary to make oneself a man; from childhood one learned to capture moments as they came, and to exploit them one by one. But what if the ultimate goal of life were laziness, to lie still and let the moments come and visit one, to sit on one's shoulder and then fly away again, on and on into eternity? It was of course as a challenge to his contemporaries that Schlegel called laziness the ideal. A prettier name could be found for the experience, but the desire to tease old and rational people arose when man discovered that there was a special kind of

30

wealth, the door to which could not be forced open but which came like the passing moment and lay in one's thoughts when one was quiet.

There were no limits to experience; every new discovery threw open portals to new worlds with wider horizons, and the further the explorer went, the more profound became the actuality which he experienced. He who once penetrated beyond pleasure and pain felt that never before had he been more than half alive. The soul of life consisted of those experiences which were neither pleasure nor suffering, since they lay deeper than the source of tears, as Wordsworth expressed it. Those were the times when ecstasy and severe pain were intermingled, and no one could say which was the more necessary and which the dearer, but only that the moment partook of both. For the new generation life had its nuclei in those moments when the greatest bliss and the deepest anguish threatened to burst the heart. When a youth could say, "an unknown feeling oppresses my heart: is it joy; is it pain—I know not," it was then that he matured into a man. The old dream of pleasure without pain was overcome; not only had strength been found to despise such vapid pleasure, one had attained a realm where the word *pleasure* no longer meant anything.

The new generation rediscovered eternity within itself; or, one might say, it discovered a new eternity that really corresponded to the name because in it that which has been fathomed expands eternally into something unexplored. "Sail out," says Schiller, "where the breeze blows no more, And Creation's last boundary stands on the shore," and from the unknown before one comes the answer: "Thou sailest in vain. 'Tis Infinity Yonder! 'Tis Infinity, too, where thou, Pilgrim, wouldst wander!"[3] The soul, which previously was an ego standing at the focal point of thoughts and wishes, has become a dark chaos on whose border the ego stands, almost helpless. Out of the vast darkness sweep forces over which I have no control. Storming impulses whirl me into deeds of which I have never dreamt. The impulses come from within me, but I am quite as much surprised by their power and content as any spectator might be; yet precisely because they are mine, I am as much in their power as a midge whirled away by a gust. Destiny is powerful because it rises within me out of experiences and dreams, joy, pain, and despair which a moment ago I did not know but which now are essential to my ego. Into the soul has come a whole new world different

31

from that in which I was reared; and yet the new fantastic world is both nearer and more real than anything tangible. If for a moment it leaves me, I stand in the noisy everyday world, calculating and comfortable; the next moment I hear myself laugh at the poor pedant who walks in worn-out clothes and smokes Canaster; and the pedant stumbles in the shadow of this mystical man who laughs. At times the two wrestle just behind the veil of my consciousness; and the everyday self walks about smiling and conversing, but in dreamy expectation, in absent-minded uncertainty, because the wrestling within may at any moment eventuate in a decision which will overthrow all of society's calculations about me. I can account for myself, for I know where I went to school, what I studied at the university, and what my degree allows me to expect of positions and domestic fortune; but the man within me has experienced endless fortune and misfortune, he has assumed guilt, and he has committed himself to plans which I cannot comprehend but for which I am nevertheless responsible. My inner self lies so deep that I cannot survey it, or indeed even see its countenance. That countenance lies far within the darkness; but it *may* emerge one fine day and confront me, and then I, terrified, shall stare myself in the face.

The old psychology was exploded that had analyzed its way to the soul by constructing tables of the various "emotions" and "feelings." The ego which the students of the eighteenth century had explored was only a part, and a small part, of the soul of man. In the new era, man was dreams, and man was revelations which came out of the depths, from no one knew where. Man was the unexpected who suddenly appeared and in a night or in an hour created an entire new ego, its goal, its will, and its premises. Man was eternity, and man was the moment. Man did not shepherd a herd of emotions; he was the blinding storm of the moment, and not before he saw the back of the driving storm could he say "I" in the old sense of the word. The new doctrine of the soul became a poetry of the soul; the new psychology was proclaimed by E. T. A. Hoffmann, the master and the forerunner of the psychologists who were to come. Man was not everyman. Each soul was a world unto itself. The average man did not exist; there were only individuals, and he who would write about the soul had to study the individual. How solitary an individual like Byron or Chateaubriand felt himself to be; he was like a pillar rising about the desert. He felt that pain exalted him above communion with the surrounding world and gave him a soul with peculiar privileges. There was a difference in kind between the average man who lived among everyday things, and Cain who suffered the agony of the universe and grew so large that he comprehended his own nature only when he hovered like a particle in the midst of the infinity of chaos.

Experience also proceeded outwards toward nature. Man had walked and spoken with nature, had thought for it, and had articulated whatever such intercourse had developed. Now a more sensitive generation perceived in nature a wordless spirit which swept over the mind so that there arose in the soul a breeze of feeling, a mood, which to be sure contained nature's meaning but which was born neither by, nor for, words. Gray sat in a churchyard and reflected on an old saw, to wit, that earthly glory becomes dust; but into his mind crept some of the darkness in which trees lead their own peaceful lives, which has nothing to do with defunct generals. From his mind the darkness crept into his verses. Having savored the power of the mood, men searched the nearby woods and fields and gentle hills, and then the frightening ravines and dizzying waterfalls, and ended upon fields of ice. There they heard an echo to the new yearning, and nature's reply sank within them and brought forth a reverberation from hitherto unknown longings in the soul. At first the mood meant little more than a sentimental enjoyment of the surge of melancholy, even though this required new and pompous words. The experience was not so strange that it could not be transmuted into solace and encouragement. But as the feeling for nature deepened and the secret longings of the soul continued to be called forth to light, the mood became more and more ineffable; it revealed a meaning which defied not only words but thoughts. For Rousseau, mountains and waterfalls were as necessary as friends; he could still "enjoy" nature and experience it as a source of great, surging, lachrymose emotions. He sat on a stone by the shore and saw with rapture that his tears dripped down and made rings in the clear water. For Shelley the mood became a destructive passion. In *Alastor* he described himself as drawn to death by the unfathomable and indispensable which at each moment stood before him but at each moment was gone. Of an evening it rose before him like a woman who

33

phrased in song his innermost thoughts about life, while the mountains played an accompaniment of warm colors—and then he awoke to the grey, cold sheen of the glaciers; he was not poorer than before because of his rich experience, and he went on, teased into a further search for actuality. Nature became a reality by being merged with a new set of experiences. Unknown forms were needed so that the new mood could be expressed: the image, the myth, the *Märchen,* and finally the melody—and still the experience was never entirely consumed.

The confrontation produced such poems as the one Goethe wrote on the top of the Ettersberg. There he sat and looked out over the motionless woods, filled with their own ebullience and with never-resting life, while the silence descended suddenly almost like a voice, and he felt the same silence steal into his restless, teeming soul. That moment, when the words and his own soul descended into silence together, lives forever in "Über allen Gipfeln." The experience of the peculiar unearthly power of silence when restlessness sinks to rest, the ineffable feelings, as full as if all eternity were gathered into the moment, live in the little poem, and people recreate them again and again as their own, in overwhelming moments. Germany is full of songs which with the simplicity of half-chanted verse say what had never been sung before: songs like Brentano's "Singet leise, leise, leise," or Mörike's "Gelassen stieg die Nacht ans Land," or Wilhelm Müller's "Hier und da ist an den Bäumen"—all songs which Schubert set to music—or even Heine's: "Leise zieht durch mein Gemüt," which in a few words encloses the surging and yet solemn joy of spring. These poems are comparable to the eulogies of God's revelation in nature that were composed in the previous century, but they contain an eternity with which the Renaissance was not familiar, a momentary eternity which is achieved by a rapturous meeting of the soul and something external to the soul.

Finally, man had so extended himself that his experience threatened to rend his soul asunder. Step by step he discovered himself in nature, bit by bit he was forced on, until he was confronted by something which teased him like a ghost. To explore would no longer suffice; in agony and tears he must grapple with the unknown thing; and he found that he had conquered himself.

As soon as men began to find themselves anew, they looked about for others who had experienced the intensity of life. They recognized themselves in the peoples of distant times. Old books acquired new life; in them were visible the same great feelings which now swept through souls, the new force. The Greek poets and the Old Testament had been studied for centuries and hitherto readers had believed that they understood very well what they were reading. Samuel Johnson read his Homer as he read his Pope, with the same spontaneous pleasure. The thoughts of the ancient poets were considered to be as valid as other sound thoughts, to be independent of accidental or local prejudices, and an ancient tale proceeded so naturally that it nearly translated itself. Actually only a few differences in costume and house-furniture separated Achilles and Dr. Johnson; mere historical details did not obscure the words. Wesley, too, liked to read Homer as he rode from place to place to preach judgment and salvation. True, the evangelist was not so certain as the doctor of the spiritual freedom in Homer. He could not close his eyes to the obvious errors of the ancient sage, who was inexcusably full of heathen superstition; nor in the opinion of a reasonable person was it probable that Odysseus could swim for nine days and nine nights in the sea. Nevertheless Wesley, like Dr. Johnson, formed a favorable impression of Homer's morality and humble fear of God; and for the very reason that he respected Homer so highly, he particularly deplored that such a rare spirit should permit the gods to speak in a way that would make a drayman blush. But to a newer generation Homer and the Old Testament revealed completely novel contents because the new men read their own way into the books and found new answers. They found in them the "poetry of the heart," for which the soul was crying. David and Sulamith were free agents moved by great emotions, who never asked whether it was right to have feelings. They obeyed the heart's command, and could obey it freely because there was no prosaic society to hinder them from being children of nature.

One now read of Achilles' sorrow, "Would that in any wise wrath and fury might bid me carve thy flesh and myself eat it raw, because of what thou hast wrought, as surely as there lives no man that shall ward off the dogs from thy head,"[4] and shuddered, marveling at a hero whose natural feeling was so spontaneous in its grandeur that his passion required the most violent words for its expression.

Now that the portals of the time were opened, a swarm of people entered through them, enticingly exotic in appearance, and evoking confidence by their passionate spontaneity. Macpherson fascinated his contemporaries with Ossianic heroes and heroines who sat solitary on the heaths of Scotland and bewailed their sorrow while the spirits of their forefathers dragged cloaks of fog over the ridges. In the folk songs appeared a world in which life did not flow like a quiet stream but tumbled from one great moment to the next. And finally, the Middle Ages gained a mystic fascination; from the world of the monastery and the tournament came echoes of everything that the ear wanted to hear: dreams, the supernatural, the eternal, struggles in which life and honor were gambled away at one throw, and a divine laziness which felt the breath of eternity in ecstatic dreams.

The same hunger which drove men to nature pursued them through all the kingdoms of history. That which was strange became alive, for it was revived with ardor and vigor. Quiet scholars translated, edited, and described; fervent souls through poetry identified themselves with history, experienced the defiance of Prometheus, the sullen brooding of Cain, and the exaltations of the Huron on the prairies. Previously people had written—or usually, talked—about the past; now they assumed the roles of titans and heroes with their whole souls. In Germany every poet became a bard or a minnesinger; in England Byron donned Oriental clothes in order to ensure a suitable color to his bitter enjoyment of the pains of passion.

Posterity has looked askance at the tone of a masquerade which characterizes much of the writing of the time, the reams of verse intoned over the grave or celebrating an Indian's nostalgia. It is true that the poet often played roles which exceeded his talent, and he did not always achieve solemnity when he appeared bearing one of the harps which his forefathers had lost in the Teutoburg Forest and chanted bardic verses. In a Byron, in a Chateaubriand, there was not a little vanity, or perhaps even mere youthfulness that enjoyed being misunderstood by smug villagers. It may be added that Byron knew exactly how to wear his exotic costume so that the spectators did not forget that under the gaudy garment there was a real nobleman of an ancient line, who could sit in the House of Lords if he wished.

We nevertheless do those men an injustice if we bestow no more than a passing smile on their affectations. It was the need in their souls that forced them to flee from themselves over land and sea, and to search for new egos in strange lands. All the poets who are now forgotten, or who are only remembered for their idiosyncrasies, were pioneers who helped vanquish older, preconceived opinions about beauty and who achieved experiences which our generation cannot do without. These poets are superfluous now and we can laugh at them, for we have inherited what they strove to acquire.

Byron was surrounded by an army of witnesses; he and they were driven by an insatiable hunger to know the people of the world and to penetrate their hearts. From the Middle Ages back to antiquity, from the folk songs to the Edda, to the Orient and the aborigines of America, to the Greenlanders, the Lapps, and the Finns—farther and farther men went, asking about new songs and strange dreams. One may become giddy at the thought of a single generation that tried to embrace a whole world. All the peoples of the East and the West testified to the right and beauty of passion. Every word they spoke proclaimed that life becomes real when it is experienced in its entirety—in fact, they said exactly what the new generation of the nineteenth century was trying to say for itself. Passion was real and poetry was an actuality. If the poet of the people did not have to force his words to make them poetic, it was because he sang the life of the people as it was lived from day to day. There were regions where life itself was poetry; and it was true that men should and could live so that the soul itself was wholly and fully a thing of passion. The folk song passed proudly from one tense moment to the next, so that it seemed to us poor human beings as if a man of the plains suddenly were jumping from mountain top to mountain top. But the hero did not live in the plains; for him life was sublime, and the prosaic was only a pause and not as in Europe the melody itself. The man of nature lived his poem; and when he played and sang, it was because his cup of life ran over and bubbled into art. His actions were deeds and songs, as Herder says, whereas modern man has foundered in a divided world: we live in the darkness of a cave and occasionally climb up with difficulty into the sunshine in order to write poetry or to reflect on life. The Greenlander in his lament does not describe his emotion; he portrays the past and lets the picture of his life be his lament; and, similarly, the warrior experiences the ecstasy of battle again by letting its varying phases take form in words.

Modern men now understand that the primitive human being used images as easily as the European uses his abstract definitions. For the modern poet fine words are a means to beautify thoughts and transmute them from prose to poetry; for the poet of the people, the image and the myth provided the only possible expression of a well-rounded experience. Poetry was once life, one had to remark sadly to oneself; once there were people who lived a life from which we are now excluded. No wonder that they could sing then so that it resounded through the ages, and century after century repeated what they had experienced, while our songs die away in a night. The new generation realized that the bonds which bound modern man to prose were stronger than they had thought; they suddenly felt that the bonds were cutting into their flesh. One could not merely poetize one's way into nature; to achieve nature required labor. Like society, the soul had become something unnatural. Before man became free there would have to be a revolution, more penetrating than the French, one which affected both body and mind. Thus there was born the cultural self-contempt which increased throughout the nineteenth century and which during the last few generations has taken the form of a demand for social and spiritual rebirth.

That is, like nature, the poetry of an earlier time seemed at first the answer to a modest demand by the heart for deeper feeling and for passion; but in the end it created new demands and suggested possibilities that had slumbered within the soul.

The generation sought itself in strange lands and desired to find there nothing but itself. It demanded purity and innocence, nature and passion—and raised objections the moment that passion and nature exceeded the bounds of the poetic and threatened to destroy civilization. Actually, when they said passion and nature they meant only passionateness and naturalness. It is no wonder that they were taken aback when folk poetry in all simplicity answered with something which went beyond what modern men could accept, and which they therefore called savagery. They did not want to grow coarse, but rather to inoculate humanity with nature and let the force of passion ennoble fine forms. Without knowing it, they revised Homer and the Old

Testament, while they read them, quite as much as any man of the age of harmony had done. They rejoiced that Achilles in his great sorrow did not suppress his emotions but permitted passion to drive his speech as far as language could go—and still more were they pleased to see a child of nature defy any decorum; for to be a child of nature who bade defiance to form was the desire of the new generation; but it was understood that the hero did not mean literally what he said. How deeply poetic and deeply human is Achilles at the cremation of Patroclus, when he lavishes wine and jewels on the pyre: so does sorrow force us to forget that he whom we love can no longer speak or feel our caresses. Of course, Homer could not have meant that the dead Patroclus should drink the wine from the earth! Had they understood that the cremation of Patroclus was ordained by established Greek custom; had they understood that the mourning Achilles was not a weak human being, beating with bloody kunckles on the portals of Hades, but a Greek who wanted to give his deceased companion peace in the grave by sending dead enemies down to him bearing the requisites of life—certainly they would have shuddered over Homer. Goethe was offended by Antigone because she says that her brother meant more to her than a husband or children, since a husband can be replaced and new children can be bred. He sincerely hoped that some one would discover this passage to be an interpolation, so that a fleck could be washed from the robe of Sophocles. He expressed his conviction clearly: "After the heroine has given the most splendid reasons for her action and made clear the nobility and purity of her soul, she adduces on the way to her death a motif which is quite unjustifiable and which borders on the comic."[5] The great Graecophile did not understand the need in the hearts of Antigone and her sisters, and therefore he found something comic and ugly in a sentiment which reveals the innermost secret of tribal feeling among the Hellenes, as among all other natural people. Like Antigone, to this very day all over the world a young woman will sigh for her brother. For her his death is a loss to her community of blood relatives. She knows that a child who dies is a broken twig, and that the branch can send out a new shoot and fill the gap; but a brother, especially an only brother whose parents are dead, must continue the family and cannot be replaced. The civilized man was offended by such unnatural feeling.

39

Similarly, he felt himself to be nature's interpreter when he praised mother-love as the highest in the world; those who did not agree with him were unnatural and inhuman.

In the same way that Goethe did his best to defend Sophocles against the charge of "poor taste," the collector of folk songs endeavored to clear his heroes of suspicion by explaining their doubtful utterances as not genuine. When pure, natural taste degenerated, unimaginative people introduced giants and trolls into the elevated society of heroes where, as anyone can see, they cut sorry figures. The giants, the perpetrators of violence, and the magic castles in old tales were in Macpherson's eyes sad evidence that the older poets were mired in childish superstition: "the contents of their tales have, like all romantic composition, many things which are in themselves unnatural and consequently are disgustful to true taste but, I do not know why, they engage the attention more than any fictitious tale which I have come across."[6] It was difficult to speak in defense of the noble savages, for not infrequently they behaved inhumanely before their patron's very eyes. Then it was the patron's duty to endure the accidental ignorance of the times. A lover of antiquity had therefore not only the right but the duty to erase the evidence of the lack of culture of the departed. When folk poetry descended into "barbarism" the collector *consciously* revised it in accordance with his own sure taste. When he felt a need to alter and smooth both contents and form, it was in order to do justice to antiquity and to revive in the work of the skald the nature and truth which had inspired his poetry. These refinements meant that Macpherson's heroes—as we see with painful clarity today—resemble Dr. Johnson more than they do the old Celts. The Middle Ages which inspired both literature and history at the beginning of the nineteenth century were not, as the real Middle Ages were, an evil, proud, and beautiful time of prelates and barons; they were a modern pastiche that resembled its model no more than a stained glass window lit by the moon resembles the human race struggling in the light of common day.

Hellas was treated in the same way. The antiquity which nourished Goethe and his disciples consisted of a one-line poem by Winckelmann: *edle Einfalt und stille Grösse*. Where the glory of antiquity rose before Winckelmann he sought himself in the statues of its gods and heroes; and in the serious, contemplative quiet of the wrought marble he found once more the ideal man that he and the Renaissance could not do without. The figures of antiquity became for Winckelmann a norm which determined what he should strive for and what he could achieve. He never grew tired of preaching imitation as the only means to salvation: beauty, absolute beauty, had been discovered once and for all by the Greeks and if we wish to find beauty or if we wish to express beauty, it is far easier and above all far more certain to imitate the Greeks than to go forth and look at nature with our own eyes. One could see in Rubens what happened when men tried to look at the world for themselves. The discovery of a whole new world in Hellas was not to Winckelmann a demonstration of the potentialities of man; he saw in it only a new and more certain basis for the universal man. He had no need for the belief that the Renaissance had been the apex of creation—as the Renaissance had assumed—for he had achieved the alternative conviction that man had reached his zenith long before: he knew that we could climb the heights again by imitating the Greeks.

The Hellas of Winckelmann and Goethe was just as modern as the Germany in which they themselves lived; the cultured, complex Greek with his self-imposed limitations and unlimited striving, his bacchantic enthusiasm and his resignation, the Greek who continually asked new questions but never accepted a thought before he had made it blood of his blood—that man was as unknown to Goethe as he had been to Voltaire.

Nevertheless, Winckelmann's great and serene Greek—like the mystic knight of Romanticism—by virtue of his familiar appearance brought a new world into nature. Winckelmann was the first who discovered the Greek to be a different kind of man, and by the discovery he enriched the times as much as if he had constructed a new world around the old. By reducing an almost painful richness to a simple formula he made it comprehensible to his contemporaries. Hellas had been an Arcady within the poetic Elysium, where the soul found recreation when it was tired of reckoning and counting money. The pink dawn of Arcady now faded, and daylight showed a real land with men who lived and wrote—of course—independently of the taste of a later time. The miracle had already taken place in Gray's Pindaric odes: the imaginary mountains had turned to stone. Gray tried to elevate his own feeble thoughts and feelings by clambering on the back of Pindar's eagle, which bore him so high that on the horizon he saw a land with mountains that cast dark shadows, and with "woods that wave o'er Delphi's steep, Isles, that crown th' Egæan deep, Fields that cool Ilissus laves. . . Where each old poetic Mountain Inspiration breath'd around: Ev'ry shade and hallow'd Fountain Murmur'd deep a solemn sound."[7]

But every new experience blasted out a place for another, still more violent. As the sympathy with folk poetry grew, it aroused premonitions of experiences yet unknown. The premonitions engendered yearning, and the yearning by magic drew up wealth from the depths of the heart. There was a continuous interplay between discoveries in nature, in the soul, and in history, for after every new rebirth men saw hitherto unknown beauties in folk poetry. The sweet but painful awe of nature which could not be brought in accord with time-honored metaphors found its release through the folk song and folk myth. Goethe's "Erlkönig" and "Der Fischer" incorporated this mood so that what had been half-won through anticipation achieved form and became a thing possessed. Nature acquired new life, and suddenly men understood that the simple barbarian who had watched a fairy girl dance in the moonlit meadow, or had trembled as a giant moved thunderously among the mountains, wrote as he did because he had seen more and experienced more, inwardly, than the provincial bourgeois who carried his picnic basket into the meadows. The dreamer moving in the everyday world of prose suddenly felt a kinship with the poet of the people; he realized that the folk songs had power because they were created with the senses, with the heart, with the whole soul —indeed, he realized that myths and legends were not the products of artistic excogitation; they had written themselves. And by realizing his kinship, the dreamer was encouraged to be himself and to assert his imaginative wealth in the face of all the world's unimaginative common sense. There was an actuality behind material reality, even if it could not be measured or weighed; and spiritual actuality contained a deeper truth than the palpable world, for to the children of nature the soul in things was more important than their utility.

Thus men came to understand the enchanted castles and the supernatural beings who moved obscurely in the background of nature.

They did more. They continued to explore until they found their doubles in history as in nature—men who had voices like our voices but different souls, people who thought differently from the way we think about justice and injustice, who felt revenge to be the most profound ethical command, and yet who revealed themselves as men through the rich beauty of their poetry. History was transformed; from a series of illustrations of great and good deeds and comparable villainies, it developed into a revelation of the overwhelming wealth in the human soul. The discovery of the self now led no further; the discoverer of the soul came to a boundary; facing him stood a stranger whom he must overcome and make into himself.

At the moment that the explorers suddenly stopped and saw that they were confronted by a creature different from themselves and nevertheless a human being, the modern humanities were born. There was only one man at that time whose sharp eye immediately saw the problem in its entirety. Herder understood that the historian should not sit in judgment on peoples. His duty is rather to identify himself with the alien peoples; and until he has learned to see the world with their eyes and in this way to understand their thoughts, he has no right to speak. The historian must move into the homeland of the strange tribe and satiate his eye with the nature which has left its impress on their thoughts. History is full of nations whose thoughts and customs differ markedly from ours because their experience was of quite a different kind. The people close to nature use myth as the direct and honest expression of their experience of nature, because they see something in it different from what we see, and therefore cannot express their knowledge in physical formulae. "They dream because they do not know, believe because they do not see, and act with all their rude unpolished souls,"[8] as Herder put it. For them it was truth that the dawn acted and lightning jumped; in their eyes nature had not been dehumanized, and had not degenerated into the dead machine within which we now move. With the sober eye of a visionary, Herder saw what soon would come. There will be a new history, which will not consist of events set in chronological series or of moral truths marching toward an ideal society, but a series of studies of the souls of men, and which will gather its raw material from the confessions of the peoples

43

in stories and songs and moral traditions. It will not be a history which examines only the mind, but a physiology of the body politic: the peoples' spiritual and social life will be studied like an organism that is born and grows by the struggle of the spirit with its surroundings. History as the moral experience of a people, rather than as the schemes of kings and prelates: that is the goal which Herder sets for the future.

Chapter III

The Struggle for a New Harmony

HAVING ATTAINED self-knowledge, the generation confronted a more difficult task: the creation of a new self out of its new-found spiritual wealth. All was chaos: passion and reason were at odds because nothing knew its place or function. Passion sought the place of reason, and hurled man into madness; reason tried to conduct itself like passion, and the spirit was dissipated in grandiloquence. The old harmony had given cohesion and strength to the soul. When it finally burst under the new pressures, men became titans who stormed upwards to topple the gods from their thrones—and swooned at the first stirring of an emotion. The generation is represented by heroes like Werther and René, who at one moment feel as if life were doubled within them, so that they have power to create new worlds; yet at the next moment they feel existence only as a vast loathing or a delicious languor. Not only the soul was confused; the world was chaotic. The old harmony had extended from man into the universe. Nature had mirrored the thoughts of the soul; nature was governed by those laws of justice which gave strength and cohesion to human life; everything rejoiced in performing the will of the Creator; everything had a purpose. Now nature became a power with an obscure will, which effervesces unpredictably. And as it rises like some mysterious and meaningless beast, it manifests a raging desire to swallow all that it creates in the mood of the moment. It is like the force which stirs ants into continual unrest, and moves them incessantly to build elaborate structures—and lets the lifework of a thousand of them collapse under the foot of a passer-by. Now a chaos stretches out, limitless, through the soul and through nature. The universe lies groaning in labor, and the soul aches.

As the generation discovered, one cannot long subsist on rebellion. Clearly, a new cosmos had to be erected, a completely new harmony. No one had shown the way or even suggested it. The ideal was latent in the chaos that surrounded the generations; from a confluence of forces, it was to arise as that form in which thought and passion, dream and yearning best revealed their mutually complementary strengths. Such a generation is both rich and poor; and for the same reason that

45

it has everything, it has nothing. What will become of it no one knows, but one thing is certain: it will suffer much pain both within and without. Such a generation has no ideal to seek, but it is driven by a force stronger than the attraction of any goal: it has a need.

For them a new world lay within the chaos, and from this new world the religion of the future was to proceed. There was to be no mere renewal, but a creation. Chateaubriand's attempt to arouse interest in the old forms and formulae was a sterile diversion. He lured men into a church by standing outside and expatiating on the architecture and the poignancy of the tolling bell. He invited spectators of taste to observe with him the impressive appearance of a servant of the church—to note the exaltation on his face, the majesty of his words; he himself was passionately moved when he called attention to the holy man's peace of soul and his elevation above all passion. Can one imagine anything more beautiful than a woman as a link between the eternal and the secular, or beauty as a relation between divine majesty in its just order and human nothingness crying for grace? And that woman, at the same time a trembling innocent virgin and a sheltering mother—what higher and more arcane symbol could God use for redemption! Cannot you hear that she is eternally surrounded by the music of harps and the rustle of candid wings?

Yes, this church with its eternal music and the rustle of snowy wings invited weary men and women to relapse in sweet repose. And there were many weary men; and ladies came in carriages to the church, ladies who were dressed in the latest fashion but who nevertheless did not think it beneath their dignity to kneel like ordinary persons. More holy water was used than in the memory of living man. Emperors thought of their Creator and threw men into dungeons; and kings held prayer meetings with real princesses and baronesses. If these may be considered significant events, then indeed there went a Pentecostal storm through the lands; but one must also add that a bad summer succeeded that Whitsuntide. Outside, the world lay in chaos and called for workers; and because of the noise from the ensuing toil, the rustling wings, as well as Chateaubriand's falsetto, remained unheard.

On the threshold of the new era a prophetic figure proclaimed a world of unlimited dimensions. Blake's poetry suggests the possibilities which then existed for those who would build a new world, and may warn us of the direction in which introspective experience necessarily must lead. Blake—a poet and an artist—by himself and by virtue of his own inner life emancipated himself from the attitudes and thoughts of the Renaissance. His poetry is unique in its naïve directness and its respect for the manifold splendor of life. Rejoicing, he sings the tiger that flames in the darkness, with muscles of iron and claws made to tear living flesh; he rejoices in a beast of prey in a time which consoles itself by a belief in the justice and goodness of the laws of nature and which therefore does not dare to look with open eyes into the virgin forest. He sings of the summer evening as if poetic descriptions had not been written before, as if it took no thought to create an experience nor a poetic subject to create a poem. He sings of everything that meets his eye, large and small, beautiful and terrible, with the same joy that something so small or that something so awesome exists. He is not aware of a harmony that gives every thing and every living creature a fixed place in the world; he knows only abundant life. Fixed laws transpierce everything from plant to man, said Blake's contemporaries. No, every creature has its own law, said Blake. "One Law for the Lion and Ox is Oppression."—[9] "The apple tree never asks the beech how he shall grow; nor the lion, the horse, how he shall take his prey."—[10] "The sea fowl takes the wintry blast for a cov'ring to her limbs, And the wild snake arrays the pestilence to adorn him with gems & gold, And trees & birds & beasts & men behold their eternal joy. . . . Arise, and drink your bliss, for every thing that lives is holy!"[11]

In the middle of this teeming multitude stands man, a world within a world, following the law within his own soul and casting a glance to the reaches of infinity; his life can embrace whatever the infinity of infinities may provide. He does not always realize his wealth. The true life belongs to eternity—a word which for Blake is identical with the imagination; in it everything is equally near: the past is as near as the present, and one is as close to Socrates as to one's wife. For eternal man the senses are always open, and they permit the soul directly to experience the infinite life, beauty, contents and depth of the sun, of animals, and of plants. He does not see with his eyes but through his eyes, and he experiences in nature all that poets imperfectly express; he experiences it face to face, life to life. Most people, how-

47

ever, close their senses and for them nature is only something that one can weigh and measure; and he who once has closed the doors can experience nothing more; he cannot comprehend that the actuality which his senses admit to him is only a limit. His part he calls the universe. Nature has become his prison, and his prison diary is called science, and from his one fall follow all the fruits of sin. In his prison he constructs laws. One animal he calls good, another he calls evil. He calls himself good at certain moments, but at others, when his deeds are of a different cast, he calls himself evil. For him there is no whole; he cannot see that life has many facets and that in this, strength subsists. Therefore he takes the peculiar characteristics of his prison and makes them his ideal. Everything else he fears; in this way he saps his own strength. But one cannot fear without hating. In order to maintain his prison law he must force all things to bow beneath it. In the wake of law there is wailing, hypocrisy, and cruelty. When law is perfected, man is dead: a living corpse. The church, the prison, and the brothel are his monuments.

In the saint, on the other hand, the law is perfected, and therefore he dies a second death. Only he who can sin can be saved; because the sinner can understand that a life subjected to limits is hell. Hell is beautiful, great, fascinating, frightful. Its god is Satan, the powerful, the magnificent, the dreadful. To live is to suffer hell, with a suffering that mingles joy and pain, rejoicing and weeping—the fullness of life. Only through the sufferance of hell may man achieve salvation. Eternity is not empty and characterless; it is not the opposite of hell; eternity consists of forms, colors, animals, the sun, and man. Hell is grand because it is eternity delimited and imprisoned. No man can be saved by denial; the law is death, the way to freedom lies through passion. Only by being oneself completely, and by taking Satan upon oneself—loving, hating, and following to their ultimate reaches the mighty impulses of the body and the soul in work and in pleasure— does man find his eternal self. And the eternal self is selfless, the end- less love which knows no limits because it is all-embracing. He who knows only passion as egoistic enjoyment steals the bread of life and eats it hidden behind a curtain, as Blake expresses it—he never achieves freedom.[12] He who revolts is more tightly chained than any prisoner. True passion, on the other hand, is the perfected state of all capacities

48

of the soul to immerse and merge the self directly and naïvely into the eternal life of man.

Blake proclaims the limitless expansion of the self as the way to salvation. His religion is identical with life itself. Eternity is God and it is man—what else could it be, and how could the one exist without the other? This god-man descends at the Fall to become Satan, the spirit of limitation; and he rises through the agony of life to the true life, unless he denies the splendor of life and subjects himself to law. To live is to experience and to call forth. The true man is like a poet, he also creates a reality. He is not a slave of conditions and their interplay; he is a rapt player of a game.

Blake takes his images from many sources: from the Bible, from Gnosticism, from the Mystics, and from Swedenborg. He refers to Jesus as He who descended and took up Satan's burden and by way of the cross became God. But images are for him only the ways by which men have expressed experience, or the impulses to express those thoughts that accompanied them; in the fire of his own experience he reshapes images and makes them new. For Blake there exists only one reality: the individual soul's struggle as Satan, its suffering as Jesus, its splendor as God.

Blake however did not become the prophet of the nineteenth century; his voice died away within his own infinite world, and there was silence. Not until the turn of the next century did the break with the past he had announced become fully apparent; and men recognized him as a prophet only when they stood and fumbled at the doors which he had opened long before with complete assurance; and in his words they then recognized the experiences which they themselves had acquired at great cost.

Although in the age of Werther and the Romantics the harmony of the past had ceased to act as the highest law of life, the influence of traditional ideals continued to hover over the creative process. A worldorder does not disappear from the minds of men at once when inwardly the soul has exploded it. The formation of a new order must take place during a struggle with the old, a struggle which again and again ends in compromise or even surrender. This struggle is external, because any generation contains both radicals and reactionaries, and because the old order lives on within a large number of individuals; it is also internal, insofar as the old habits within the soul—even in the most zealous revolutionary—continue to attempt to dominate the new content of the soul. The generation of a time of transition carries deep within it a longing for the simplicity and clarity of harmony. Herder, Goethe, and Shelley looked back to the ideals of an earlier age and sought even in their most mature works to pour into the great old commandments new life drawn from the wealth that the expansion of the soul had brought. Even the new men often could not tear themselves away from the old ideals. Those who revolted, by their revolt became aware of their individual selves. If the world had been changed in conformity with their demands, they would have fallen to earth, faint and empty. Men like Byron and Chateaubriand were not revolutionaries but birds ominous of storm, borne forward by the gust of revolution. Shelley drew all his ideals from the past; his poetry lives and breathes as part of the struggle between the new craving and the old reality. Throughout his work a strange dichotomy exists, as if there had been two poets, a seeker and a prophet. In his *Alastor* and "Intellectual Beauty" he proclaims his experience. Like the Romantics in Germany, he senses a world behind the veil of nature, a complex actuality in whose wealth all beauty germinates. He sees himself within that world, but with a strange face; in the unknown realms his desires have taken on substance, but the mysterious soul teases him by always withdrawing into nature when he reaches out his hands. He can evoke the new world so that it stands between him and nature, but it will not itself come close to him or merge with him. In his verse there resounds the complaint of the lover whose heart has sought an ideal in the distance and remained there. His life is like the leaves of autumn carried aloft by the breadth of the approaching storm and hurled into the dust of the road or upon sharp thorns. By the time he writes *Prometheus Unbound* all pain has vanished for the prophet, and he sees a new world rise, radiant, from the sea: waterfalls tumble from the mountains above which the eagle hovers, the old dragon that called itself God crashes into the depths, and man, who hung patiently waiting, nailed to the cliff of suffering, descends into flowering meadows. But the beauty of the new world is not the enigmatic splendor which Alastor-Shelley sought throughout the world; the new earth of Prometheus which arises after the fall of the evil god is a world ruled by justice such as the men of the Renaissance had imagined, but radiantly transfigured into a more essential magnificence. He populates the world with men and women who have simply shed the old vices and expanded the old virtues to perfection. The passions have been purified in thralldom so that they now wander freely without doing harm, as tame as fawns that have been fed in a park. The blessed draw and paint without daemons in their soul, they build temples, and make statuary and conversation; what they are to paint and to talk about, the gods no doubt decide. Together with the unlicensed emotions all ugliness has vanished: the clawing beasts that stained the earth with blood, the ugly toad that made the sensitive recoil, these have been transformed in a miraculous fashion, as if hideous sloughs fell from them and they became good and beautiful through a mere change in shape and color. The Elysium which Shelley the prophet proclaims is nothing but the heaven of the Christian Renaissance transformed into a secular Eden where the gentle, purified teachings of Jesus have conquered; and only Renaissance men who are not bored when the devil and suffering and ugliness have been excluded from the realm may dwell in this paradise. The complete happiness which Shelley praises is based upon the Renaissance beliefs that paradise appears the moment evil has been cancelled, and that the soul of evil is lust for power, personified in the tyrant who chains and torments the free, naturally good, gentle, and just man.

Shelley never found a new harmony which could unite his ideals with his desire for experience. The old and the new man existed side by side at the depth of his soul, and alternated in directing his pen when he wrote. What Shelley did not succeed in doing before he met his death at the age of thirty, Wordsworth accomplished. Like Shelley, he sensed the spirit behind the forms of nature, and he learned to rest in it and, through a silent and pregnant absorption in the moment, to allow the Eternal to speak within him.

Wordsworth early achieved familiarity with that spirit of nature which had teased Shelley during his short life; from childhood it was closer to him than his own heart. He had grown up among hills, and from the time he had first opened his eyes his soul was filled with images and impressions which, layer upon layer, created him. One may say of Wordsworth what he said in his poem about Lucy: when

51

she watched the graceful motion of the storm cloud, her own figure was molded by silent sympathy. When she put her ear to the murmuring rivulet, its beauty passed into her face. He saw nature, he thought it, he felt it when as a boy he ran his traplines on the hills at night or climbed the crags in search of ravens' eggs. He was as sensitive to the shifting moods of the sky as the waters are: "From Nature and her overflowing soul, I had received so much, that all my thoughts Were steeped in feeling."[13] So deep were these impressions that they even prevented traditional mythology from imposing itself upon him like a suit of armor. He was unable to see the spirit of a little child, sitting and crying under a lonely hawthorn, nor could he see a fallen warrior's shield in a wet and glistening stone on a mountain; he was unable to discover a nymph in the waters of a spring—he required a countenance and a configuration, not human, but peculiar to the spring. Into his intimacy with nature crept far-reaching presentiments when a familiar vision, suddenly, through new enlightenment or the antici- pations of his soul, overwhelmed him, as if the sight had never existed before; when the banks rushed spinning past the skater and suddenly it was as if he saw the earth roll through the spaces of heaven into the dying sheen of the sunset, and then a moment later the sheet of ice lay like a dream upon an ocean which no movement had yet penetrated. He felt the quiet of the evening as a weight of joy which held him fast to the spot; his sight rested upon the landscape until it saw noth- ing; but the visions possessed him. In fact, his life was most profound at those moments when his soul and nature united to form a prolonged and silent mood: In these hours a holy quietness descended upon my soul, so that eye forgot to see and that which I saw seemed to me something inside, a dream, a vision in the soul.[14]

When his sojourn at Cambridge tore him away from this inter- course with the hills and heaths of his native countryside, he felt as if something hardened within his breast. He wandered in intolerable emptiness and disgust, as if life itself had been extracted from him. When he revisited Cumberland he was most clearly aware of his mis- fortune. He hastened home full of expectation, but the charm was broken; the hills no longer answered, or at best there came a flickering glimpse which only sharpened his bitterness. As young people do, he sought to explain the error as his own, he accused himself of frivolity and shallowness and vowed both penance and reform, but neither his sin nor his remorse availed. His soul was shattered. His enthusiasm for the French Revolution buoyed him up for a time, but when he saw his ideals fail there also, he exhausted himself in an attempt to disentangle good and evil, himself and mankind, and to discover a firm moral foothold. In the end he threw up his hands in despair and surrendered—and behold, at the same moment his old soul arose and folded him in its embrace. The sanity of his childhood returned and nature stepped forth in all its splendor. He went back to his native region, built himself a lodge in the shadow of the venerable hills—and that is the end of Wordsworth's story.

From that time he dwelt within the wisdom of his childhood. He had learned that the depths of the soul, which expand mysteriously in silent hours, are wealthier than the consciousness, the common light of day, and he remained quiet so that these depths might speak to him in their power. He is convinced that the wealth of the moment does not come through the process of learning but through the integration of experience in the depths of the soul. Experiences must be transmuted to wealth in the depths, there where the soul is not a chaos but an incessantly shaping energy. Within the mind impressions are received and are superimposed upon one another, layer upon layer, and an image rises through the laminae; it acquires substance, selects and absorbs memories, and enters the light no longer temporal but eternal. He also finds that his soul is linked to a soul external to himself, or that it expands into nature and through nature into the unknown. He experiences the universe as a complex of spiritual galaxies; we stand on the periphery of our life, and impulses come to us from regions beyond the system which is illuminated by our sun. All faith has been made needless by the direct wisdom of experience.

None of the usual labels suits Wordsworth. He bears the radical characteristic of our culture: he knows of no other riches than those felt through the senses; even the most ineffable moods which remove his soul beyond the limitations of time and space have come to him by way of the eye and ear. Ecstasy, vision, the inner light, the inner sense —these are all futile phrases when they are used with regard to Wordsworth's experience, which he expresses with a psychological keenness and a poetic vision that elevate him not only among the great poets but also among the great reporters of psychic phenomena. His closest congeners are Goethe and—at a slightly greater distance—Friedrich Schlegel, in his descriptions of those passionless moments when the soul opens and allows external currents to flow in, so that a unity of thought and feeling forms, "that serene and blessed mood, In which the affections gently lead us on,-Until, the breath of this corporeal frame, And even the motion of our human blood Almost suspended, we are laid asleep In body, and become a living soul; While with an eye made quiet by the power Of harmony, and the deep power of joy, We see into the life of things."[15] From his poetry there emanates a new concept of the soul as a unity, rich but amorphous, which can be concentrated wholly and entirely in an instant.

Nor are the religious formulae applicable to Wordsworth. For him God is much more actual than any words can express; His eternity and complexity defy all formulae. Whether He is personal or impersonal, whether He is subject to conditions or not, become laughable questions to those who have known Him; Wordsworth does not even call Him God; the immediate reality of experience supersedes all nomenclature. "I have felt A presence that disturbs me with the joy Of elevated thoughts; a sense sublime Of something far more deeply interfused, Whose dwelling is the light of setting suns, And the round ocean and the living air, And the blue sky, and in the mind of man: A motion and a spirit, that impels All thinking things, all objects of all thought, And rolls through all things."[16] Through his own experience Wordsworth rediscovers harmony. The ethical demand he makes is that man must find his way within Nature and her vast rhythms; he must let himself be carried forward on those great waves so that all his life and all its deeds bear the mark of eternal peace. When experience is allowed to germinate in the quiet of the soul, it arises not only as nourishment but as a force—a deed of kindness and of love stems from the quiet beauty of a flower seen many years before; love and loyalty grow strong because they do not know whence comes the strength to love and to hold fast. The substance of the newborn human life can naturally be arranged under the categories of the old virtues—goodness, justice, and the rest.

Wordsworth has neither run away with Satan's booty nor made truth out of the passions which Satan has been allowed to distort into lies; the daemons in the depth of the soul occupy as little place in Wordsworth's world as in Shelley's. It was easy for him to feel at home in the older England. Those who see him sitting with bowed head during divine service, or speaking outside the vestibule in defense of time-honored custom, accuse him of being a reactionary. They do not take into account the fact that the older institutions and ideas have been transmuted in Wordsworth's mind and in his poetry so that they form a new wealth and possess for him new and greater possibilities. He has constructed his harmony on a new basis, of which the radices lead down to the depths of the earth, even though he rejoices to include as much as possible of the walls of the old house above the ground. The older harmony still has sufficient power to soothe and bind him so that he is not perturbed by any recognition that the new life requires new forms. He can moralize in as smug and squeamish a fashion as any old maid, but he has provided a plinth for the old maid's moral code which raises and equates the dicta to the creative powers of natural law. Wordsworth has seen duty as a goddess who protects the stars from wrong and keeps the heavens fresh and strong, while flowers spring up where the god walks, and fragrance embraces his path. He leads men to a spring which gives them strength to keep the law—and at times the strength to destroy the law in accordance with a greater need. Within the soul nature gives birth to an abundance of beauty, and a fullness that must find an efflux and at every trial elevates the ideal still more. The new basis Wordsworth provides is more valuable than his message; that is, his experience is richer than his thought.

Like Shelley, Wordsworth shows how firmly the culture of harmony was entrenched in England. By looking at these two poets, one can more easily understand the strange fact that after a few decades had passed, life in England flowed on as if there had been neither revolutionaries nor explorers.

Chapter IV

Herder

IF I SOUGHT to explain myself to myself, says Herder, I should remain eternally an enigma. For I can express in words only a small part of that which I am, and I know that the ineffable part—the images which come without being called, the feelings which sweep nameless through my soul and which lame or exalt the will—this ineffable part is the stronger. From the depths of my soul there resounds a roar from an ocean, an ocean as inexhaustible as it is mighty. Enough images arise to suffice for a long life; moods arise which can make people seem infinitely beloved or insufferably distasteful. These forces act incessantly, they mould my thoughts; but their vitality is not exhausted in thoughts alone, their abundance overflows into dreams and visions. They take the senses into their service, force the eye to see and the ear to hear when no one has called from without. The reason for this restlessness in the depths of my soul I cannot seek within anyone else, for no one else is like me; indeed, even in an insane asylum I should be insane in my own way. The distinctive quality of a life originates in the mother's womb; independent of all other human lives, it functions in the depths according to its own plan, and sends forth a dreamer or a man of action, a creator or a slave. Nevertheless, as idiosyncratically as this life-force functions in the soul, it is at every moment controlled by its destiny. It has originally nothing within itself and must acquire its substance from without. If it withdrew from the surrounding world, it would brood for all eternity in tedious darkness and silence like the quiet of the grave. Only through the channels of the bodily senses does it reach the light and the realm of light, and being insatiable, it must make use of whatever its surroundings have to offer. It does not experience nature in the abstract but in the particularities of its milieu: not Heaven, but a mist-shrouded peninsula round which breaks a gray sea, or a sunny world reflected in an azure ocean. It struggles with a humanity whose concepts, like environing mountains, have been built and broken arbitrarily time and time again; it is constricted by a social order and a consecrated tradition, so that no generation, no man, ever confronts the surrounding world and sees it pure, bare, as it is. From the world which destiny has prepared for it, the soul absorbs a continuous sequence of impressions, which clot into laminae and are steadily pressed by their successors into the depths.

It is fortunate that dark night broods over these ocean depths, for if a man should hear their dull roar continuously, fear would deprive him of his self-confidence. Energies rise from below as images and feelings, and are shaped into thoughts. From below comes the power to think, and from below also comes the material from which thought is to be created. Without the intellectual labor by which clear unity is created from obscure multiplicity, the soul would become a sterile chaos. The life of the soul consists of the reception of impressions and their shaping. The soul rules by virtue of the collaboration to which it coerces its refractory vassals, the emotions and inclinations from the depths.

The beginning of freedom is the recognition of slavery. Through the interplay of the outer and the inner, of life and what life brings, the soul grows. It *is* not; it strives ever to *become*. The goal does not exist outside of life; it is within, in each moment and its possible perfection. When perfect interplay has been achieved, the contents of life direct its energies towards the achievement of a still richer harmony, a more sublime realization of self.

The soul, then, cannot disengage itself from its surroundings. Everything which happens to mankind casts its influence into the depths as sorrow and happiness, suffering and exaltation. It is not merely that men are bound together so that one man's folly may drive a society into misfortune; anything one man has thought enters the depths of another's soul as a new energy and there aids in the shaping of new thoughts. Endlessly upward and endlessly downward extends the chain of history, and at every point the same law is in control. Each individual is his own goal; he struggles to achieve the highest beauty within himself, yet at the same time he is the condition of a new ideal that will goad the souls of others. Every society endeavors to find happiness by experiencing a harmonious interplay between its own forces and the demands of the surrounding world. A culture is the beauty in which a society sees itself realized. A culture is also the common ground upon which, after pioneers have broken down the old boundaries and, by commerce or conquest, achieved a new horizon, a later

57

generation gathers and prepares to seek a new ideal which will bring
into a new harmony the abilities of the soul and the possibilities of the
world.

That which has been never recurs; beginning is eternal. Nevertheless, the struggle is not repetitious. The law demands not only a
forward but also an upward movement towards continually greater
beauty. There is no external goal, for the goal lies within the struggle.
Man has sought a principle of existence and has deceived himself with
empty words like *progress* and *improvement*. In this connection the
most serious error has consisted, not in man's deception of himself by
a belief that he can grow more clever and more reasonable through the
succession of centuries, but in his being mean enough to be satisfied
with progress in reason alone. History is the unfolding of possibilities
which have become actual by having compelled human souls to give
them life. The goal of man must be described by a word which is
spacious enough to include not only all that has been made actual but
also that which yet remains ideal; it must be called *humanity*.

Looking down through Nature, Herder sees everywhere the same
law which he found when he considered human life; he sees that the
law rules all the realms of life. Each living thing seeks that form which
fits it best and most completely and in which it is most capable of acting
reciprocally upon the environment. Plants and animals develop inherent ideals that lie within the range of their possibilities, and the ideal
itself strives to exceed the momentary limits of the existing form. The
creatures do not constitute fixed categories of being; life merges into
life. In the veins of all living creatures there is a pulse which streams
upward, and ever more purely towards a higher life. The demarcations
are so uncertain, the similarities so great, that—metaphorically speaking—it seems as if nature employed but one pattern, and by means of
the intrinsic possibilities of the material advanced toward an ever more
clear fulfillment of the pattern, from plant to animal, from animal to
man, and from man to higher, unknown forms. Each creature, including man, strives to overcome its limitations. In the human soul
there is an urge which cannot achieve harmony in earthly life. Our
desire for friendship and love, the yearning of the self to surrender to
something greater, our search for truth and for inward beauty, all these
transcend whatever we have been able to mould into reality within the

limits of our existence. The unachieved ideal presages new forms of life.

Herder's world expanded into the depths, and he never ordered the depths to close against him. Life demands riches, and riches in the depths of the soul demand peace; he who fears ferment and motion within himself, and always wishes to fix the shape of things by dogmas —he shall see his thoughts wither away. He will never experience those great moments when a word, a tone, or an odor affect the depths of the soul and the soul responds with an exhilaration that recreates all things in new vigor and strength. If passion did not constantly recreate man by maintaining his relation to the depths of his soul, he would be in danger of growing askew, just as a body which receives sufficient nourishment only in one of its parts becomes monstrous.

Herder hates the Renaissance because it wished to obstruct the path to the depths, and thus to obstruct the flow of strength; but he retains the old desire for clarity and self-control. The law of life sanctions the peculiarities of the individual and enjoins him to strive constantly for enrichment and expansion—not to progress, not to improve, but to ennoble the impulses and desires of the soul. Life demands growth. In youth the soul must have quiet, it must grow in a sheltered place. The schemes of childhood, the dreams of youth, the aspirations of maturity —all sink down in the soul and are lost until a crucial moment calls upon the depths or the depths surprise the moment. He who is true to himself in his youth need fear no spiritual poverty in his age; his soul will produce a drama of tones and moods and images which will pre-occupy his hours. The inwardness of experience taught Herder the same profound wisdom that Wordsworth had extracted from the soul. But life also requires effort and struggle, for the mind must mould the material that grows within it into an harmonious and integrated whole. Let the stream of life flow through the breast, but make sure that it rises purified through the marrow of the reason and becomes spirit. Herder despises the wild, lawless geniuses quite as much as he hates the slaves of virtue. A hero driven mad by passion and a rational man who has reasoned his heart away are in Herder's eyes equally contemptible.

Therefore he feels no necessity to break down the old forms. Purity, truth, goodness, and beauty are not merely words that he cherishes;

they remain for him the words which express all things. At no point does he alter the old boundary between good and bad; never for a moment does he erase the difference between god and devil. In his ideals the earlier era could have recognized the qualities it prized: clarity of intellect, insight into life's basic laws, exalted sympathy with one's neighbor, and respect for the intellectual freedom of the individual—these were exactly what the men of harmony had endeavored to cultivate within themselves. And when Herder proclaimed to mankind, Forward! Upward! cast off all that is inhuman, strive for truth, goodness, and godlike beauty![17] they would have approved the program as one which led away from the bestial and the sensuous. The outlines of the past had now been given life, and their beauty did not possess that peace which stems from conquest; they possessed a more profound beauty, that gained by man who has transcended his passions to achieve self-control.

Thus Herder achieved a harmony which preserved the nobility of self-control, while at the same time it was able to include all his new-found wealth. The overwhelming power of passion, the spontaneity of the soul and its infinite receptiveness—to all these forces he gave unlimited play; but he calls upon them to aid in the creation of as stable a form, as absolute a clarity as his forefathers had enjoyed in their best moments.

Without the wealth of multiplicity Herder cannot live. In his eyes, each human being constitutes a world in himself; and every nation is humanity. The individual (that is, either a single person or a culture) looks at the world in his own way and sings his own songs of what his eyes have seen. A warrior people chants the ecstasies of battle; the shepherd watching his flock whistles melodies of love; acute minds ponder enigmas; a people terrified of nature invents ferocious gods; and no one can demand that men be other than they are. For all his delight in individuality Herder, a man of harmony, did not abandon his desire to find a unity beyond multiplicity; indeed his emphasis on coherence exceeded what his predecessors had conceived. At every point the human being is bound to his fellows in an organic solidarity which no will can destroy, but a destiny which the conscience accepts and employs. Herder probes so far into the human soul that in the end he attains that great and divine sea into which all thoughts flow.

Nothing true or good is ever lost; in mysterious ways it reaches God— it enters the great mind of creation—and from there it may be recalled and integrated within an individual.

Herder ridicules all the historical ideals of his times: the happy belief in the excellence of one's own culture, the belief in progress and in the deity of progress. He derides schoolmasters who give prizes to the great men of the past if they have furthered virtue. He allows ideals to disport themselves in their complexity before the eyes of his contemporaries: the efforts which undermine one state build up another, and one society swears by virtues which have no value to its successors. The industrious Egyptian, who must follow the example of his forefathers and irrigate his fields on schedule, cannot subscribe to the same virtue as the adventurous Phoenician who ingeniously in fragile ships undertook to conquer the Mediterranean and make the cities along its coast pay tribute to commerce. Thus, ideals differ from people to people, but no one ideal is truer than another. What then becomes of that morality which is to advance continuously towards perfection? And reason? Millennia have passed and millennia have come, burdened with experiences, but no one has observed the human race to advance in intelligence. The Right Reason on which Europe prides itself has come about through a long series of historical accidents; it can only be justified on the ground that it is the kind of reason we need in our particular situation. If the older men reply that the wisdom of history is revealed through the European and his clear reason, Herder asks what would have become of our wisdom and our ideals if the colossus of history had gestured the other way at the decisive moment and the Scythians instead of the Greeks had become the intermediary between the Orient and Europe. Political history, the succession of people upon people, is no more than a sequence of accidents.

But hidden in these arbitrary events lies a deeper necessity, an inexorable law which links man to man, people to people, and allows the wisdom of humanity to appear in the accumulation of experience and the increasing impetus which impulses receive. Whether people follows people in one sequence or another is of little significance; but whatever the series, no individual can be different from or more than the assumptions and possibilities which the experiences of his predecessors have allowed. The driving energy of history does not consist of a perfected

61

ideal which hovers above the earth and little by little is embodied in humanity; the energy lies within the events themselves and it is through their inevitable sequence that the ideal evolves. Through history man perfects himself in a continuously enriched form, and through history there are created possibilities for the realization of future glories which we now can scarcely conceive, as a plant is unable to conceive of human beauty.

The course of history is not directed toward a certain culture but serves a continuous expansion of the possibilities of the soul. It has no goal; and thus disappears the *petit bourgeois* chatter about progress. In place of progress Herder puts development, and he gives this word a richer content that it has ever had before; indeed, he recreates the word. In place of reason or virtue or bliss, as the goal of man's endeavor, he puts *humanity*: the highest form into which a man can mould himself, given the conditions of his time. If in this vague word Herder can state his secure hope of a more abundant future, it is because of his indomitable belief in the nobility of the will to live, as it eternally surges forward in dreams and longings, through blind groping and clever calculation, and drives man to transcend the limits established by the prejudices of his day. In the life of the soul nothing is a matter of chance; all is law. Law holds vigil in the subconscious, innermost life of the soul, and its strength is called passion; it binds man to his fellows in organic union and forces him into ventures which endow his entire race. Simultaneously it motivates the proudest self-assertion and the most selfless humility. Therefore *Humanity* is the right word, for its meaning grows with the increase in riches of experience.

There is no other ruler in the world than this law, and no other ruler is necessary, for none greater and richer can be conceived. Herder speaks of the creator who implanted the law in all his creatures and made man a restless, striving being; but "creator" is only an old word applied by Herder to a new experience. Everything that can be called the highest being is subsumed in law, the passion and the soul of living things.

In this way, Herder brought forth in a form freed from narrow limitations the Renaissance belief in a complete harmony, both external and internal. He sees man and God and the world anew, in greater beauty, by virtue of his recognition of his own spirit, its experience within itself, and its sympathy with the experience of others. History throbs within him as his own abundance: he is a "poor fellow who thinks that the stage upon which his life is played is the only one in the world."[18] Within his own inward experience are born Herder's profound and secure insight into the historical limitations of the spiritual life and his reverence for that which is purely individual, and his intuition concerning the creative significance of direct quiet energies, and his clear view of the role of great personalities in religion and culture.

Chapter V

Goethe

IN HERDER'S FOOTSTEPS came a youth who himself experienced the conflict between life and the surrounding world and who during his lifetime developed his own ideal from the possibilities which his birth, his breeding, and outward events prepared for him. Young Goethe's soul is the resounding abyss. He can embrace all—and more; he advances into life with a desire to exhaust the world's ability to give. Restless, he turns toward light and sound so that nothing may pass without being recorded by his senses. Restless, he changes his surroundings in order to outwit the destiny which attempts to force men to accept the gifts allotted to them. Nature and human life, poetry and science, classical marble and Gothic fantasies in brick—he sucks riches from all things and all men. He is not content to admire and to savor; he would enjoy everything as a woman is enjoyed, and he would enjoy women as well. Destiny conducts a long series of rich intellects across his path—Herder, Lavater, the men of the *Sturm und Drang*—and Goethe does not let them disappear again into the darkness before each has displayed the riches of his heart.

Ecstasy and pain—these are the terms in which Goethe praises life. He demands abundance from life; there can never be too much. The height of good fortune and the depth of pain, even the nadir of despair, all are life and its abundance. Yearning and the unachieved, they, too, are life and therefore ecstasy; it is ecstasy to feel the soul reach out for the unattained and the unknown. Paradox itself is the welcome sign of abundance: the search for truth and the joy of being well deceived, deep painful pleasure, strong hatred and mighty love. Yes, it is joy to stand alone, to be the man whom God has chosen to empty the vial of despair, whom He has created in such vast dimensions that one may not join the host of the blessed and taste the stimulant of faith. What have rules and laws to do with the abundance of life? Life stands above all laws; under its dominance Goethe hurls himself against the rules of society. Sin: I have tasted it in all its divine rapture, and my heart has been soothed by the balm. Does not fire destroy as well as warm and illuminate?—and should man be less than the element? Goethe feels the ecstasy of struggle, suffering, and enjoyment in his relations with men and also—perhaps more strongly—in his intimacy with nature. It occurs first as a dreamy presentiment, then like a pain which is highly pleasurable but remains pain—as he cannot express the experience directly, it steals out in poems that are half melody and half symbol. Again, nature stabs into his breast like a question at the day of judgment: what am I? He does not know the answer, though his life depends upon it. Or nature storms about him as an accompaniment to his own passionate feeling, and he bursts out in dithyrambs and in his superhuman passion enters the play of the elements. But for Goethe at all times nature is strength, nourishment, and stimulation; at sunrise doubt disappears before resolution; in his utmost need he casts himself back upon nature to draw strength like a child at the breast.

Goethe's world became a chaos, confused by its very multiplicity. From time to time he had to stop and think, to reflect, and to consolidate his conquests by conjuring them into the form of poetry. He became intoxicated in chaos, and when his condition grew intolerable, he sought air by writing poetry. In his poetry he laid the past away in a crystalline form, as riches for the future. His *Werther* sprang up from his aesthetic need to comprehend what he had himself experienced. He meditated on his experience until it had worked upon all the facets of his soul and dissipated its force; only when he had understood it thoroughly did he allow it to descend into the depths as the very basis for the future.

In the chaos of his youth there were glimpses from time to time of a cosmos wherein everything would have its place and therefore its beauty. But his world was never finished. His predecessors, the men of harmony, had been created once and for all; they assumed that the mind was formed as the result of one mighty commandment, "Let there be light," let there be order; and out of this "Let there be" came a soul in which the day's work and the night's rest alternated incessantly. To be sure, it was not enough to create; life consisted of an unceasing acquisition of culture, so that what had been credited would be supported and perfected. But with Goethe enlightenment was replaced by genesis; he could feel his soul grow. The youth changes as the laminae of experience accumulate, and by their mergence he becomes a conscious ego; and in the next year's growth his former individuality is submerged in another. The man is born of the youth, but he seeks an even fuller revelation. Each link is organically connected with the preceding, although the growth permeates so completely that the change can amount to a new birth. "I am different than I was a year go; this I consider to be my birthday," Goethe exclaims again and again in his letters from Italy.[19] To be sure, genesis is labor, but while self-education had previously been a labor that the ego performed upon the soul, for Goethe it is the soul that functions, and the ego is only that which consumes the fruits of labor and grows treelike, ring by ring.

In Goethe the course of growth is not a regular progression; there is a point in the transition to manhood when it stays, indeed when it turns back upon itself. While in youth a man desires only to stride outward in order to encircle the multiplicity of the world, in manhood he fends off the confusion of figures and sounds which oppress him. Instead of the youthful prayer, everything at any price, there comes from the lips of the man the severe "entbehren, entsagen": gather a bit here, discard a bit there, but seek above all to mold a unity; and exclude mercilessly whatever you are sure you cannot make coherent with the whole. In his youth Goethe saw the world as his kingdom; his realm was infinite, and in infinity only gods feel themselves at home; but in his heart he felt the power to become a god or godlike. Nothing less could satisfy his yearning; in his need to embrace all things he was destined to achieve the highest. Now having matured, Goethe knew that man must not put himself on a plane with the gods but choose between standing on earth while the oak tree nods above his head or becoming a feather bandied by drifting clouds. His longing to live in all things has changed to a fear of "destiny"; that is, of the surrounding world, which irresistibly grasps and wrenches the soul. For man there is only one salvation: he must fight his way out of the current and use the surrounding world without being used by it.

The ecstasy of life has given way to wisdom: the wise man preserves his own freedom while he levies tribute on the surrounding world; though he seeks intellectual sympathy with men, he does not link his life to theirs. He draws the richest into his circle in order to nourish himself upon their wealth, but he is careful not to bind himself to them in loving devotion, for fear that such devotion should force him to participate in both their pleasures and their sorrows. Against those events which cannot be controlled, the strong and clever man protects himself by acknowledging the power of destiny and by basing his wisdom on reality. He has achieved resignation; he dupes fortune before fortune dupes him.

He no longer has any use for grandiose and effervescent feelings; on the contrary, he avoids everything that can brew a storm in his soul. He has a need of experience, but it must be experience which undulates quietly through his mind; when the rhythm becomes painful, he dulls it by turning away his thoughts from the dissonance. Even a death in his family is for him an opportunity to practice resignation—not to loss itself, but to the erosion of sorrow. Thus he disciplines himself in the enjoyment of restrained emotions. While he would enjoy their energy, he will not allow himself to be dominated by them, to be helpless in their grasp.

Goethe the man is tormented by the multiplicity of the world and that ever-receding profundity of things which had thrown the young Goethe into painful joy. Now when his eye rests on the landscape, his soul is overwhelmed by the thousands of intersecting lines, and he likes the moonlight because it conceals many details with a cloak of shapes. His soul is restless until it learns mastery, and the mastery of the fullness of the world must be gained through simplification. The multiplicity of human life rides him like a nightmare: passion reveals itself to him first in a toga, then in a smock, then in pelts, and in each phase its quality is fellow to its garment.

The force with which the reversal comes is proof enough that it was prepared in the depths. It is Goethe's truest self that rises through the chaos of his youth and extrudes a cosmos completely different in character from what one might have supposed would be the result of the spiritual storm. Werther tempts an unrealized future; the *Italienische Reise* proclaims the rightful mastery of the past, it proclaims his father's or rather his family's conquest of Goethe, the arrogant youth who had left his home to search for a new world, unaware that he carried with him the paradigm implicit in the yearnings of his kin. In his youth Goethe had known that multiplicity and contradictions were riches; he had understood that a pain caused by a friend was worth more than the pleasure of a solitary existence. Now he desires unity as his ancestors had desired it, even if it must be achieved by amputation; now he would exclude suffering even if this means that he must shut out effervescent ecstasy. His conversion does not come as a miracle; in the depths of his mind throughout his youth harmony had lain gathering energies. Beneath the *Freud und Leid* which roused his enthusiasm in his youth, there was concealed real, old-fashioned pain, for harmony feared chaos and felt ill at ease among irreconcilable opposites and longed for the "composure in one's self," which generates security and purposeful action. If one examines carefully the expressions which the young Goethe used about his *Freud und Leid,* one discovers here and there hints of a fear of dissension; in those hints resignation lies latent. These are the passages which one may cite if one wishes to prove how little that Goethe needs to be a Christian; as a matter of fact, he sometimes speaks about his temptations almost like an orthodox saint, he shifts the blame to his fantasy and his abnormally intensified sensuousness; when he is cast between heaven and hell he cries out for peace of the blessed and signs: how long must this my agony last on earth? It is *halb Kinderspiel*; it is also half in earnest.

When the resilience of youth diminishes, a new struggle begins; now it is not a matter of conquering multiplicity but of taming it. Goethe's glance flits restlessly over the multitude; it searches until it discovers beyond some nexus of details the lines which constitute a face. He suffers and struggles, until salvation appears to him as a vision while he stands in the park of Palermo. He saw then that beyond the innumerable species of plants there stands a prototype of which all are variations. He saw then that it was the type which is intrinsic, although it may not be sought among living plants, for it lies within the forms of them all as the true reality. The multiplicity results when the original type takes on various and innumerable shapes, though in so doing it always remains itself. It does not hide behind the plant like a nymph who hides behind the bole of a tree. It is the plant itself, but the plant is not it, except as the individual revelation of a creative thought which uses the form in an effort to emerge. The single plant is only one among thousands of attempts. Incessantly creation struggles with the form to achieve a perfect clarity and completeness in expression, and in all its attempts it imposes its infinity upon the finite. What happens can only be expressed in images; first Goethe speaks of a creative spirit, the reflection of which is visible in a thousand different forms; then he speaks of nature which plays with form and thus generates multiplicity; then again he invigorates his observation by the image of the infinite which repeats itself again and again in individual shapes, without allowing itself to be bound to any form and thereby losing its general validity.

Goethe's vision provides a tremendous simplification in all areas of life and nature. He does not stop with the plant. In the same way beyond the individual animals, indeed beyond the single landscapes, he sought and found the prototypes, and finally he merged them all in nature's grand *Urphenomenon*.

And at this spot in the great panorama of nature is man; within the realm of human existence, beyond innumerable variations, there lies man in the "state of nature," a state which is identical at all times and in all latitudes. In order to discover the "state of nature," one need only glance away from the results of the superficial acclimatizations caused by geographic conditions and the modulations of history, and fasten upon what is essential and lasting. Strangely enough, in the great realm of nature the *Urphenomenon* is hidden by a rich variegation of form and never casts aside its disguise, while within the world of man it once appeared in a pure or nearly pure state as an historical configuration, namely, classical antiquity. In nature Goethe found the prototype as soon as he realized that it should not be sought among living plants. In the realm of man, he retained his belief that truth would step forth to meet him, wearing flesh and blood. Surrounded by nature he had the most profound moments of happiness when he glimpsed the *Urphenomenon* beyond multiplicity, but in society he, a man, confronted men in their multitudinous variety. Hellenic antiquity shows us a natural man harmoniously developed according to his surroundings; even the folds of his clothing complement the lines of his body. There is only one true culture, one true man: the Hellene. The body of a Greek possesses the perfect beauty of his type; by his hygiene he perfectly cultivates his type; his costume has nature's own ingenuity; his social forms evolve in accordance with the needs of the soul, as his clothing with the needs of the body. All his actions accord with the development of Nature; all his feelings accord with her serenity. When he writes, he is content to reproduce his experience in sensuous imagery;

he makes no attempt to plumb the reactions of the soul during the process of experience. By means of this fictitious Greek, who had been invented by Winckelmann, Goethe proclaims himself as one who has overcome multiplicity; by learning to submit to destiny and to exploit the possibilities delineated by the conditions of man's life, he has conquered destiny. When he ceased assaulting his own limitations and demanding the impossible, he obtained as his reward the quiet beauty of harmony in his life. Goethe found in Winckelmann the solution of all problems; Greek literature and art should be the paragon for all poets in all regions at all times.

Now that Goethe has satisfied his need for a norm he makes simplicity the law of his work. He who once exploited his own experience to give life to his poetic works, he who took his intimate knowledge of his friends as the material for his poetry—he will now admit into his work only the types of man, freed from the limitations of time and individuality and seen in situations and positions which evince their enduring characteristics. Within a nature flowing in pure lines there moves a world of man which is related to its surroundings as figures to a landscape: the old man leaning on his staff speaks words of wisdom, the mother nurses her child, girls go to the fountain with their pitchers—these are natural types, ever-valid situations; and the poet must restrict himself to this universal validity. He must not portray a man but *the* man, and similarly he must not describe a city but the city that may lie everywhere and anywhere. In his zeal to introduce the universally valid in his work, Goethe slips into the allegorical forms of the eighteenth century. He who in his youth indicated as the artist's secret the reproduction of the external through the internal world; he who took up the traditional materials, and compounded, kneaded, and re-formed them in order to proffer them *in eigner Form, Manier* (as he himself expressed it)—he now busies himself with pastiches of Greek models.

The sudden access of the zeal with which Goethe swears by Winckelmann clearly indicates his impatience to find the universal man who will provide the pattern for the design of his own life. Superficially viewed, his relation to Winckelmann is one of complete dependence. After his intimacy with Herder his new enthusiasm is almost incomprehensible, but in reality his humility as a disciple rests on a deep personal dedication augmented by his spiritual consanguinity with his new teacher. The ideal of the master is the god-sent answer to the most devout prayer of his heart.

Thus Goethe regained the ruling concept of the Renaissance—the fixed and the unchangeable—without surrendering the newer experience of the infinite progression of life. Life in its multiplicity is a consequence of the struggle between the soul's immutability and the modifying power of conditions. The eternal must break through the forms if there is to be a revelation. Now Goethe enters confidently into nature, since he has learned to see it, not simply, as something unchangeable, but rather as something that is necessary—which despite all variation and development in its aspects remains fixed in itself. Nature has lost its terrors; Goethe can lose himself among its wonders, having learned that one can master it by taking up one's stance upon the "concept of the sempiternal" and thence glancing down transversely through the seriations of the cosmos. The informed analyst feels an increasing pleasure as he clambers through the wealth of forms towards the type, towards the splendor of the *Urphenomenon*; or strides downward and outward into variegated beauty. In nature as in the world of man the individual has found its true function when it demonstrates that it is not something arbitrary, directed only by its own will, but that it exists in inner truth and necessity according to the law of the type to which it belongs.

Thus the past and the present are united for Goethe; manhood with its demand for perseverance absorbs youth with its craving to enclose life's multiplicity. Then for the man *entsagen* is possible; he may be resigned to his limitations and seek his happiness in useful work under the conditions offered him by his surroundings without sacrificing the horizon of eternity. Goethe takes his stance in the finite so that he may stride outward in any direction to the infinite; for man the only path to eternity is labor.

Manhood and youth were reconciled, but manhood was the stronger. The abundance of the world had to become subjugate to unity, as Goethe's poetry demonstrates. In order to live, youth must sacrifice its love of what is individual; it must sacrifice its ability to surrender, and the ecstasy of surrender.

Nature is the life of the spirit. When Goethe pursues it upwards through the realms of plants and animals, he sees how perseveringly it strives for greater and greater perfection, and that through all obstacles it moves toward men as the highest goal or the highest form of expression so far attained. In this apex of creation there exists everything that occurs singly and fragmentarily among the lower creatures, but here united in a harmony; and in man the momentum of nature is guided into new paths. How the development occurs, Goethe never clearly suggests. As a rule, he is content to allude to the molding influence of environment, and his single attempt to explicate the theory of adaptation produced only insignificant echoes of those contemporary speculations which we now associate with the name of Lamarck: such notions as that the desire to hear better creates sharper ears; that a marine mammal which leaves the sea must develop legs because its heavy body, previously borne up by water, now flounders helplessly in the mire. Actually, Goethe's explication is controlled by his scrutiny of the life of plants, from which he fetches his most personal images of the course of development. The prototype is to be found in the leaf, for everything that the plant develops, even its fairest flower, develops through changes in the leaf. When the seed germinates, the plant bursts from the surrounding night; it towers up joint by joint, becoming constantly more lobed and divided; and when the leaf is perfected the energy is guided into the rigid stem, again to divide itself among the polychromatic leaves of the calyx. And in the same way a segment of a tapeworm develops a head, and the vertebrae of an animal a brain; the bees achieve perfection in their queen and a people in a hero.

The contention between spirit and form Goethe approaches from the standpoint of history. The forms compose a chain in which each individual link has as prerequisite the entire preceding series. But though Goethe's view is temporal it is not historical, in the usual sense of the word. The concept of progress through generation after generation has validity only within the realm of form; the attendant spirit does not change; it remains eternal, beneath its variations; it is not carried on the wave of form from one epiphany to another. The prototype itself exists in all the forms, and the creative energy of each form stems directly from eternity. Actually, every single configuration emerges from the depth of the *Urphenomenon,* being conditioned in its appearance both by its predecessors and its surroundings.

Goethe's *Urphenomenon,* like Herder's world spirit, can be interpreted as law; it *is* the law in all living things, but it is not a mechanical law. It is an energy, because it is life and contains the luxuriance of life. Further, it holds within itself all the fertility of life and life's unbounded potentialities; finally, one must add, shape is one aspect of its being. The *Urphenomenon* is distinguished from the temporal by its freedom from particular form, and the temporal is distinguished from the *Urphenomenon* by its necessary restrictions to fixed form.

The *Urphenomenon* is the glory which is reflected in all life, the beauty in nature and the beauty in man, the radiance of eternity. In the refraction of light the perfection of color is made visible; so, in the practice of virtue a creator reveals the attraction of beauty in order to entice men beyond sensuality. The struggle of the *Urphenomenon* with form explains the existence of ugliness and malformation in the world, without reflecting upon God. The beauty of form depends upon the relative completion and harmony with which the outward and inward are intermingled. The amount of ugliness in existence may be ascribed to a refractory Nature which the infinite cannot overcome; only where the spirit succeeds in creating a completely efficacious form can its beauty break fully into light.

In the *Urphenomenon* we grasp the hem of God's garment—as much as we ever can. In form He is half hidden; in form He is half revealed. The form is wholly God, but He is not the form. Everywhere we are confronted by the unfathomable, which irresistibly draws us beyond the boundary of the sensuous. Bit by bit through cognition we conquer God in nature, though we never attain the abundance of the divine. And other than gradual cognition, there is no way to God. In order to bring Himself within our vision, He has wrought the variegated garment of nature, within whose folds we may see the lines of the immortal form, at once adorned and hidden.

When Goethe explained his experience to Schiller, Schiller exclaimed, "That is not an experience, it is an idea."

"It is strange that I can see ideas with my eyes," said Goethe, slightly offended.[20] Of course Goethe was right, and Schiller was wrong. Goethe experienced the *Urphenomenon*; he found his reality, and therefore he was certain that no accident could have misled him. He had rediscovered the vision of his forefathers, who everywhere saw the species before they saw the individual; but within the species Goethe had found individual abundance, so that for him nothing is lost in unity. But to experience nature as it is, is not simply to observe it; to see eternity, the soul must purify itself, must rid itself of desires and lusts, must empty itself so that it may be filled anew. Nature is exacting; as long as man tries to augment his experience by his own impressions, nature jealously conceals its being from him.

Silence signifies a union of nature and the soul, so that the two intermingle freely. This pure silence is precisely the passionless quiet which strikes and fills the soul, without jarring it because of eagerness to achieve a predetermined goal. The soul waits until its energy is transmuted into action, and by action it finds or creates the true goal. Then the man experiences in himself the same profound quiet which broods over nature as it takes on form. Thus nature creates beauty with somnambulistic certainty, in the inspired moments of the artist. But really to experience nature and through nature really to experience oneself, good will and emotion are not enough; here the highest reason, alertness, and strenuous thought are necessary. Observation must be thought and thought must be observation, says Goethe, and here he expresses the confluence of the elements of his soul and the things outside it, whereby nature becomes not an object of his thought but the thought itself. In order to achieve this junction with nature, man must prepare himself laboriously. In his letters from Italy, Goethe has suggested the bitter struggle which the process of purification demands. Pencil in hand he steals up to nature. Again and again he announces an imminent triumph, when he will capture the abstract shape of man. He alludes to a mystic line which he will discover: presumably, he searched in nature in the spirit of Winckelmann and the eighteenth century for the ideal line in which all lines are concealed. Strangely enough, when dealing with man, he takes Winckelmann's short-cut to the *Urphenomenon* by studying antique sculpture instead of the throng of men about him.

This was the law: obedience above all. Man must not learn more than what reality discloses, by peering behind the veil; nor may he take before to him 'tis given. But by the feeling of unity which silence

74

brings there is fostered within the soul, as a mood, the essence of the thing. Nature has a meaning—or a soul—and he who has not seen the soul, shattered by refraction from the thousand facets of Nature, is no better than a brute.

When Goethe broke with his youth and sought a stance in the finite and the limited, he suddenly retreated many paces, searching for firm ground beneath his feet. For a time words like *God* and *immortality* lost all meaning, and when he heard them spoken by others, he felt a need to deride them, in an attempt to convince himself that he belonged to the world of tangible facts. Cautiously he advanced until he again achieved the profound experience of eternity within the finite world, so that the words *God* and *immortality* again took their places within his vocabulary.

In his manhood, Goethe constantly advanced from the finite farther and farther into infinity, and nearer and nearer to the eternal. In *Faust* he has proclaimed the achievement of his maturity: through self-development to defeat, through defeat to effective limitation of self in altruistic labor, and finally through discipline of the self to a new birth which reveals God in unanticipated splendor. Goethe's mature work contains no hymn celebrating a victory won by suffering and death; rather, that work is a weighty rebuke to the presumption of youth and a promise of reward for him who learns to despise lust and to seek happiness in faithful labor. In the hour of death the heavens open and the *Urphenomenon* irradiates the world with its brilliance. There God reveals himself to Faust as never before; nevertheless, the form of his revelation is no other than it was in the soul's hour of need. Here and there the *Urphenomenon* reveals its splendor by breaking into finite configurations: love, purity, and truth (or the loving, the pure, and the true, for form and content are indivisible), but now its splendor is projected much farther into eternity than any human eye previously had seen. One by one these images of the divine—Pater profundus, Pater seraphicus, the blessed boys, Gretchen—appear to Faust, and by their help his soul rises higher and higher toward infinity. How far, neither Faust nor we know. But we know what awaits him: he becomes more of God, and he participates in the creative energy of God. He becomes the highest form which the *Urphenomenon* has yet achieved; and through Faust, we ourselves gain an insight into the beauty of the eternal God who never rests in any one configuration but tirelessly moves forward from splendor unto splendor.

In order to express this experience Goethe must utilize myth, and he finds in the Church's accumulated treasury of images the forms which can reproduce what has been experienced, though never beheld. But no one will ever be able to interpret Goethe's day of judgment and his struggle with Satan by studying the Church's eschatological teachings. He takes up a metaphor and recreates it, making the myth as new as if he had made it out of nothing. All successful interpretation must be derived from Goethe's own experience. When, therefore, his experience approaches the perception of faith in the salvation of the soul by defeat and rebirth, this concord testifies to a relationship in the depths of his spirit. It is still more significant that this Faust, who would win the whole world and through the greatest and most comprehensive experience gain his own soul, but who in the end overcomes both himself and his youth—that this Faust has become the god-man in whom posterity has seen its own countenance.

Chapter VI

Schlegel and Novalis

THE YOUNG MEN who followed Goethe were a generation unafraid. They did not feel the master's need to be sparing with experience but said, as he himself had said in his youthful enthusiasm, "All pain in its entirety; all pleasure in its entirety!"[21] For these young men—Friedrich Schlegel and Novalis—and when they are mentioned Caroline should not be forgotten—life was a tempest of contradictions. They would live it no other way, for they could not and dared not be content with less than actuality. They did not want to diminish the joy of reality even though it threatened to burst the heart, and they could not do without its pain, which they felt to be man's badge of nobility, for they had discovered that the soul is changed by suffering. The opposites lay close to one another, indeed were interwoven. A smile could border on unspeakable anguish; abandonment to pleasure could co-exist with quiet anticipation. They had looked so deeply into suffering that they recognized the kinships between sensual delight, pain, and cruelty which others either evade or mourn. It was precisely because these young men lived so profoundly that they could afford to be realists without trembling and without cynicism. They found life to be complete only in the moments of highest passion when ecstasy sweeps through the soul, for then pain and joy are inextricably united.

Therefore love was for them not only the great experience, but the type of all those great experiences which are man's sublime right. But bacchantic ecstasy was not the only kind. They knew rapture which went beyond the storm of passion, a holy quiet in which the soul hovers, open to all influences, a simple mood in which feeling is thought and thought is feeling. This experience, passive in its unlimited receptivity and active in its instinctive creativeness, is the moment of inspiration; then the individual is dissolved, the individual who thinks distinct thoughts and has distinct experiences, and the place of the centrifugal urgency of self is taken by the clarity of inspiration. The moments do not include either pleasure or sorrow; they are moments of endless yearning which exists for its own sake, of endless sadness which broods on the abundance of experience.

The experience of the young men expanded their souls so widely that in order to express them an interplay of tragedy and farce was necessary. The young men felt a new consanguinity with Shakespeare, who had made the hero and the fool inseparable brothers. They even reverted beyond Shakespeare to the Middle Ages and concurred in the medieval pleasure at the antics of the fool in the Gospel plays. And the soul was not merely a depth; in man a path wound inward which linked world to world in mysterious infinity. In those inner worlds figures moved and mountains towered and there was growth and blossoming and reverberation in as real a mode as in the other universe served by eye and ear.

About the young men there lay an inexhaustible world, and they knew its abundance, for they had attempted to exhaust it. Nature and man, history and the present, the great harmony and the confusing complexity—all of these were real and indispensable. Yet how should they capture the opulence of the world? It was a screen upon which beauty might play, or a soul, or an idea which deceived the eye and drew the soul down into grievous yearning. Experiences taught them that the opulence, which seems a dark and gaping abyss to the eye of reason, became a world replete with latent energy for him who lost himself in passion. From nature there came response after response; each stone and tree became an intimate. Impassioned, the soul awoke and became one with nature; it saw itself as a flower, as a spring, as a landscape. Then they saw that the meaning inhered in the mood, not in the dead substance; beauty was reality, and the form was only the vehicle of reality or its symbol. Love opens man's eyes because his passion rouses passion in his beloved; ecstasy ensues when life joins life. The beloved does not become real prior to communion, in the literal sense; and similarly, through scientific communion, nature opens her soul in the form of mood.

What is closed to the meditative scholar springs open for an ecstatic youth because his soul arrays itself in nature as if it were an extension of his body, so that he experiences its inner movements. In this overwhelming experience there occurs a merging of the soul and the world which casts light both inward and outward. Marveling, a man sees a real, visible world unfold within his soul during the act of love, and marveling, the successful scientist sees a world extend beyond the stars in an effervescence of energies; and when a man knows both experiences he can understand the mighty commandment, "Let there be," which resounds not only in the human soul but in all that exists, and which transmutes chaos into forms and colors.

The experience of passion revealed to the young men that there is no line of demarcation between the inner and the outer; what happens in the soul, occurs in nature; what begins on one side undulates immediately to the other. In sympathetic intoxication, the young men embraced all nature and inspired it with the life of their own life. In all nature, wherever they turned they saw themselves. Novalis called a flower earth's most profound language; man is the consciousness of the planet, the eye which the earth raises toward heaven. At first glance it seems that for the Romantics the universe had simply become a man of gigantic dimensions; but the first fleeting glance does not notice that at the moment when man sees his own image in the surrounding world, the surrounding world becomes a part of him. He projects himself into the whole of nature, but he also draws the whole of nature into himself, so that he begins to suffer or rejoice over things for which he previously had no sympathy. In these new men there was born, through the baptism of passion, a vast new soul, at once human and superhuman. The soul first learns to know itself when it looks within and without simultaneously. Without, it sees the tranquillity of nature: individuals grow, bloom, are broken and wither, while nature stands impassive—and nevertheless, everything which is born and dies is a part of nature. His heart moved, man looks into the distant majestic countenance of nature, and in so doing he becomes aware of the tranquillity within himself, a tranquillity as distant, as impersonal, and as rich in moods as the tranquillity of nature. His thoughts and feelings rise and fall; there is no mere part of his soul which can rejoice, or mourn, or feel fear, for the whole soul is involved in this experience. But during this impersonal meditation the harvest of the future is conceived. There is no distinct thought or distinct labor; but the feelings converge to thoughts, and as they surge through the soul, they gather power which will compel intense labor in days to come. And behold, nature also creates, in impassive tranquillity. It plays, dissipates itself and restlessly forces into life form after form from plant and animal up to man. The ascent traverses death and suffering; at each stage life meets with resistance, forges forward, and is crushed. If we again look inward, we see that suffering is also the destiny of the soul; moments of pain are moments of growth. The free play of the soul strikes on all sides an obstructing and imperious destiny. The soul strives to conquer all that is alien to it in nature, in the community, and in the consequences of past events; and it learns agony by being small and yearning for abundance while in penury. The soul must conquer; man must have his will of woman; and behold, in one moment he loses his ego and gains a higher self, exalted love. Thus man's greatest pleasure is to fulfill his will, but his pleasure causes pain, since the will loses its slough, its bounds, and assumes a larger mould so that it may live not alone but for another. At one and the same time man conquers and is defeated. He conquers through defeat and destroys himself for something greater.

When man is most truly himself, intoxicated with the urge to dominate, he is closest to destruction. Both within and without the soul, death is the condition for life; through continuous self-creation and self-destruction the soul and nature stride forward to a more sublime reality. In all its aspects life advances through contraries: the soul confronts the body, the tranquillity of selfless inspiration opposes the centrifugal personality, man forces woman. Without strife life would be savorless and powerless. Life exfoliates into abundance because it always presses on its boundaries; and in love's need for that which is beyond the self, it surges over a boundary, founders, wakens, and sees the boundary again before it, but farther onward than before. The unknown is fate, for it is external; nevertheless, at the moment that I conquer it I know that it is myself.

Life is suffering; life is sickness, because in sickness the soul exceeds its limits and strives with its old shape. Life is pain, for the form which I now possess is the highest that I know, yet inadequate for my future being. Pain is dear, for it presages the breakthrough of a new abundance. With the will as an ally the self struggles with its environment and when thwarted by the environment struggles with the will in order to subject it to severe laws given from without. But in place of the self there appears (simultaneously with the breakthrough of a new abundance) a spirit which advances toward and merges with the necessity of the universe, and feels it as its will. Instead of a self that can only

80

say "I," there appears a spirit which, even in its most intimate thoughts and with its most profound energy, is as impersonal as destiny.

What is the little ego which struggles for its own survival? And what is the larger self which dominates and effaces the ego? Are they not both the spirit which reveals itself in all that lives and in all that rests in quiet beauty? The same fight is fought in nature that we experience within us; there too development advances through suffering and death to the victorious appearance of higher forms. The soul of nature seeks its own image; as it slumbers in undeveloped splendor within multiplicity it observes itself and seeks to assume its proper shape. During the crises we ourselves discover how sharply the spirit pierces when the self surrenders to the unknown passively and trustingly, and is destroyed unaware of the new ego that is being conceived —indeed, surrenders without any assurance of a successor. The same spirit strides forward from form to form within the great soul of nature.

Closely related as they may seem at first, the inward experiences of the Romantics distinguish them from Herder and Goethe. Herder looks back upon nature as a series of monuments on the path which the spirit has pursued up to the point where he stands. The Romantics see themselves in nature; they even see themselves in stones and trees, and they discover their inmost egos in the dreaming silence of nature. For Herder the spirit reveals itself gradually throughout history; more and more clearly its noble features become visible as it pushes matter aside. For the Romantics the spirit is equally accessible everywhere, in the landscape as in the human soul; therefore, man can comprehend nature by introspection and understand himself by observation, just as he can comprehend himself by recognizing his thoughts and dreams in the heart of a friend. The Romantics do not wait to achieve unity before they observe the nature of the spirit; for them, it dwells integrally in each human soul. Herder strives in hope; he knows what has already been accomplished, and on this he bases his secure faith in a higher ideal that will be realized beyond the life on earth. The Romantics do not need hope, for in their opinion the ideal lies dreaming in all human life as well as in the life of nature, in individuals as in the whole, and it realizes itself both in pleasure and in pain. Here on earth, rather than elsewhere, is the highest plane of spiritual life. The Romantics do not anticipate an eternity which honors the pledges of time; but neither can they rest content in Herder's assurance that history demonstrates the spirit's advance toward a higher goal. For the Romantics, labor is a personal responsibility. In each man the eternal life must be completed, and each soul stands responsible for the victory or defeat of the world-spirit. Herder and Goethe had to resign themselves to limitations that constituted an extrinsic force, a destiny which turned back the striving soul as soon as it attained the boundaries which the moment had raised about it. For the youthful Romantics, form did not constitute coercion; for the outer is spiritual as well as the inner. Only by the fragmentation of extant forms does life ascend beyond them.

In the common soul the Romantics found suffering and labor. The first characteristic which the soul recognizes in itself is its imperfection; perfection can be won only by conquest and abundance. Novalis can be undecided; he stares inward, and he gazes outward; within, everything is so familiar that the experience is more profound than its instigation. And what is outward multiplicity other than a repetition of the play of the soul at the bottom of the heart? Novalis finds himself in the external world, and again he finds the whole world within himself, and for him, who carries an ebullient vitality in a disease-racked body, there are many moments when the crystalline fountain in the realm of night tastes so strongly on his tongue that he exclaims: "After such a draft who would return to the land where light flickers in eternal unrest!"[22] But the temptation to retire into dreams is interrupted by the command of nature: work and use. And he obeys because he knows well that if dreams are not continually recreated, they will wither. Schlegel, on the other hand, has never known vacillation. For him there is only one way to the true life, *Bildung*—as we might say, enrichment, or expansion. Nature, history, living men are means through which the soul gains abundance and finds itself. Schlegel assumes as a sacred duty the study of the past and of the spiritual life of far-away countries because it brings nourishment for the soul. In order to become a true man one must wander through "all three or four continents, not to sharpen one's thoughts but to expand one's view and gain for one's spirit more freedom and inner variety and therewith more originality and independence."[23] A strange human soul must be wooed until it has become mine and I live wholly for my beloved in the same way that my life is dedicated wholly to myself. Thus all is won, so that my heart throbs throughout the entire world. The symbol of the living man then is his "sense" for what lies about him; for the "sense," or as we might say, interest, is the dawn of sympathy with what is strange, at the beginning of its subjugation. Interest puts in the soul a seed which grows, and brings forth flower and fruit; and its growth marks the death of the old man but the birth of a new and greater man. Ecstasy and dreams are not sufficient; work and thought are necessary, and philosophy as well as poetry, if the soul is to achieve its proper splendor. To be sure, the condition of all work is the full exertion of the soul, for one can only carry on the work of the spirit when his soul is wholly awake. And the full force of the soul is called passion. The way in which the young Romantics defined labor passed a death sentence upon the scholar, who assumed that he could create spiritual values while three-quarters of his spirit enjoyed the sleep of idleness. All the forces of the soul must be exerted, all the components of spiritual life must be directed towards the work, for the goal is universality and complete harmony throughout the spirit. Not reason alone nor imagination alone, but the immediacy of instinct, is the most profound revelation of the soul in the whole of nature. Inspiration, which in the imperfect human soul is extraordinary, will occur continuously in the perfected soul. The soul must be trained to live in an undivided consciousness in which all conditions, and indeed all changes, are simultaneously present; in which all thoughts are present and imbued with an all-embracing energy of feeling; and in which knowledge and action are identical.

Divine egoism is Schlegel's term for the most intense desire of the soul, its urge to surpass itself. Unresting, the soul proceeds from conquest to conquest; but this advance is also a homecoming. When the soul fulfills the dreams of the spirit, it achieves the tranquillity of nature, the immediacy of the child. Nevertheless, the highest perfection is not a simple return to the blind instinct of nature; during its upward struggle the soul, through inner dissension and reflection, wins the twofold power to be at once unconscious instinct and conscious will. It becomes conscious of its unconsciousness without losing the latter. The description may suggest that an experience of "conscious instinct" is complex and might even cause a schism in the soul; in reality the experience is simpler than the most common psychic state; only, its infinite breadth makes necessary the forcing of language to the utmost or the formulation of a paradox in order to express its entire scope. The union of the conscious and the instinctive is simply what Goethe called the soul's pure dispassionate state, which by his own confession is required for the productive dominance of inspiration.

When the soul has thus achieved its highest exfoliation, it has conquered multiplicity and can live expansively in its abundance without suffering division. His new power allows man to devote himself to the particular without losing his grasp of harmony, and all his deeds and words now bear the stamp of eternity; they cluster about the goal, and they signify more than they reveal. The deeds of earthbound man are fragmentary: he loves in order to be loved, he works in order to earn; that which should be a means to growth becomes an end in itself; his action is sterile, for it achieves its goal but plants no seed for the future. But the perfected human being loves in such a way that the loving pair become a revelation of the wealth of eternity, and their love has eternal effects both within them and around them. "A genius" is Schlegel's term for man's highest form of existence; and the genius is recognizable because he confers eternity upon everything he touches, large or small. He makes a meal a sacrament; he makes his own labor a work of God, which hints at beauty as does the wind sighing in the woods. Wherever he goes he kindles an ideal from which the hearts of men take fire, so that flames rage among them. Like lightning his words burst forth from the harmony of his inspiration, which can never attain complete articulation. Though the words fit a momentary need, they contain such a wealth of implications that their meaning is never exhausted. The words of genius are like those of the fool when he says, "Tom's a-cold."[24] The fool utters the common words as if the need of the moment overshadowed all his thoughts; nevertheless, the words make the auditors shiver at the thought of all the cold within and without mankind. Such glimpses by the spirit Schlegel calls *Witz*. In imaginative literature *Witz* may be a song, a drama, a *Märchen,* in which all the overtones are heard and the words convey more than they express. Such an example of *Witz* Schlegel attempted in his novel *Lucinde*, and Novalis with greater artistic control in *Die Hymnen an die Nacht.* Schlegel desires to write in *Lucinde* about the sport of man and woman in such a way that the reader will understand that his relationship is more significant than the most serious problems of the day. Smiling, the man and woman revel in their youthful energy and discover one another like strange worlds; they are consumed by the desire to embrace the unknown, and their painful longing drives them into the unconsciousness of self brought by passion, so that they are both transformed and live in a new conjoined and transmuted ego. Their play is energetic and painful because a greater force is playing through them. In the two human beings the dynamic soul of nature rises to the surface; the two feel that they form a universe struggling to become conscious of itself, for they partake of the same soul and the same pain that strive in nature to break out of the conscious life of plants and to surge upward from form to form.

In his fifth hymn Novalis paints with the old mythological images the world in the bloom of its youth, where the gods dwell on earth and divine power flows in sparkling wine; but death strides into the poem and banishes the gods into the night, so that men can do no more than shroud death in flowers and give it the more pleasant name of sleep; in the middle of the world lies the night, eternal night, a sign of the reign of unknown forces. The gods die; lifeless and doom-ridden, the world spreads out around mankind. But in this new world death is born anew as the brother of men, in the son of the Virgin. He gazes ahead into the unborn future, disregarding His days on earth and their harvest of destiny; and through Him a new life germinates in death and in the grave. This hymn should not be taken as an historical account (any more than Oehlenschläger's poem "The Golden Horns" should be taken as an archaeological treatise); it is a symbol of the moment of crisis which comes again and again in every man's, in every people's experience when they believe they are traveling to destruction but awake to the knowledge that a new and greater ideal has been born in the moment of their tribulation, when the youth discovers that the death of his childhood dreams is the threshold of a richer life.

The abundance of implication in this poem demonstrates the difference between simile and mere allegory as imaginary modes. A simile cannot be interpreted, because it suggests more than it expresses; it can have an eternal soul in a mortal body because the eternal vitality of genius assumes the flesh of form. The profundity of *Witz* does not stem from vague allusions: provided that it proceeds from a soul which has experienced eternity beyond the finite, the more original a symbol or the more witty and sharply dramatic a figure, the stronger the suggestive power of *Witz*. In this discrimination is perhaps most clearly indicated the difference in experience which separates Schlegel from Goethe; and even though Schlegel, like Novalis, was unable to give his experience aesthetic form, it gave him a completely new comprehension of the Middle Ages and of mysticism, of Dante and of Shakespeare.

Witz sounds paradoxical because it comes from a world which is broader than the prosaic world, and therefore contains contraries which in petty, conventional society seem irreconcilable and hostile. Actually the entire life of a genius consists of *Witz*. The genius lives as a member of society, he acts at one moment as a pater-familias, the next as a citizen, then as a friend, then as a poet. He functions conventionally as well as anyone else, but he is not bound by the illusion of convention. He has his own certainty within himself, and therefore he can make light of his dignity, ridicule his love or his civic virtue, his friendship or his art, or parody himself until the average man does not know what is jest and what is earnest. Thus when Socrates walked through Athens, Alcibiades admired and loved him; Plato admired and meditated; the people admired and hated. "Irony," the *Witz* of life, complete jest and at the same time complete earnestness, represents the perfect man's mastery of himself and his recognition of his freedom.

When the goal is reached, and the soul has exceeded the limitations of the petty individual, then it is free, because it participates in all and feels destiny as its own will. It is not bound by history, for it has expanded until it is coterminous with history; and it is a part of every action which takes place by virtue of its own law-inspired freedom. As long as we withdraw into our little egos, everything from without sweeps powerfully over us and carries us along, the slaves of destiny. By *Bildung* and expansion we introduce infinity into our actions, and make the world our instrument. The genius is not subject to the wear and tear of passion; he accepts every impulse and feels certain that whatever happens is both natural and inevitable. He attempts everything because he has no specific goal. He does not live in the moment but in years and centuries.

The Romantics have the courage granted by experience, and they do not recoil from any ideal. God wants gods, says Novalis, or in other words, life requires godliness of us. If the spirit is to achieve divine abundance, then the duty and responsibility of human beings must be to strive to become a god. It is not that the paths of a thousand souls will run together so that all the individual souls amalgamate into deity at the end of their paths—each of the thousand can become a god and feel the world to be his body. A god's duty consists of creating the world, nature, and history, and making these a true expression of the soul. Man has the mission of conferring upon the world *Bildung*, that is, of humanizing it. For Novalis there are no impossibilities; the mastery of the body is not perfect until we can destroy it and reconstruct it as we will, and even create bodies and force the senses to bring forth shapes as they now bring forth images. And in the control of the body lies the mastery of all nature, the second revelation of the soul. Ultimately we become all in all; the realm of nature becomes a realm of the spirit; its tranquil instinct, genial harmony.

The religion of the Romantics rises immediately from their spiritual experiences, and they fearlessly draw the ultimate consequences. God is a word the meaning of which has been lost to the world. Every man has his own god in the ideal which lives in him and which through his life he makes into reality. God is everything in which life lives in its fullness, and thus it follows that nature is God. If we must speak of a god that is the basis of all human life, then it is only a phrase for the highest soul, an "abyss of individuality, the only infinite abundance," as Schlegel puts it; and in his vocabulary individuality means the individually moulded soul with its endless possibilities for exfoliation. This "abyss" is nothing other than the spirit which dreams its endless, infinite dreams both in nature's force and in nature's formlessness, and which observes itself like a human face in man and is perfected in the genius. Schleiermacher, who in his verbose and evasive *Reden über die Religion* expressed the experiences of his friends in the way he thought would be most acceptable to the "cultivated" reader, can from the standpoint of traditional usage be called an atheist just as well as anything else. The belief in a personal god, in any case, is in Schleiermacher's opinion no necessary part of true religion.

The Romantics are fully conscious that they proclaim a religion of the future; they are equally revolutionary in the realm of religion and ethics. The more richly a man lives in their sense, the more irreligious and immoral he becomes in the traditional sense. Despite the world's judgment and condemnation, they proclaim a new morality and a new religion, which will conquer by an historical necessity. They are themselves only geniuses who experience the future in advance. They do not hesitate to play the role of prophet or to provide a new bible. Their relation to existing religion can be described as enlightened rejection. Protestantism expresses the ideal of the poor, narrow man: absolute sobriety, pure morals, complete self-abnegation. In its breadth the new religion will reflect the entire soul; there will be room in it for both the highest tragedy and the most unrestrained comedy; it will demand the orgy, a divine service which encompasses passion and ecstasy; and it will demand myths such as the great man of Nazareth once created, myths that in the pregnant form of *Witz* express the incredible abundance of reality; it will embrace both poetry and science, it will embrace all that is human. No divine service can become more than the daily life of a true man. There is nothing in the world that cannot serve as a mediator between man and eternity and transmit the pain and passion through which his soul dies to rise again in a more abundant life. Man can encounter God in a stone or in a tree just as well as in the communion. To him who knows not love, a woman is nothing; but he who surrenders himself to love meets God in her, a God who destroys his self-limitation and leads him into a more abundant and more responsible life. Thus, the experiences of the Romantics turned them into revolutionaries in all areas of life and made them merciless critics. Conventional morality they termed licentious. They demanded that ethics should be based upon reality rather than convenience. But first and foremost ethics should have its basis within the soul itself and not upon external laws. The ethical consists in activity or what Schlegel calls *Bildung*, that is, a constant struggle to bring new wealth into the soul from nature and from human life. And the principal commandment is that man should live according to his abundance, be completely himself, and in so doing live completely for others. No higher commandment can be given, for to obey this law is to attune all one's actions to the eternal and allow them to serve the petty goals of this world only in passing. Man cannot be ethical unless each of his actions arises from a need of the soul, so that the action need not be justified by transient lust or a skill become almost automatic. Accurately speaking, sin consists of that which is accidental, of everything that stems not from necessity but from the moment and is of the moment. Inversely there is no other characteristic of virtue than that it serves the growth of the soul. But no one can regulate the manner in which something grows; and as the truly ethical man's action can arise only from his inner needs, his ethics must seem paradoxical and often offensive to people of a different persuasion. The genius cannot live without offending and bringing confusion into the accepted morality of society; but by being true to himself he serves to make the world more moral, and he opens the eyes of his fellow men to the wealth which they have forfeited.

The ethics of the Romantics represent a radical intensification and spiritualization of all the relationships of life, and in their minds many of their thoughts were already translated into matters of conscience. A marriage which does not rest on inner necessity is mere whoredom; and inwardness is no matter of the heart alone as people usually think: the sensuous, the flesh, must be ennobled in the same degree as the soul. Marriage is an embrace, from the physical union to the most secret intertwining of thoughts and feelings.

Necessarily these ethics must have significant results in the organization of society. Law and politics are immoral; the single valid group is the civic association that rests upon organic sympathy and therefore takes on organic form. The basic types for human society are friendship, which produces corporations, and the family, which expands and becomes the state. That merging of individuals through a struggle which sanctifies marriage must be established in the relationship of the estates. Just as man through the pain and tenderness of love overcomes his narrowness and learns to know woman both in her reticence and her affection, so the distinguished man must learn to become like the servant, and the poor man must share in the rich man's consciousness of wealth. But complete similarity does not come from leveling; it can be achieved only when each man, having taken up a firm position within himself, strides outward until he has learned to feel what his neighbor suffers and what his neighbor enjoys, so that all his feelings are imbued with sympathy. The perfect state is an aristocratic democracy where each citizen feels the state within himself, and feels the interests of the state to be his personal interests, so that he suffers and rejoices, sacrifices and acts for the state as for a friend whose destiny he cannot separate from his own. Above the aggregate of men is a king whose power and rights stem only from his feeling that he is identical with the state, wholly and at every moment. The king must be so comprehensive a genius that he has made the thoughts of all the citizens his own, and he must have made his will so comprehensive that no conflict can arise between him and his kingdom. Outwardly this society expresses itself in practical solidarity, with common dwellings and kitchens, and in the public evaluation and recognition for the work of each citizen. And a new beauty will come into life through the creation of ceremonies which release experience into the connotative forms of *Witz*. When the wife really becomes the queen of the home, then marriage becomes a solemn consecration of the woman to the honor and responsibility of her new dignity; when marriage really becomes the beginning of greater pain and greater pleasure through the establishment with another human being of a completely new entity, then the ceremony of marriage and the coronation of the bride will have a meaning—then the need for a festive consecration will be felt.

It is an art to become a human being. If you do not become an artist, you will never enter the kingdom of God, the Romantics could well say. For them as for Goethe art is the highest manifestation of life; for all life consists of making manifest the striving of the spirit; and even to recognize nature, it is necessary that man enter into and become one with the creation of the spirit, so that the creation is born anew within him. The artist "creates" in the literal sense of the word, and if he succeeds, his work will become as true as the productions of nature—so far Goethe and Schlegel agree fairly well. But the Romantics expand the terms "art" and "genius" to pertain to all of life; one man is an artist in verse or paint, another in trade, a third in statesmanship. The state, morality, trade, and craftsmanship must all be made poetic, Schlegel says, and by this he means that life as a whole must have that depth and inwardness which poetry hitherto alone has had. The merchant must carry on his trade, the craftsman must use his tools, with the same truth of inspiration which moves the head and hand of the poet writing his poem. This is the meaning in Schlegel's statement: morality and genius are identical.

These young men, who have the reputation of being unrealistic dreamers, were exactly as realistic as men must become when they possess an inward, overpowering, unresting experience which continuously calls forth their thoughts and sends them abroad with ever more precise instructions. There is nothing fanatic about them except that they demand truth as the first requisite for real human life. It is not enough to act from conviction, not enough to discipline the will; the soul must be disciplined so that only truth can possibly come from it. Because they had such a severe master within them, these young men could let their enthusiasm take them to the zenith of heaven and the nadir of hell without losing their association with their native soil. As naïve and utopian as their thoughts may seem, many of those thoughts have demonstrated their vitality by rising again and again to demand fulfillment.

Novalis is a youth who has gone beyond the horizon and entered a whole new land. He does not know where the paths lead, but he must hew his way through brushwood and swamp until he discovers firm ground in the midst of the quagmires. He did not succeed in following his ideas to their conclusion and in discovering how much in them was profound and how much no more than the barren play of fantasy, before at the age of twenty-eight he sank into the night which he had so fervently celebrated, and drank from its cooling spring and forgot all the flickering unrest of light. Frequently enough it happened that in his zeal he threw the reins upon the neck of fantasy and let himself be carried precipitously onwards at full speed. But he never lost his way; he was always able to return to reality; the moment after he was completely enveloped by the blue vaporous wreaths of dream, he was again amidst realities, perhaps not those of today but of tomorrow—where Schlegel was always to be found. In his youthful zeal Novalis often tries to force truth to appear to him, and therefore he advances into conclusions almost as crude as caricatures; but the wavering quality of his writing cannot be ascribed only to youthful inexperience. He lacked the prudent balance that Schlegel possessed to an unusual degree: Schlegel combined rich experience with a clear head; but on the other hand he possessed nothing like his friend's lightness of touch. In addition to the essay Schlegel discovered his proper genre in the aphorism, which his ingenuity and his cumbrous, apparently naïve weight of expression gave the impress of mastery. He never learned how to complete a work; *Lucinde* is good only because of the aphorisms—brilliant, profound, perfectly wrought aphorisms—that he inserted with great labor into a frame unworthy of them. His ambition drove him to evade the limitations of his natural form and to attempt the novel, a genre idolized by his contemporaries. Had he pursued those paths which his thoughts trod most easily, he might have met some persons who avoided him because all the world said that Schlegel was a cynic and frivolous to boot. Later generations have had no use for his thoughts, and the historians of literature have not had time to read him; they have been too busy assuring their neighbors that they also are scandalized by his frivolity and his reactionary tendency, so that no one will have a chance to believe that they are less virtuous or critical than all of their confreres, who have not had time to read him either.

To judge and distinguish between Schlegel and Novalis is often difficult and always unjust. The younger of the two was always dependent on his friend, by whose thought his own youth had been redeemed; but on the other hand, Novalis had given generously of his own ardent soul. And as the two were joined in life, we may hope they will be united in the future.

Chapter VII

The New God

IT IS THEIR NEW EXPERIENCE which makes these people new; the experience of a new world, of a new human soul, of new demands and new rights. Whatever later times may find to say about Schlegel's god, he cannot be criticized as lacking life. For Herder and for Goethe, for Wordsworth, Schlegel, and Novalis, God is not something that can be seen or heard; from within the depth of experience He arises and presses forward, causing pain and ecstasy so mighty that the soul must defend itself. For these men immortality is not a consequence which justice seems to demand, nor is it a hope to which one has the right to cling; it is concomitant to the tension caused by experience within the soul. Life is so powerful that it drags death with it into reality and gives it substance. Indeed, life pulses so strongly in these men that for them the very moment when time shatters and forms collapse is filled with the most convincing assurance of life. Everything in which life reveals itself, death can conquer; but it cannot touch life itself. The soul needs no assurance of its own immortality other than its daily struggle to express itself through dreams and thoughts and deeds. That which succeeds most sublimely and most nobly is never more than an enfeebled and reflected ray of the will which struggles to succeed. The soul greets death as a release from the strait-jacket which we call the beauty of form, and judging by what already has been created, the soul feels confident that it can now create something superior to all the splendor of the senses. Whatever aspirations a man may fulfill through his highest striving are but a fraction of those which lie and press upon his soul—that is Herder's immortal certainty. Again and again Novalis expresses a yearning for death which is like a child's impatience to grow up. With delight the young man feels his foot slip on the brink of the unknown, and half in delight, half in terror, he feels a temptation to throw himself beyond the brink and capture the wonder of death.

Life drags death with it as the day the night; not as a darkness that extinguishes its light, but as its own fulfillment. The night is not the death of light; in the silent intensifying darkness light finds that fulfillment which it did not achieve in the more limited complexity of day.

93

"More heavenly than those sparkling stars seem the infinite eyes which the night has opened within us."[26] We call it night, we call it darkness, because it is something other than the light; it is not a nothingness upon which we turn our backs as we turn away from something which merely ceases. Nor is night merely a continuation of the day; it is a darkness wherein life shows its power to function without calling upon light for help. In the day, light is refracted by the many who receive it; in the day light washes over a thousand details and from them calls forth reality; night is the one, the eternal, which cannot measure its magnificence in the rays of the sun. "To light was apportioned its time, but the realm of night is outside time and space."[27]

Novalis discovered that the world of night has rights equal to those of the world of day, but is more profound as the simplicity of eternity is more profound than the multiplicity of time. When he praises the holy, ineffable, secretive night, he praises it as the mother of the light and the day, and his words are not beautiful images which he evokes merely in the hope that they will express more than they denote. Poetry is myth; in the mouth of a genius *Witz* always becomes half-chanted imagery and immediate truth. Novalis can experience eternity in the night because everywhere the eternal lies directly below the temporal, because the eternal is as near as time and at every moment pushes its actuality through the thin shell of reality. Standing at the grave, Novalis feels eternity break through there, where the shell of life is worn thinnest. "I blew the grave before me like dust, the centuries were like moments, I felt their nearness and believed at each moment that they would step forth."[28] Therefore he finds in night an eternal abundance which entices him towards death. For him the darkness becomes the great womb of eternity in which the soul sinks to rest, where it is freed of all its creative energies and engenders living thoughts, as gods engender worlds. It is the same yearning to beget in the unlimited fullness of eternity that lifts Faust up toward a participation in the creative energy of the universe. The river plunges into the deep; from the eternal creation which surrounds man, the lightning flames like a message of divine love and arouses in the sensuous soul a desire to be overwhelmed by fervor. By desire the soul is cast upward toward bliss in the oneness of the all, where the metaphor of transience ceases and the ineffable gains actuality.

These men are certain of victory because they do not grope blindly after an unknown immortality of which man can have at best a presentiment. In their most profound moments they have already experienced an eternity in which the soul subsides and gives up the peculiarities of self and all the will, in order to enter perfect activity. Goethe has moments when his soul is void of desire; things stream over him without becoming experiences, but the *Urphenomenon* exalts him into pure cognition. Wordsworth continually recalled the moments in which his vision rested, and what he had then seen remained the nourishment of his soul. Schlegel and Novalis speak and sing about moments of ecstasy when they, by seeking themselves wholly, find a pain which engulfs them; and they speak of still more profound moments when the soul rests in itself freed from all longing, when everything is perfected in them without exertion on their part. And they all look back upon the selfless moment as the womb from which the rest of their life wells forth.

None of these men was a dreamer, none of them was a questing soul who wandered about looking for something other than reality. What they had found, they had found by living. They had captured eternity in the common day, and they harbored no fantasies about a salvation which one can achieve by mortification and fasting. They found salvation in the actuality of the day; on the field of the day it must be won if it is to be possessed. Goethe derides men who believe that they have gained immortality as a kind of prize because they let themselves be born. Men become immortal according to the dimensions of their spirit, and there are innumerable men who never gain more in life than the bare necessities for the three or four score years which, at best, nature doles out to man. More incisively than anyone else, Schlegel preaches that the day is a talent which the good and faithful servant must multiply; the soul must construct eternity within itself. It is not enough for man to know that the spirit lives in him; if he himself does not share in the spirit's struggle to develop, he sinks back a shell, and the spirit works on without him. Strongly as they feel the power of eternity behind the forms of time, they sternly disallow an eternity which can exist in its labors and struggles, free of actuality. Schlegel establishes a responsibility so great that it requires a new ethic; Wordsworth and Herder find new power in the old commandments and a new reason for their authority: none of them is a stranger in the world of law. None of these men ever sings the song of a pilgrim who wanders toward a paradise beyond the world and avoids hard facts along the way. "I gladly work diligently, I gladly watch everywhere that thou needest me; I praise the glory of thy majesty, I let my eye unrestricted survey the beauteous unity of thy artistic creation and reflect on the laws of the game which innumerable spaces and their times so wonderfully play."[29] So Novalis speaks about the day's great light in the middle of his amorous hymn to darkness.

Thus eternity is reborn as reality; thus God is reborn. Compared with this inward experience, doctrine is inconsequential. The belief in the supernatural was dead, but eternal life arose within experience; "The eternal makes itself felt in everything," says Goethe.[30] Life is rooted in the tangible, even if it extends beyond time; and therefore these men need not call upon any presentiment or hope borne of faith. They need only to wax in the actuality in which they have been planted, to move as they grow, and to burgeon in the unknown future. Life itself corrects the established formulae; when actuality is too widespreading for a single principle, a series of formulae must be established in order to express the breadth of the experience; and these are all equally true even if they seem incompatible in the eyes of people whose logic proceeds from narrower experience. Goethe can profess to be a pantheist and a polytheist at the same time; Herder can be a pantheist at the time when he worships God as Father and Creator.

Herder and Goethe each created for himself a new harmony, in which there was room for the experiences which he had gained by struggle. Each created his new harmony in such close association with the old that for him the ethical ideals by which his ancestors had lived retained their dignity. Herder felt no need for a radical revolution in the realms of either morality or religion. He accepted contemporary forms and used them according to his needs, quite unbound by tradition or the interpretation of others. Goethe is like a self-assured examiner who at first nods in friendly encouragement to the Evangelists because of their high morality, but then sweeps their successors aside with an impatient gesture. Children and childish souls need aid because they cannot lift themselves to the natural, primitive religion; and for them an official church is absolutely indispensable. It would therefore be heartless to make changes in the existing order, other than slight improvements. As is right, the sage of Weimar has often been acknowledged by pious churchmen who value the recognition which the famous skeptic occasionally implies. And Goethe has rightfully been annexed as a good Lutheran witness, for he is a full-blooded Protestant with a Protestant naïve indignation at all the ways of Rome.

Quite otherwise, the Romantics. For them religion is not simply emotion, and not simply reason, but the fullness of the human soul; it is a passionate and at the same time a tranquil activity, like a dream, "a bright chaos of divine thoughts."[31] Therefore they are hostile to ever-rational Protestantism, which cackles in bewilderment over its chicks; they require a new and more intense fear of God, together with a liturgy more tolerant than any the world has yet seen. The revolution is in their blood, but their revolutionary inclinations are counter-balanced by their gentle comprehension of all that lives. Their experience forces them to sympathize with all the shapes which the spirit has assumed in history, and they see the classical religions as well as Christianity as necessary expressions of the life of the soul. The old orgies and mysteries are quite as comprehensible as the Christian stress on sin as an antecedent of eternal life; sickness and suffering and death are life's own way to salvation. The worshiping of stock and stone, the belief in the God-man Jesus, the adoration of the Virgin, and faith in the sacraments hold no enigmas for men who experience the radiance of God both in nature and in a woman's smile.

This moderation Schlegel inherited from Herder; indeed, all the Romantics drew from Herder the inspiration for their profound experience of history. It is this sympathy with the Human in all its forms which distinguishes Herder and his successors from Goethe and his disciples. For Herder all religions are true as long as they incorporate and formulate a people's experience, and religions are valuable to posterity as evidence of those experiences which each of us must undergo anew. Herder cannot accept a religion which is pure speculation or pure morality; for him religion is something man lives into with all his senses; religion embraces the entire man; and to live a religion is to endeavor to ennoble the entire soul. God is in the songs of the people, and in its sacrifices, in its revenge, and in the will of its chieftains as much as in the yearning of the soul, and for this reason all ethical commands have their origin and their avenger in the god known to the people. Religion is both in dreams and omens, in the wonder and speculation caused by the light of the heavens and the course of storms; it is conceived in the awe of nature and the might of the soul, the awe which generates passionate words and powerful images. Religion is poetry and myth, the visions of wisdom and the fantasies of fools; it has grown under the adroit supervision of priests and prophets, and by their crafty exploitation of the deference of the people. In the myths and pious conventions of religion men are united organically with the great events in nature and in human life; and religion, as it traditionally descends from father to son and meets the child as he enters into life, acts as a shield between a man and the outer world, and prevents him from beginning for himself, face to face with nature.

All this is God's revelation, and Herder knows no other. There is no difference between the chosen people and the others. If Jahweh revealed his thoughts to Moses, the Greeks learned to sing from Apollo; and the God of the Greenlanders has placed song upon the tongues of the kayak-paddlers, and dreams in their minds. If the thoughts of Indians about the world and God are nothing but myth, the Pentateuch is also myth: therein consists its nobility. The proper method of interpretation of the Book of Genesis he finds in the poetic and metaphorical language of the prophets and the psalmist and Job; their songs of the coming of light contain the nucleus of the history of creation. And in His highest revelation God speaks through the chosen men whose souls plumb the depths of life and whose language gives the purest expression to the awe of the heart. In God's voice as it reverberates through the ages, when the father whispers his wisdom in the son's ear and that son in turn in the ear of his son, in tradition, there resounds a nameless nobility which conveys a blessing through the sequence of souls. God affects man only through chosen, greater men. Herder does not admit that there is one true God among many false ones.

In Herder's account of the series of revelations, the philosophy and poetry of his own time enter naturally; and he feels no need to alter his own spiritual life by the aid of superseded formulae. Inevitably, he treats the old formulae and symbols as expressions of their times, valid expressions for the earlier generations, valid expressions of their searches and discoveries, and for later generations no more than dignified monuments to souls who have existed in God's great chain of history. That which shall nourish a time must grow in the mold of that time: "Was für die Zeit geschieht, muss in der Zeit geschehen."[32] As naturally as he breathes, he thinks of the Old and New Testaments as parts of history of which the treasures reveal themselves only to him who can live a life under the limited horizon of the prophets and the apostles. Religion is a fact, and the fact is history, the history of God in man from generation to generation.

Goethe is narrower than Herder. He found all his needs satisfied in Hellas. Herder, like Goethe, had seen Hellas; he described the intellectual life of the Greeks in a few pages which exhibit insight superior to anything found in Goethe; but Herder, unlike Goethe, did not need a model, and his scope was too wide to allow him to be satisfied by loving a single people. Goethe's enthusiasm for an idealized Hellas fostered within him a stubborn dislike of barbarian times and made him shut the door to primitive culture which Herder had opened wide. According to Goethe, the poet can receive impulses from folk poetry, to be sure, and can gather the treasures of emotion and feeling from the literatures of all peoples; but before he elaborates motifs, he must take them back to classical models through whose purifying influence he can make the motifs universal. He reveals no deep understanding of the Old Testament, or any real sensitivity toward the New Testament, as human documents. In the good old Renaissance fashion he interprets official religion simply as a system of dogmas and morals; the latter are absolutely necessary for the people, and it is therefore risky to tamper with the former, absurd as they may seem to the sophisticated man. Biblical criticism—that is, the attempt to give again to the Bible the life it once possessed, which for Herder kept the concept of God alive—like all other attempts at revolution, made Goethe skeptical. As firmly as any rationalistic clergyman he insisted on the high morality of the Gospels and the necessity of the average man's believing in revelation.

Chapter VIII

The New Germany

THE ROMANTICS threw a torch to the world, but the world did not catch it. The artists could not lead society from its immoral state of spiritual lawlessness; the new era belonged to the politicians who trusted in good old institutions which do not depend on anything as unreliable as experience and inner truth, but are maintained by the police. Novalis died before he really found himself. Schlegel lost heart and sought in the poetry of the Catholic Church a surrogate for the wealth of the spirit—in this he was the first of many. For Clemens Brentano literature came to mean sad songs of longing and phrenetic hymns to love that teach the soul to find a bride's blissful repose in the bosom of the heavenly spouse. Thus died the soul which the Romantics had created; and all was still.

Certainly an experience like that which split the nineteenth century from the past cannot be forgotten. The grandiose pictures which E. T. A. Hoffmann painted of the soul show how profoundly men had been affected. But the experience was hushed momentarily into a gentle enthusiasm for nature; it lay dormant in the depths of the spirit, gathering energy; for a time it seemed that the liberators had struggled in vain.

Everyday actuality was too stable to be swayed by the visions of a few dreamers, even if those visions were prophetic and their fulfillment would create a new heaven and new earth. The experience of the soul runs ahead of life's conventions; sooner or later it draws outward realities after it so that society conforms to the new ideals and images; but only too frequently, as in this case, the dreamer must die before his soul can merge with the outer world and arise with it.

To all appearances there had been no change in Germany. The prince had his government and the citizen his business, and at neither the court nor the shop did any reasonable man feel a need to exchange old ideas for new. To be sure, Germany had experienced an era of enthusiasm which had inspired in many young hearts a hope of rebirth. To many it had seemed as if God were about to fulfill the predictions of the prophets. The Wars of Liberation, in defiance of Napoleon, had swept the country like an evangelistic revival. Young men were carried away by their enthusiasm and became poets and heroes. The people, long no more than a tool in princely hands, suddenly and in amazement saw themselves as makers of world history; when they returned to their hearths, they only too naturally supposed that the flaming creative energy which possessed them would imbue their peaceful tasks. But the peace did not recognize the heroes who had sung and fought for it. Disappointment overwhelmed the people when they saw men of high rank take over the entire realm of government, as if the eighteenth century had crept unobtrusively along with the times. In the crucial hour the prince had made a covenant with the people which assured them the free man's right to self-government in a new society. Of course it was not the prince's intent to break his word, but he who best understood the people's real interests could not endanger society by allowing uninitiated men to experiment upon it. After the people had been disciplined into maturity it would be possible to accept them as partners in action and responsibility. And all reasonable men agreed with the prince, for they had been bred in the old aristocratic culture which believed in government by paternal despots, landed proprietors, and *philosophes*. The enthusiasm aroused by the Wars of Liberation vanished like water spilled on sandy ground.

Having been baptized into a new life by suffering and ecstasy, men rather understandably clenched their fists when the paternal despots, who wished to continue the education of the people at the old glacial rate, in accord with their conception of the spiritual needs of the people placed Jesuits and policemen as auditors in the public schools. Chamisso wrote the bitter watchman's cry:

> Hört, ihr Herrn, und lasst euch sagen,
> Was die Glocke hat geschlagen:
> Geht nach Haus und wahrt das Licht,
> Dass dem Staat kein Schaden geschicht.
> Lobt die Jesuiten![33]

But is was not political misery which drove the finest spirits to self-effacement within Roman Catholicism or the Nirvana of art. The end of the eighteenth century had been a jubilant roar. The bonfire of the French Revolution was reflected brightly in many young eyes; the explosion of popular power was an overwhelming symbol of that desire

101

for freedom which young men felt within their hearts. Their souls had glimpsed eternity; but at home they found that there had been no change. And now a diurnal round of meaningless drudgery and sluggish repose settled down like a gray pall over the minds of men. In effect, the old culture remained unchanged; but everything became grayer and grayer. The slight insight which men had gained into the poetry of primitive peoples had given them a taste of a life where toil and festivity were not separated, where the burden of the day and the joy of the spirit together inspired the mind, so that the worst drudgery took on the luster of song. They had seen men who worked and fought for honor at the same time they strove for happiness and the bare necessities of life. They had tasted a repose which was a festival. And they did not need to go to antiquity or heathendom for examples; at harvest time the peasant could work sixteen hours and then dance away the other eight of the day, intoxicated by the golden wealth of the grain. Men had seen enough to make them imagine new possibilities in human existence; they envisaged a life which did not fall apart, with all the prose on one side and all the poetry on the other. They understood that to achieve actuality, literature must be the poetry of life, and that it presupposes noble work—not work done for the sake of a wretched piece of bread, salted by the sweat of one's brow, but work accomplished for joy, with some black bread simply thrown in for good measure.

It was his desire to see culture as the unifying principle of life that inspired Novalis to praise the Middle Ages in *Die Christenheit oder Europa*. In them he found what his own culture lacked: a principle which joined all the parts of life into one organism; there he saw how quotidian reality can permeate art and religion and pass through them into the depths of eternity. He felt the split in his own culture so deeply that he was led to idealize and exaggerate the medieval virtues; but his ideal sketch is informed with a surprisingly clear understanding of what was central in the organic era that had awakened his envy, and with an incisive recognition of the flaw in his own culture: that is, he understood that in modern culture, wherever there is a choice, material considerations always take priority over spiritual requirements, and that by the dependence of Protestantism on the Bible, religion is transformed from life into philosophy. In rapt words he prophesies a new time—

102

not the old returned, but a new creation in which deference for the past and the desire for freedom will intermingle. A world will come into being where peoples meet in mutual understanding and in work, discovering that what is earthly is a sacrament, the bread and wine through which the energies of eternity stream into the soul. Europe will abolish boundaries and erect a state of states; and the resurrected Europe will share its wealth with all mankind. "When? Do not ask. Only have patience; the time will come, the time must come, the eternal peace when the new Jerusalem will become the capital of the world. And until then, confidence and courage, ye who share my faith. Proclaim in word and deed the divine gospel, and keep unto death the faith in truth and eternity."[34]

Schlegel and Novalis dreamed of a business organization, built upon cosmopolitan brotherhood and including booksellers and printers, which would be devoted to scholarly and literary activity, and would make artists and thinkers independent of the commercial schemes of publishers. Utopian as this dream may sound, like the vision of an organic federation of states it will be fulfilled in time, because it is based on practical necessities. But the Romantics were alien to the times, and the heavy wheels rolled over them.

In Europe men alternated between drudgery and rest from drudgery. More and more strongly, reality denied the possibility of a life in which ideals would be woven into the routine of the day. It is terrible to watch the men of an entire continent learn to think of work as a curse, when they have nothing else which can take the place of work; when they feel themselves to be a horde of slaves and have as their only wish, as much free time as possible. The worker no longer looks upon his work as a means, or looks through it to a beauty that strives to rise to the surface; he is so much concerned with keeping an eye on his customer that his hands must work mechanically. In the course of a few decades work was transformed into industrial production. To make his business thrive the merchant had to concentrate his attention upon the possible, and as time passed ever greater advantages accrued to the select few who could order their lives for the sake of the profit of the moment. He who could best satisfy the customer's taste, speed up the tempo of work, outdistance his competitors, find new markets where new and useless demands could be created, and even encourage bad taste and persuade the customers to buy what could be produced most easily and cheaply—he was the victor in the race for gold. The Renaissance had possessed a culture designed for and dominated by aristocrats, in which the inward and outward life were in harmony. The central figures in that culture had been the leaders: the landed nobles, and merchants who fed their men, oversaw their relation to God as well as their games, thought for them, instructed Providence to treat them the right way, and wrote poetry for them—or had it written. Lesser men had been organically related to the culture through their leaders, who really felt them to be extensions of themselves; members which they could discipline, adorn, and honor. In the day of Novalis, all men—leaders as well as workers—were born to be slaves, machines consisting of human parts, and differing from machines only in that some were happy while others were not; and this cultural development could not be stopped by the elevation of morality or the magic of art. The reality of culture was so strong that it could distort Herder's crowning idea to its service.

Herder had experienced history, and he had infused the concept with meaning for his contemporaries. At one stroke he had transformed history into the psychology of the human race. According to the new ideal which Herder established, the historian must have a discriminating knowledge of souls and an inexhaustible love of humanity. He has no fixed and neutral base on which he may stand to dole out praise and blame; he must throw himself into the experience of each cultural epoch in order to understand how it shaped its own destiny through its ideals and its sins. If he grasps and examines a man, a single link in the chain, he discovers in that single soul the infinity of history in the motives determined by the past and actions preparing the future.

Herder opened channels through which an ocean surged. By his vision he became the herald of a whole new series of sciences. He demanded a history of religion, a history of culture, a psychology of culture. He pointed out the necessity for archeological investigations in the Orient; nothing in man's past should be neglected as insignificant: every legend and every song in the mouth of the people should be written down; every stone in every monument should be studied until it had borne its witness of the people who deliberately stationed it to mark the grave of a hero or a place where God had wrought marvels for his people. Gradually Herder's demands have been fulfilled. Unfortunately, the new sciences have not inherited the prophet's vision. In later generations only Friedrich Schlegel knew Herder's joy over every human formulation of experience, and his ecstasy in abundance and his intimacy with all the forms of life. One man alone was draped in Herder's cloak: Friedrich Schlegel felt Herder's joy and saw with his eyes the multiple facets of history.

But there was one aspect of Herder's vision which posterity could understand, one concept in his writings which later generations could share: that was his law of history. Nothing occurs by chance. Therefore the historian searches the past in order to explain his own times. An idea can be supposed of greater virtue if it existed in the Middle Ages; an institution increases in dignity when its roots have been followed back into the distant past. The law-bound, the law-enchained, may be easily recognized. All that is, exists by law: the law of its existence is organic growth. It *is* because it must be, and it cannot become other than it is. That which is in actuality is right. Everything develops according to strict laws, and therefore anything which is, may be assumed to be its own justification. No man can change the order of nature; to alter religion and the state, justice and privilege, in order to improve them is like digging up a tree and planting its branches in the ground. If the world as it now appears cannot be called the best of all worlds, it has the advantage of being the only possible world; and when the belief that the forms of society are inevitable has been accepted, a conviction of their excellence will soon bloom.

One may learn another thing from history: that culture as a whole is the vehicle of all ethics, justice, art, and all other goods, and one may see proof of this dogma everywhere about him. The individual has no significance today except as a cog in the machinery of the state. Everything the individual undertakes succeeds only in as far as he fulfills the possibilities latent in society; this view became clearer with each decade to Herder and his successors. What is accepted by society is the norm, and the individual becomes a rebel as soon as he formulates independent thoughts. This situation does not result from any despot's desire to rule; it is inherent in modern culture; so that out of history's paean to the diversity of human life one may make use only of the refrain, which praises the unifying force within a people. It is the good fortune of the individual to live his life encysted in the body politic: so says history, the great prophet. And at the mid-century the needed philosophy was proclaimed: a new science, the so-called ethno-psychology. Why ask about the individual, why investigate the slight movements within his brain when we know that they lead nowhere, and when we no longer assume that history can be deduced from the study of petty human motifs? Since it is the group that thinks the decisive thoughts, let us study the group-soul which decides, creates, arranges, and gives us all life; let us study the soul of the people and its laws by observation of its products and culture.

In his authoritative way Goethe illustrates the strength of the existing structure and the adherence of minds to the old culture. He regenerated the old ideals so that they became new wisdom. He proclaimed the gospel of work, the duty of man through work in his calling to overcome and transform his longing and slowly to advance through the finite to the infinite. At peace with "destiny" and gladly accepting and yielding to his environment, a man can by faithfully executing the nearest tasks enrich his soul and grow useful. By subjecting himself to the conditions that exist, he can ensure that they will guard his outlook to eternity.

This was a doctrine for fortunate men who wished to protect their fortunes against untimely leveling. To the humble this wisdom recommended obedience, industry, fidelity in small matters; on men in high places it conferred the noble responsibility of rule, and fidelity in great matters. In his old age Goethe proclaimed that beauty consisted in utility or in conformity with the environment, and that such beauty is a powerful aid to the preservation of society, being effective against all sorts of revolution. Goethe no longer needed any upheavals, as in the days of his youth when his name was Werther—neither in the social nor the moral realm. Let everything stay as it is: the benevolent despot, the landed proprietor, is truly a father to his people, and the peasants who bow and doff their hats will get grafts for their orchards from his arboretum, and scions for their home fields from the same high source.

Goethe transmuted the abundance which his generation had brought forth into a form that could be used in the ordinary commerce of life by any man sufficiently prudent to conform to reality. From it an ethic could be evolved which would develop rather than destroy society. In

Wilhelm Meisters Wanderjahre the newer generation found an Utopian representation of the very education which it needed—an education in discipline and in honor, in human fortune, and in profound reverence for and blind obedience to the existing institutions and their representatives. Under the leadership of vigorous authorities and the protection of their constant vigilance, young men were to learn to subordinate themselves to the whole, and function as useful members of society. Goethe did not wish to transform, but to ennoble: as satiated friends of progress now phrase it, he desired to reform within the existing framework. He wished to elevate the status of work and give back to duty the qualities of nobility and joy. In all his reforms he was looking backward: he admired the old ideal of the craftsmen directed by authority; he was scarcely able to envisage any progress that was not directed and continuously supervised from above. And in close parallel to the eighteenth century's aristocratic culture and its deference for the ruler of the land he demanded special rights for the exceptional human being like himself. Of others he required acceptance of the conditions into which they had been born; for himself as the exceptional individual he reserved freedom and the right to determine how far he need conform to the requirements of society. He demanded solitude, but a solitude surrounded by clients and retainers. While Herder's life proceeded equably both internally and externally, it strode forward through a continuous interchange that bound him inextricably to his fellow men; Goethe's solitary life was so exalted that he was willing to use people, but not to be tied to them; he was willing to give gifts, to be sure, but not give himself with the gift. As the century advanced and all men became slaves, from the highest to the lowest—and for that very reason imagined themselves to be heroes—Goethe became the prophet exalted above all prophets.

And Goethe had yet more wisdom to proclaim. He gave society a solace, in art. Work *is* the poetry of life for him who accepts necessity; it must not be *made into* poetry as the intoxicated enthusiasts had proclaimed. And art in its higher forms is not thereby lost; on the contrary, it becomes a proud tower attached to the low, secure dwelling—a Hlidskjalv* where men may seek refuge from the ugliness and baseness of the world. The course of Goethe's life was in marked degree

---

* A high seat in the dwelling of Odin.

determined by the fact that his aesthetic desire to depict life was equaled in strength by his human desire to live. When in his early manhood he suffered from multiplicity of nature and life, his purely human pain was increased by his inability as an artist to reproduce what he was experiencing; and even in his youth he found that the way to natural beauty lay for him in the imitation of nature by brush or pen. He felt himself to be a higher being, an artist; that is, one whose work is a creative act of the dynamic spirit of the world. Actually, the artist is on a higher plane than nature, in regard to creative energy, for he can overcome that resistance of the material which often cripples the world-soul and causes unbeautiful abortions. The artist is God's interpreter, for only he who can enter into the working of nature and recreate it within himself can participate in the soul of nature, and comprehend the secret which lies behind the multicolored life of the universe. Here again the Renaissance extends into Goethe's love of the well-rounded and the beautiful and his fear of the irregular, and into his view of art as something patrician, above actuality. But on this point he shares the tendency of the times, and this prevents him from following Schlegel on his wild utopian path when Schlegel attempts to overcome prose with poetry.

Goethe gave to the nineteenth century precisely the art which it asked for. As long as the culture of the times remained but an outlying province of human existence, art had to have its own realm. He who could make this neighboring realm as valuable as possible, and tie it firmly to the slum of fact while preserving its autonomy, made the greatest contribution to the times. Thus art can build upward without incommoding people who are convinced that what the time needs is the practical, the attainable. The dichotomy still exists today; literature and art form an independent state, with its own parliament, its own religious conflicts, and its own journalistic feuds. Our poetic republic has a prototype in Goethe's artistic life, in which his clashes with colleagues, scribblers, and critics necessarily developed into a world-war in verse and prose; the clashes even penetrated into *Faust*.

The cultural dichotomy is still deeper, however; the cleavage empties intellectual life of actuality. Compared with that burgeoning of intellectual life as a whole which took place in the nineteenth century, art was isolated; but this had little significance. A culture which teaches the human being to live one life in his own chamber and a different life outside, with the most conscientious kind of double-entry bookkeeping, makes the historian of culture who has seen a little of the world beyond Europe rub his eyes and ask, "Have I come to another planet?" Of course, in such circumstances the intellectual life becomes a delusion, for man can live only on the basis of facts. There where he sees truth, there his heart will be. The true "artists"—in Schlegel's sense of the word—whether they work in verse, in anarchism, or in the crafts, must become great rebels filled with hatred of the ugly actuality to which their society confines itself. They become prophets who herald a new god and a new earth in which resides not justice, but something above all justice which they call love or beauty or brotherhood or something of the kind. But in the nineteenth century their time did not come until the dusk had grown so dark that to many it seemed night.

The entire century is marked by a double life. It became a sign of nobility for a man to say about himself, as Jacobi did, "I am a heathen in my reason and a Christian in my heart, and thus I swim between two bodies of water that will not combine to help by bearing me up, but while the one continuously holds me up the other lets me continuously sink."[35] And the further we proceed in the century, the more numerous become the "fighting" or "searching" souls who enjoy this dichotomy and make of it a surrogate for inward experience. The church worked faithfully in the service of culture; it invested all its energy in an attempt to divorce its spiritual content from actuality, so that, having conserved eternal truths, it could apply its abilities to the practical needs of the state. And outside the church, there was no religious life. Men could share and value Goethe's practical views, but the eternal energy which Goethe fetched from actuality—this they had no use for. Religion flowed sluggishly from the eighteenth century in variously tinged currents—a little so-called rationalism, a little so-called pietism, and a great deal that lay between the two.

In the sphere of religion the contrast between the reality of the spirit and the reality of culture was particularly noticeable. The facts of the spirit had a different character than practical facts. In the spiritual realm, thoughts were controlled by different—and fewer—laws of logic; demonstrations could be made by a looser association between cause and effect; the observation of phenomena did not demand the same precision as in daily life. In general, there is no compelling connection between theory and practice; pure ideals should be constructed and supported by the basic laws of metaphysics, religion, and ethics, but it would be utopian to demand that they be of decisive significance in the course of culture. How ridiculous or how pitiful would be a politician who brought his private life into parliament or who made reference to his most elevated ideals during a debate about a social problem or foreign policy; it is precisely his claim to honor that in practical life he is only a politician. It is easy to make accusations of hypocrisy, but all charges against the pious rest upon a misunderstanding of the nature of our culture; modern man cannot be the same in all situations, because he lives in two worlds—he resides in one and pays fleeting visits to the other. There were thousands of pious men—pious clergymen, pious merchants, pious lawyers, pious statesmen; if one were to mention an illustrious name, Bismarck probably deserves the honor—men who could truthfully say that were they not able to withdraw into the solitude of their chambers to find their God, they would never be able to bear the burden of the day's work. It is dreadful that these men could fear God, honor, truth, love, beauty—that they could be quite honest in their devotion to the unreal—without feeling anything strange in their daily life. Poets and artists are now no nearer to reality than clergymen, whether they write about passion and honor for the evening recreation of tired citizens or wear themselves out in helpless ridicule of philistines and despots. They all know that the spirit and beauty about which they write cannot be transmuted into social reforms, better techniques for workmen, or anything practical. It is simply that the dichotomy is more noticeable in the realm of religion because religion ought to be, and under normal conditions is, the highest expression of the spiritual force of a culture.

As long as the pious quietly occupied themselves within their own world, they did not see that the actuality of the church had become isolated and continued only by virtue of the testimony from earlier times that religious verities did indeed exist; but the world of the pious was constantly threatened from without. David Friedrich Strauss hewed through its props by simply subjecting the Gospels to a critical examination which was meant to suggest that the reports about Jesus' life did not have the credibility which the historian should require of his sources. Nothing more than a *Leben Jesu* was needed to cause dizzy panic and a paroxysm of anger. The only remedy was to arrange new props, and it is touching to remember how grateful the church was to those scholars who demonstrated that Strauss was not as good a critic as he pretended to be, and that the historical evidence was actually not too weak. Believers needed only a helping hand—then logic allayed their doubts. A demonstration that most of what Strauss said was wrong allowed one safely to conclude that nothing he had said was right. And thus one could also thank God for Strauss, since he had become an instrument to show those of little faith that they had nothing to fear from higher criticism—and moreover, had been sent as a useful castigation of those Christians whose lack of faith caused them to be frightened by the encroachments of so-called science in areas which lay beyond its competence. But to allow their doubt to suggest the query: have we any religion? This they did not think of—to be sure, doubt made them *say*: we must now build on the actuality of our faith!—but that ended the matter. In defeat or victory, in fear or confident consolation of the afflicted, our religious life necessarily appears as a peculiar province; for security its boundaries must be rigorously closed, or at least protected by alert customs authorities. The church confesses aloud its lack of proper actuality based upon immediate experience; nevertheless, it makes no attempt to comprehend the streaming life of modern scholarly and scientific thought, except that it notes with joy every instance of scientific failure, and every instance of an honest and significant scholar, preferably an unbeliever, admitting one of the divine truths.

The result must be that the pious in their world always are beset by a lonely fear, and that doubt always lies crouching at the border. Believers assume the role of sufferers, and exhibit a patient endurance of injustice; every attack upon the substance of their faith, indeed every critical inquiry, they greet with indignation: it could only have been inspired by a demoniac hatred of the truth. They solace one another by saying that it ever has been thus; history is an unbroken series of attempts by the natural man to thrust God from His throne.

The religious catastrophe of the century developed out of the clash over Ludwig Feuerbach's book, *Das Wesen des Christentums*; for it became clear to everyone that believers and unbelievers are brothers in the spirit.

In Feuerbach the indefatigable anti-Christ came once more into the world, a more dreadful epiphany than ever. He preached clearly that all religion is self-delusion: that man elevates his own desire into a god, and falls down and worships the creature of his imagination. Why does God have the countenance of man, except that man compensates for his weakness by imagining a being who possesses all the power he himself desires? He who has any understanding of intellectual life, and of European and extra-European history, will consider it idle to refute Feuerbach. That the concept of the divinity in a living religion is not merely the reversed image of human weakness cannot be demonstrated simply, because the conclusion becomes too apparent before the demonstration is complete. The positive ideas in Feuerbach—and there are many of them—are as false as only the truth can be when placed in the wrong intellectual context. But that which determines the result of Feuerbach's analysis is the kind of religion which he finds to exist in the actuality about him; and all his words bear the mark of accurate observation. He describes what he has seen: men throwing on the white screen of eternity chromatic images of all that resists realization in their culture—and calling it Religion.

Schopenhauer, building upon the basic ideas of Goethe and the Romantics, provided the best religious solution in the spirit of the times. If God, the spirit, is the only actuality and man's life is a delusion, then man should show his nobility by withdrawing from that life and obliterating that god by refusing to be putty in his hands. Let us oppose the will to life, let us impede its modulation into action; let us kill the self through asceticism, let us stop begetting children—so that this god will be driven from existence. The only possibility of joy lies in art, where we can imagine life without being caught in the snare of actuality. To be sure, Schopenhauer was careful not to follow his own theory—otherwise he would not have been a trueborn child of his times. To an Indian who thinks consistently so that he can act consistently, Schopenhauer's thought and life must seem a grandiose farce; but in Europe such a contrast is nothing more than the natural result of the fact that actuality and the intellectual life have nothing to do with one another. To this very day no European finds it strange for a man to build a tower on his house but to live in the cellar; a tower is not built to live in. The great pessimist was more closely akin to the worthy theologians than he would have liked to hear. Together they announce the new Germany that chose the will to life but let the spirit take its own course.

One group of theologians at least made an honest attempt to establish an association between culture and religion by undertaking stylistic improvements in ecclesiastical thought. Schleiermacher repaired Protestant theology by inserting Romantic profundities in its dogma, so that at least it could serve as a temporary dwelling for modern men, should any of them seek shelter. As early as his famous *Reden über die Religion an die Gebildeten unter ihren Verächtern* one notes his conciliatory mood, which in fact is indicated by the title. He is not a prophet who proclaims truth with authority, but a scholar who attempts to arouse interest in a subject among the influential in his congregation, in the hope that the multitude will follow them. Later theology continued the work of the great master; but its reinterpretations lack force, as one might expect when scholars must assume in advance that their work possesses no practical meaning for culture as a whole and will have not the slightest effect on the actions of men. It is characteristic of the modern position of theology that there exist two completely different spheres of evaluation. Within the circle of theologians men speak with enthusiasm about this or that attempt at mediation, which no one outside the circle has ever noticed. A clever professor can modernize hell into something in which everyone is committed who will not be saved by Jesus; he can demonstrate that Jesus has the power to save by discovering that the Saviour united spirit and matter without sensuousness, since he was born but not begotten. Though the professor's ingenuity may be admired, the world remains about the same. Outsiders may be surprised that anyone should in this way patch the holes in his coat with cobwebs, and may ask why it would not be better to use a piece of new material; but the theorist is cleverer than his critics, for he knows that new material would tear along the seam, while cobwebs never rip out.

Now that culture had more or less muzzled the dreamers, or had driven them into the outlawry of fantasy, now that the new world with its gray oppressive compulsions had locked men in and accustomed them to its atmosphere so that they did not seriously consider the possibility of another existence, the church could even begin to dispense with cobwebs. Men looked back, not to Luther, who was too much alive, but to post-Lutheran dogmatism. That was something tangible, a satisfying contrast to all the cobwebs. That was something substantial. And with the truths inherited from earlier generations one could strike heretics resounding blows; but a man must be either naïve or defiant to eulogize such dogmatism as of higher value than life.

Life by itself and ideals by themselves; viewed historically that means life today and ideals in the past. One could harmlessly indulge in impotent enthusiasm for the glory of the past, a golden age when gods or at least heroes trod the earth. The imagination had complete freedom to create in historical perspective everything the heart desired, for it was freed from all considerations of reality. And science obeys the same rule as art; it serves truth when it is firmly related to diurnal life, but it creates an unstable truth of its own as soon as it is removed from the service of actuality. Historiography, which, if it had advanced in the spirit of Herder would have become religious revelation, was transformed into the most magnificent will-o'-the-wisp that any swamp has ever produced. All the primitive poetry, all the pious simplicity which did not seem to have any immediate use, was ascribed to the golden age. In their histories Schelling and his eager disciples drew a picture of sentimental inhabitants of ancient India and Greece who to a disturbing degree suggest benevolent despots and their duly appointed village clergymen, clergymen who felt quite as much at home when cultivating potatoes as when expounding the mysteries of the catechism. The wise men of Egypt went to Thrace with the original mystery of revelation in order to civilize barbarian tribes, and missionaries wandered in Grecian dales, clad in white garments, lyre in hand. The lyre was to accompany the poetic sermon, but it was also for the people a tangible symbol of the lyre in the heavens, put there by God for the spheres to play their music on. These wandering white-clad priests spun profound myths about the sun and the moon, about the world-soul and its emanations. They packed so much profundity into stories, sometimes rather unseemly stories, that one must master all modern logic and philosophy in order to disentangle the profundity and bring it to light again. It is almost incredible how much an ancient Egyptian

114

could say in a few sentences. His secret was to give a short tale from four to seven meanings; for he was a priest as well as a sage and a philanthropist. He would let all partake of the good tidings, but he understood that if his purpose was to be fulfilled, he must take into account the wide range of popular intelligence, and therefore he made sure that in a myth there was something for everyone, both the educated and the simple. He told the myth of the flood, and by it suggested the truth that the sublime world-soul may be at once both stern and good, since inundations are harmful to evil men yet enrich the soil as well as any fertilizer. If the common man discovered nothing more in the sermon than veneration for the Lord together with a good idea of the value of fertilizer, his hour had not been wasted. The sacrifice of domestic animals gave to the soulful listener hints concerning the course of the sun through the zodiac, the union of god with man, the corruption of the flesh and the eternity of the spirit—and from it the peasant could learn to be kind to his ox and thankful for his workday diet of porridge.

Like history, these profundities had little to do with ancient times, but one relation may be noted, the fact that they were inspired by the popular philosophy of later antiquity. When the gods of Olympus had played out their roles, and the chasm which separated the cultivated men from the masses had become an abyss, the philosophers, the conciliatory theologians of that day, tried to build a bridge by inserting a meaning in archaic religious nomenclature so that educated people could sympathize with simple men and yet maintain their intellectual integrity. According to the *philosophes* the old myths which seemed to be naughty stories about the loves of Zeus, were *realiter* profound symbols for the truths of natural science. In other words, the Neoplatonic myths were the cobwebs of their day. When Zeus is said to commit bigamy, it is because Zeus is the sun and the earth is a goddess, and when the earth proffers herself to the blessed rays of the sun she casts a long shadow into space, which forms of course a second goddess.[36] And behold, everything offensive has been blown away! In such pedantic visions Schelling and his disciples discovered a natural theology which was as unrealistically poetic and as prosaic *à la petite bourgeoisie* as the time required. And there was no difficulty in ascribing this natural theology to the golden age. Schelling had learned from

Goethe and Winckelmann that all that was Greek was sacred; ancient Homer in the dawn of time and the neo-Platonists of the Christian era —all were Hellenes, all exceeding genial; as if Herder and Schlegel had not described Greek intellectual life historically and had not shown that its beginning and end were almost as widely separated as the Edda and Grundtvig's mythology. On such a broad basis more literature could of course be written; and model and copy become one to such a degree that it would be as difficult as it is unnecessary to determine exactly who decided that Hermes, ecstatically observing Ares and Aphrodite *intime,* is a symbol of the creator rejoicing in the consummation of his labors.

In any case, the Romantics were willing pupils, quite capable of carrying on the method. In the North as in the South one could discover relics of the most sacred belief of primitive times, which God himself had instilled in the hearts of men during the naïve childhood of the race. Loki and Heimdal are the end of time and the beginning of all things, and they destroy one another at Ragnarok in order to teach men that by the nullification of time, beginning and end will be one. So Uhland discovered in the Edda the Romantic concept of primitive revelation.

Into the lap of this new science there fell like a golden apple the Rig-Veda, which became known in its entirety to Europe only in the early nineteenth century. In the ancient Indian sacrificial hymns the scholar found the pure religion of the childhood of man, filled with lisping profundity. Max Müller drew the Indian of the Vedas in a picture that was strikingly similar to the spiritual heroes of the mid-nineteenth century, who sought the mystery of the infinite at the point where actuality ceased. Primitive man meditates in the morning of time, stares toward the horizon, and asks himself what lies beyond; and in his childlike soul rises the concept of the infinite behind the finite. The poor man, how could he give his profound thoughts form without myths—beautiful, romantic myths? The sun and moon, the dawn and clouds became characters in tales about tender or brutal love, because the speech of primitive man was so poetic that he could not give a name to anyone or anything without creating around it a lyrical romance. When he wanted to say that the sun rose and the dawn disappeared, he could only relate that the hero of light sought union with the rosy dawn, and she fled shyly before his fire. But when in the course of time the language changed, the poetic primitive forgot what the names meant, and thus he lost the key, the profundity eluded him, and he began to take his own stories literally. He sat puzzling over his myths about whoredom and rape, quarrels and murder, among the gods. Can anyone be surprised that he lost much of his original innocence while reflecting upon the promiscuity of the deities and their innumerable bastards, and that he finally undertook to imitate the gods in rituals of sacrifice? Thus the aberrations of heathendom necessarily and systematically arose from good and innocent beginnings. Had the good heathen only remembered that Apollo and Zeus were poetic names for the sun, he would have understood that the poor girl was only the dawn. Then life would have been much easier for him; he would never have invented the stupid ceremonies that led religion into a morass.

This history of religion—or mythology, as the times called it, since religion meant to them nothing more than myth—contained the confession of the post-Romantic era and its poetry. It attempted to insert a meaning into dead forms, which it then superimposed upon the past in elaborate configurations. The proponent of these attempts, Friedrich Schelling, was spiritually akin to Schleiermacher—though Schleiermacher was a head taller—and together they were an inspiration for the theologians of the first half of the century. And the profundities with which mythologists clad the old myths exhibited their own culture to the light of day: a little pantheism and some natural science, a little shallow poetry and some tenacious moralizing—in other words, a coarse version of the popular enlightenment of the Renaissance, a mock intellectualism bolstered with a little sentimentality. Dependent on traditional thoughts and forms but lacking their force, longing for something new but impotent to create—so post-Romantic culture appears in its poetry. And Max Müller's school demonstrates, incredible as it may sound, that the attenuation could be diluted further. Religion, the mightiest force in the world, became a pale lyric of the kind the bourgeois likes because it makes life so poetical.

Nevertheless the modern history of religion which probes so deeply into practical religious life—and which will probe still deeper in the future—owes much to the post-Romantic era. Scholarship was modernized by its contact with an actuality; it came to consider not egocentric fantasy but practical needs. The agent of the change was Jacob Grimm, who never would have acquired his naïve and gigantic strength had he not shared the enthusiasm of the followers of Schelling for the profundity of the folk-soul. From them he learned to hear God's voice in the first paradise and recognized in it those profound tones which resound through history. How wonderful it was to perceive the revelation contained in *d* and *t*, as in *Gott, Vater, gut, Mutter,* Odin, Hoder, Odysseus, Ogier the Dane, etc., etc. By taking care that there was a dental sound in all the words which should be considered consanguineous, God had unmistakably revealed in all the languages of the earth the connection between himself, his being, fatherly love, motherly tenderness, the good, and much else that is splendid. Or consider the depths which the myth about the spinning goddesses reveals to the naïve observer; battle is manly deed, and the spinning wheel is womanly need, and in the myth about the battle-spinning Norns we may through poetic symbols contemplate God's being, which unites the eternal masculine with the eternal feminine. These discoveries Grimm expounded in his youthful essays. Having exhausted the possibilities of the alphabet, he made himself quite dizzy in an attempt to decide the limit of the god-idea, for the myths fade gradually into the history of kings who slew one another *realiter,* and even there the divine dentals continue to appear, as if in history God began to extend his profundity to dynasties and dates, after exhausting the possibilities of mystical orthography—which seems quite plausible when rightly viewed.

Grimm heard God speak most clearly in his own people, past and present. What is the history of culture other than the degeneration and death of revelation? In a refined civilization it may be only faintly perceived, but the common people have preserved unspoiled the naïve soul; the peasant still expresses himself in myths and legends, and through pious customs. To an extent unknown in England, Germany still preserved in the countryside a common people with an ancient culture which had roots deep in the past; there "nature" was real and intimately known to men. The collectors of folklore whom Herder had inspired listened to the voice of the *Märchen* as they sat among peasants and charcoal burners. In the woods of Thuringia they listened to eyewitnesses tell in hushed voices about "des wilden Jägers" dash across the heavens with fiery horses: they felt themselves transported to the dreamland of antiquity, they saw men wander respectfully over fields which were God's earth and not merely a factor in agricultural economy, saw them make the last sheaf into a doll and put it in the place of honor while they danced in ecstasy about the golden harvest.

Who spoke through the people's old legends and songs if it was not God himself, or—and this was the same thing—were not poems a song from the inexhaustible and ever-inspired soul of the people? The spirit of the people was a poet which recreated its dream each time it sang. Every word and every variant was sacred, no matter how insignificant they often seemed. When the tale ends with the pious phrase, "And if they are not dead, they are still living," we hear in the simple words the voice of God; and when the tale is retold, it must end with this naïve refrain. Thus was born in Grimm the disinterested respect for the actual which is the *sine qua non* of modern scholarship and science. But if this veneration grew and made itself felt in daily life; if it could transform itself into the rigor of research, into patience in collecting, and ardor in rewriting; if it could spread over all of Europe and evoke an interest so great that colonial officials and missionaries bore it with them to the islands of the South Pacific; and finally, if there grew out of it a science which was co-determinative to the intellectual life—it was because at the very beginning of it all Jacob Grimm conceived of himself as a contributor to culture and, inspired by the vision, felt so strong a sense of responsibility that he was impelled to reach out to actuality. Germany had lost touch with its past in the unhappy era after the religious wars. The best men in Germany were constantly perturbed because their people lacked the feeling of stability which gave to England and to France self-assurance in intellectual work, and men like Lessing, Herder, and Goethe devoted their lives to the development of German culture. Grimm had found the solution to the problem: a bridge could be constructed which led directly to the glorious Middle Ages; the planks of the bridge would be the common people.

So Grimm found his way to the world again. He gave Germany what it needed: a relation to the past. His fatherland acquired a German god who fuses with Odin and Thor and reveals himself quite as fully in the old myths as in the Old Testament. By uncovering the material necessary for the study of the inexorable relations within the

119

history of monarchy and constitutional law, Grimm gave the time what it demanded: an explanation of the recent discovery that individuals are fettered by the organization of society. And by attaining actuality he gave to the history of religion the necessary energy to concentrate on observation of historical fact, so that it eventually would attain enough authority to arbitrate in the so-called war between faith and science.

Chapter IX

The New England

IN GERMANY, as in Scandinavia, Romanticism marked the beginning of an epoch, though it was essentially destructive and gave a mere semblance of richness to culture by applying an aesthetic varnish. The Reformation and the era which followed that great change had broken off Scandinavia's bond with the Middle Ages and made the region a spiritual colony of the cultures of England and France. The intellectual giants of Germany—Lessing, Herder, Goethe, and their contemporaries—labored in the conviction that they were literary and cultural pioneers, who not only must discover their own identities but must create a national genius. And they did accomplish the herculean task of giving to their people a past, a present, and the hope of a future. Because the new Germany had been reborn, its culture included an awareness of its contrast with the preceding era.

England did not need to be created anew; its history was a single current flowing from the Middle Ages through the Renaissance to the present. The coherence made it natural for the Englishman to accept impulses from the English past. When an English poet went back to the Renaissance for inspiration, he was like a person remembering his own youth. The Reformation had not broken the relation of past and present; both in the English common law and in the principles of the English Church the historical connection with the Middle Ages was preserved, and the ethics of the English gentleman stemmed directly from the ideals of the English noble. And during the Renaissance classical literature had become so closely fused with English intellectual life that afterwards the ideas of antiquity were woven into the cultural changes from century to century and were never really felt to be alien. The Englishman continued to think classical thoughts in English; he often discovered new values in them, but those values were domestic. Quiet growth from century to century has given English culture stability, so that it does not change bit by bit, but casts its slough when new impulses have completely permeated and impregnated the whole. Quietly, almost rhythmically, English intellectual life renews itself from time to time, and each renewal is a rejuvenation rather than a

121

revolution, since there is never a disruption in personality. Because of the very stability of intellectual life a rejuvenation not infrequently appears as feverish excitement; a rebel like Byron has to deny everything, to ridicule regulations and ideals, government and religion, in order to have room to discover himself. And because the old ideals are inherent within him, he must struggle the harder against them, and as a result the ideal finally achieves renewed life through the struggle. For the same reason, revolutionary experiences leave their mark deep within a man; the impressions work in the depths, and it may be a long time before their effects become visible on the surface.

In the latter way, the struggle of Blake, Wordsworth, Shelley, and their contemporaries for the expansion of the soul ended in apparent failure; it left no mark in the actuality of culture. At the beginning of the nineteenth century churchmen proclaimed the harmony of nature and of society as their fathers had done; to believe in virtue, to profess faith in the Creator, was a simple matter of good breeding. The Dissenters preached the same harmony in their own way, but gave the Devil a more generous share of the control of the universe; they preached the same morality except that they listed as sins more of the pleasures of the world. The established church, in fact, had become superfluous because it proclaimed axiomatic truths, and the chapel was a nightmare for healthy souls, who found it difficult to constrict their lives as severely as the evangelical concept of good and evil demanded. The same ideals were preached better and with more practical effect both in Parliament and in the writings of social economists. What the church added about God and other such subtle matters did not alter the picture. Nor did the people spend their time needlessly in churches. Benefices conferred upon the younger sons of well-to-do families; priests who never visited their flocks; vicars who shuttled from parish to parish and rushed through divine service with the sexton as the entire congregation; baptismal fonts which served to store candle-stubs, coffin-ropes, and other ecclesiastical gear; dilapidated churches with an enclosed pew in which during the sermon the lord of the manor occasionally took a placid nap behind the curtains: these are the things that people whose youth fell in the first decades of the century later remembered about the church.

The soul had not expanded, much less traversed its boundaries, but it had gathered wealth within the limitations of harmony. The old ideals were honored and exalted above what was worldly; but it looked as if reality had moved on while the ideals had remained fixed and now cast their light on abandoned territory. In the poetry of Tennyson the new century saw its own portrait; here was a lover of nature who took an aesthetic pleasure at the radiance reflected from the blades of grass and the wings of birds; here was a sensitive spirit who could preserve in verse the glimmering reality that he received through his senses in his soul. The world has become so rich in forms and colors, and the soul, sensitized by the vision of this splendor, has become so rich in nuances, that the inner experiences of friendship and love occasion a resonance of ever-tenderer and more mysterious harmonies. The soul takes its finest nourishment from the moods of nature; and it is so penetrated with music that the myths of antiquity and the Middle Ages arise, reborn in a poetry of mood. When Tennyson with his lyrical and luxurious art has created an enchanted world from the noblest dreams of the Middle Ages, he can provide only virtues and vices—not men and women—to wander in the garden and live upon its fruits. He dresses Knighthood and Chastity in the costumes of King Arthur's Court; and the costly materials accentuate the bourgeois cast of their countenances, so that the poet's contemporaries immediately recognize the heroes as their own ideals. But worse: it seems as if by the elaborate design the poet, in his heartfelt zeal, has made obvious the sheer un-reality of the ideals. As one reads, one has a feeling that the virtues and vices are revenants, and one asks, where are the men and women in this beautiful world? Or rather, one dreads to think how the human race may fare in a world populated by shadows who claim precedence in the enjoyment of its splendors. But perhaps men have been fore-sighted enough to arrange a paradise for the virtues in romantic castles in order to reserve the fertile regions for themselves?

Tennyson's religious poetry displays his weakness clearly. He is determined to sing about the immortality of the soul and the meeting of the divine and the human in this world; he struggles to use the Christian words and formulae as straightforwardly as possible. When his tone wavers, it is not only because he uses traditional expressions as symbols to represent his faith without any recognition of the chasm between form and content; quite simply, his tone is false because he cannot decide how much he should and may believe. Yes, in his words there lurks the fear that actuality will not turn out to be commensurate with his faith in love and justice and eternal life. The most he can say is this: I remain faithful to the ideals, even if the ideals desert me. For him the ideals are more valuable than actuality. "I can sympathize with God in my poor little way,"[37] he says with intimate candor; it is a strange basis for all the hope which is trumpeted in his verse.

As it is fitting, another man of the times appears, a prophet named Carlyle, who begins to judge the generation which claims to live but is dead. How can you paint and write poetry, he asks, when you see nothing and believe nothing? Your religion and your culture only mask the truth that you experience nothing, nothing within yourselves and nothing without yourselves.—Carlyle demands rejuvenation and rebirth; before a new life can be born within men, they must prevail upon themselves to look truth squarely in the face. They must have courage to doubt in order to discover the facts, so that life can have a firm foundation. And the foundation of life is religion. But what, then, is religion? To act, answers Carlyle; to do one's duty without asking for reward or comfort. Do it, and you will discover God's reality above and beyond all dogma; you will discover that God is just, and demands justice. But the world is so permeated with injustice! — Yes, answers Carlyle, therefore God judges the world. God remains silent, injustice increases through the centuries, and the wrong presages its own destruction. Consider the French Revolution, and understand that history is God's revenge, hoarded from century to century, and finally exacted with interest from the last generation! — Like the prophets, Carlyle preaches conversion, the transformation of the heart, as a condition for the salvation of the people. The individual must give up his vanity and emptiness and seek to follow a path of justice, goodness, and charity. If one asks what is goodness, Carlyle answers confidently, ask your own heart, and you will feel what justice, honesty, and truth are; elevate your soul beyond vanity and your conscience will rise to meet you. The common words, *goodness* and *truth, virtue* and *duty,* are for him elements in the world of the soul. God—or the higher powers, whatever they are—once differentiated between good and evil, just as He once separated earth from water and called it land. Carlyle's argument is based on his conviction that God wrote the law of justice into nature and history so plainly that everyone who wishes can see that virtue gives birth to fortune and that sin breeds death. In *Sartor Resartus* he describes the painful course which he had to follow in order to find truth. His path took him through despair, "the Everlasting No," where his fear and doubts were lost together with his slavish dependence on the Bible and dogma, to "the Everlasting Yea," where truth was given to him once more from within himself: the concept of duty for the sake of duty and for the sake of man. Justice revealed itself in him as a power which did not need to call upon a god; for in the cry of the soul for goodness and nobility, the commandment "Let there be" sounded as if higher powers were calling out of the chaos of doubt and transforming the riddles of the world into a *mysterium*. But this rebirth which Carlyle achieved through the ordeal of fire—and with the help of Goethe—was in reality both a liberation from and an adherence to the catechism. He understood its contents but disassociated himself from its *raison d'être*. The old faith, the old ethics, the old values, the belief that fortune follows virtue, these are dominant in Carlyle—when he is thundering against an evil generation.

The message which Carlyle brings is not a gospel about new and richer experiences and a world which shall rise from them, but only a warning to men that they must exert themselves if they are to become in truth what they now pretend to be. They must find their souls; but it does not occur to him that they have lost their old souls and must find new ones, or that society has changed so that goodness and justice have become empty words. Men must be true—but how can these men who no longer experience anything have a self to be true to? Carlyle is called a prophet, but he is not like the old prophets who made new demands on the people and drove them to a new life; nor is he like the revivalist preachers of the previous century who aroused "sin and the Devil" in men until, in the ecstasy of fright and salvation, their flocks shattered commandments, patterns, and decency in their search for a new life. All of Carlyle's thoughts were based on old ideas, and therefore he was afraid of all new thoughts, of science, of historical research, and indeed of everything that could disturb tradition. He hated all the men who drew conclusions based on his own analysis and sought a new footing in actuality. When some bold men struck out against conventional opinion and replaced the interpretation of the Bible—the very yoke which had been too heavy for Carlyle—with historical under-standing of the Bible, he shouted words of abuse at them: The senti-nel who deserts is shot!

As a consequence Carlyle ended in a cult of the hero, since he had no other basis on which to build than the approbation of his own heart. The great man is the revelation of the true human being, who obeys the divine voice in his own conscience without demanding signs in heaven or on earth, just as the author of *Sartor* had done. But when he must give flesh and blood to his concept of the hero, and insert it into history, the hero becomes a disguised representative of the great spirits of the eighteenth century who lived and thought for their own sake and for the sake of a people. Behind Carlyle's energetic and active hero, be he William the Conqueror or Mohammed or Napoleon, is the old lord of the manor and benevolent despot from the times of his parents. The hero is the will of God revealed in action; he is a Bible, the only Bible for humanity, but he is also the ethical ruler who sternly leads men against their will into the path of justice. For Carlyle, as for Tennyson, the ideal is above actuality, but he has the courage to defy the world and bid it to submit to the ideal. He decries science when it dares to place itself on the side of experience; every spirit that will not submit is con-demned to Tartarus and shares the fate of cowards and hypocrites.

Tennyson and Carlyle proclaim, each in his own way, that harmony lives on; and each also proclaims that it no longer corresponds to that actuality of which it should be the general symbol. Carlyle's great con-tribution consists of his disclosure of the discrepancy between culture and actuality. The world has become so vast and so complex that it has destroyed the ideals of the gentleman which once supported an har-monious culture. The shift is felt most clearly in the social area, where it had begun in the eighteenth century; in the next, it had increased with the speed of an avalanche. An entirely new people arose in the factories, a people for whom culture, so to speak, had no room. The eighteenth century had viewed the people as an entity that could be sub-jected to education, justice, or pitying satire; all these people, who hitherto had been parts of the landscape, suddenly forced their recog-nition as individuals by freezing and starving, or by going on strike and destroying machinery. Their world becomes articulate in the novels of Charles Dickens, where a warm-hearted gentleman is the interpreter of the inarticulate and expresses according to his judgment and on the basis of his experience what they must feel. But neither he nor anyone else achieved a union with the new world, which was so distant from the old that the only possible bond between them was sentimentality.

There were two peoples in England. While in Germany two cultures opposed each other, one old and one modern, in England there was a contrast between the cultured and the uncultured. Between the two yawned an abyss. An English lord might feel pity for Negro slaves and fight for their human rights; but in Parliament the same man could demand the severest punishment for striking workers, on the ground that the poor can only be kept from crime by fear.

The new world of the English workers had no language of its own; all that the people had possessed of spiritual good—games and songs, ethics and religion—they had held as a kind of fief from the upper class, which had both created and sustained culture. When that connection was abolished, the common people were deprived of their possessions, and in their penury they had no resources except remnants received from the culture of harmony. For a generation or two traditional ideals may live on as a kind of rugged feeling of honor. The common man withdraws shyly from self-created or state-created charity; he wants self-respect, he says, and he takes care that his life shall demonstrate his respectability. But without some renovation, a second-hand culture wears out. Moral precepts and the song about love in a cottage, which the man of the people learns at third-hand from Phyllis and Amaryllis, wither away; the fairs and festivals become rootless and formless. When the struggle for bread required twelve—and even up to eighteen—hours of work a day in the factories by a man, his wife, and their children, family life disintegrated. In this way the nineteenth century created the natural man, who had been sought in vain among unenlightened heathen, a man with no other law than need and custom, untouched by moral and religious discipline, as Shaftesbury defined the concept.[38] It was horrible that thousands lived in cellars and starved and worked themselves to death, but the real horror lay deeper: it was a world of men for whom actuality was crusts and rags, a world of men for whom the spirit did not exist in any form. The tragedy becomes still more poignant when one discovers that a few groups of workers held on to their cultural heritage as long as possible, that in their spare time they studied history and entomology and only gradually lost their grip and slipped into the abyss. These people were condemned to live and die in one spot. They were accustomed to their hell and needed it; if they were put out into the country again, being rootless, they would have withered away. In their poverty they were a product of the factory and the street, just as the Greek was the result of the interplay of man and the ocean, the islands, the mountains, and the battle of Salamis.

With consternation the men of culture looked down into the gulf which gaped in society. Carlyle preached conversion; he urged employer and worker to seek within themselves justice and obedience and a feeling of duty. John Stuart Mill preached education and self-education; society needed reform, and the human conscience needed reform; men should rely on reasons and cultivate their feelings. Widely as Mill and Carlyle differed in the realm of the practical—one being a political philosopher who believed in universal suffrage, and the other a prophet who despised legislation as an ethical fraud—they were in hearty agreement about the essential. Culture, the culture which they themselves represented, was identical with humanity, and it was the work of the reformer to induce humanity in the people, whether it was termed an awakening of conscience or the cultivation of the feelings. And among the many philanthropists that dire need called into being, there was the same faith in action, for they sacrificed their lives and fortunes to raise the workers to an enjoyment of the fruits of culture. None of them understood that their culture was a revenant from a vanished actuality; that the workers were a living proof of the death of culture.

Consequently, all words and all deeds disappeared into the gulf, which became greater and greater. Of what use were the old words about justice and goodness, when destiny itself was undermining culture? Within a simple society where man confronted man, the landowners and the employers themselves had constituted a revelation of justice; human providence competed with the divine to reward virtue and diligence with good fortune. But through the great new modes of industry there was created an impersonal power which robbed Providence of its controlling status and ruled the world by means of its own agents: competition, supply and demand, specialization, and all the other new demons. Men no longer worked for one another but for a destiny that automatically chained together diligence and hunger as inseparable companions, so that evil no longer was needed to bring forth injustice. The landowner was not evil when, having obtained parliamentary permission, he fenced in an old common field, where the crofter pastured his cow, and ploughed it up; he felt that he was the champion of equitable justice and also of improved agricultural methods, the value of which the common man could not see. And he was justified by the result: England was able to bear unparalleled military expenses without a groan and at the same time to accumulate capital on a scale hitherto unprecedented. Nevertheless, the worthy actions of the landowner caused the hopeless impoverishment of the common people.

To be sure, when observed superficially, culture seemed to continue on its course and to prove its truth by its deeds. A tangible demonstration of the harmonious belief that diligence, ability, and good fortune were allied was to be found in the advances of the times: machines which performed the work of a hundred men, and carriages that ran by themselves. Is not the power within coal a servant which God gives the faithful worker in the vineyard, who labors in the firm conviction that there is regularity in nature? True, the culture brought about social misery by subjecting itself to the steam-engine and capital. But at the same time that by inflexible laws it created bestial forms within Christian Europe, it brought forth the finest works of art within a small circle of people by gentle suasion. It fostered the world's finest breed, the gentleman by whom all coarse passion was unknown and—its masterpiece—the sensitive and noble lady, so modest that a man must with elegant adroitness disconcert her before she can listen to his suit; a real princess on the pea; so chaste that for her an innocent rumor is like a waft of death, unable as she is to soil her hand by attempting to ward it off. All the Victorian novels constitute a eulogy of her nobility in fear and pain, and of her faculty for creating or inspiring a milieu that becomes a setting for the loftiest human life.

The great new modes of industry that placed all of humanity beyond the basic laws of justice in order to make it dependent on the arbitrariness of competition and the market also released from material domination a fund of the noblest energy for the cultivation of life as a fine art. The same culture created in the world a heaven so ethereal, so spiritual, so unreal that most other heavens fade beside it, and a hell so brutal, so devoid of beauty, so unimaginatively real that all other hells seem in comparison poetic masterpieces.

There had also occurred a change in the world which lay beyond the society of men. In the view of the natural scientist, nature had changed from a landscape enlivened by the tribe of feathered songsters to the habitat of competing individuals that tear food out of each other's mouths and peck out each other's eyes in order to push their own young forward in the world. And it was not only that the world within the familiar horizon was revealed as a jungle of contrary wills; the so-called heathen peoples which previously had lain in the mists on the horizon now took on clear contours. As the result of colonization and commerce, all these—black, red, and yellow—started forth from the landscape as distinct peoples, not children of nature, full of poetry and naïveté, but men with their own cultures who seek revenge, take scalps, and expose weak relatives to starvation and death under stern ethical compulsion.

Like the world beyond the horizon, history also was transformed and assumed frightening dimensions. For the Renaissance the past had been an harmonious whole which, beginning in the Old Testament and Homer, advanced quietly through the classical era and the Middle Ages to the present, like the career of some happy human being. Whether one stressed Abraham or Achilles as the beginning of history, one rejoiced to meet noble, cultivated human beings, in Genesis or the *Iliad,* whom one proudly supposed one's distant relations or ancestors. Now history expanded in all directions from harmonious lines into distorted shadowy forms. Every year brought the excavation of new peoples. Previously there had lain beyond Homer only a dark void from which the German imagination could conjure the dream of a Golden Age and evidence adequate to make such pseudo-profundities plausible. Now Egypt and Babylon arose from the grave. Those cultures, which previously had been known to classicists only through rumor and through allusions in the Old Testament, each attained its own history; and the primitive priest in long white robes who poetically taught the doctrine of nature to the strains of a harp could no longer find refuge on the banks of the Nile. Previously Assyria and Persia had existed only to put history into motion and to bring pathos into the lives of the Israelites and the Greeks; now they emerged as historical entities. The history of humanity was lengthened backward so far that Europe shrank to a mere episode, and the lines of the past crossed in a jumble where previously one had easily discerned the growth of a clear spirit.

It was a still more variegated sight when the archeologist's spade became a divining-rod which wherever it was pointed conjured forth neolithic flints from the earth. There, beneath our feet, lay stony proof that our forefathers walked about armed with miserable stone axes, as wild men still strut about on the edge of modern civilization. Out there the heathen tribes of Australian aborigines and Hottentots walk about, living illustrations of that race from whom we boast descent. The European was no longer *sui generis,* with high thoughts and a pure will sprung from the dawn of time, the faithful guardian of a heritage which all the black and red and muddy-colored barbarians had discarded when they descended into superstition. Link by link, a chain was formed by the finds, from the mussel-eaters about the kitchen-middens of the Stone Age through the gilded warriors of the Bronze Age to the Vikings of the Iron Age. In other words, Europe got a new set of ancestors whose implements betrayed them as the spiritual cousins of the primitive peoples of America and Australia. And one could not seek solace in the view that the Stone Age had been buried in its own kitchen-middens so that a more advanced people might appear, for bronze and iron were intimately connected with stone through an unbroken chain of discoveries and improvements; there was no gap where a new set of forefathers could be supposed to come upon the scene with their culture and bronze vessels and philosophy in a portmanteau, as Vodskov phrases it.[39] There was something sinister in the history which contracted about Europe and made it equal to a society of cave dwellers and cannibals.

With every new discovery that forced itself on mankind, it became more and more difficult, even with the best will, to read God's goodness and justice from the book of nature, or to recognize a harmony which is congruent with the human desire for happiness, so that a man is naturally on the best footing with his neighbor. As one of the prelates of the day remarked, the world has become so large and man so small that it seems rather ridiculous for religion to dare to prescribe laws for the world. Animals tear one another asunder and devour one another, the warrior crushes his enemy's thigh-bone in order to suck the marrow, the despot treads upon the necks of the people, the tribe steals its neighbor's women, and now, before our very eyes, men are forced through hunger into thralldom by an economic fate. The history of the world seems to be a chaos, undefined and without a purpose, flecked with accidental victories and accidental defeats, where fallacy struggles with fallacy, while truth and freedom often must take refuge with ambitious men who for unworthy reasons offer them protection.

And the doubt which long has gathered in the mind now bursts out in a fearful question: is it possible that the great and basic laws do not control the world? Is justice really a basic law, at all? Animals tear one another asunder, the strongest survive, and is it otherwise in the world of men? Is life not like a mill that grinds men exceeding small without consideration for their ethos? What becomes of goodness and truth when that which is sinful in Europe is praised as virtuous in Cathay? Are good and evil elastic quantities? From everywhere, all countries, all strata of society, all religious sects, men cry out their need, which deepens to despair. It is the poet of the time, Tennyson, the cultivator of harmonious beauty, who coined the watchword of evolution when he called nature a wild animal "red in tooth and claw";[40] and in Darwin's chilly treatises there is heard the same lamentation: "There seems to me to be too much misery in the world" to allow belief in a God—a God who must be responsible for the cat that plays with the mouse and the insects that eat one another alive.[41] The same pain was felt and expressed by all of Darwin's disciples and friends; it was probably expressed most clearly by Huxley when he wrote that "if our ears were sharp enough to hear all the cries of pain that are uttered in the earth by men and beasts, we should be deafened by one continuous scream."[42] For those who saw most clearly, who dared look truth in the eye and express the logical conclusion of what they saw, the answer seems to have been clear: there is no justice, there is no goodness in the world, the attempts of men to be just and considerate to one another are but oases in the desert; the world is evil.

It is striking that the answer was a condemnation of the world and its God; for this shows how firmly the old ideals were imbedded; men would not give them up, men could not give them up. Justice and love were for them rooted in the basis of existence, in other words in actual experience, and for this reason they did not think to inquire of nature what it understood by law; instead they accused nature, naïvely, because its will did not correspond with their presuppositions, set by civilization and society. The researcher carries his ethical ruler with him; he measures nature and finds it defective on all counts, and he is shocked. He supposes that animals should help one another—and he sees that they eat one another and tread upon one another in order to advance. He is confronted with a destiny which arbitrarily scatters about luck and loss, and he is pained to learn that there are no rigid ethical laws which produce a harmony by fitting reward and merit to one another as his feeling for justice requires. By laws and plans he understands the harmony between intent and goal, and he shudders to see the blind extravagance with lives which nature permits itself—thousands of seeds are cast into the world, where most of them are trod down, so that a few may find the conditions necessary to live and grow. No reasonable man would hunt rabbits by placing a thousand shotguns about a field and shooting them, unaimed, all at once, even though in this way he would get a rabbit or two.

People and animals long for happiness as the goal of life; Nature itself has put this desire into its creatures, but it ridicules its children at almost every step; lets them sniff pleasure, then withdraws it from under their noses; or, even more evil, lets its creatures taste fortune, which turns insipid in their mouths. From birth to death the animal is in danger; it must always beware of enemies, it can never relax in security; self-preservation is its first instinct, and yet this very instinct forces it out into a struggle which is protracted into a bloody death. The world is permeated by suffering, and yet within us nature says that suffering is evil. Darwin recoils at the thought that all life suffers pain; if there were a god, and that god were good and omnipotent, he would not have created a world like this one—the conclusion is inevitable. But Darwin cannot accept the logical consequence of his own inexorable reasoning; he must seek alleviation in the hope that death comes quickly and that pain is brief. The old optimism has diminished to a decrepit solace. But it lives on, with its desire to find a justification for pain.

All these agonizing contradictions are discovered because the ideal —the ideal which the Renaissance had constructed on the basis of experience—is in man's blood, and he can do nothing but seek himself and his own spiritual constitution in nature. He must judge all phenomena from the standpoint of the experience in the human soul. Darwin sympathized with the animal whose life is spent in constant insecurity, and the dread of such a lot which he himself felt he projected into the soul of the animal. It did not occur to him that nature may preach a "happiness" different from that which requires impregnable security; that nature may teach that tension and suffering are assets, which belong to the full life. When he observed that violent death in the animal world is not the exception, as it is in the civilized world, he consoled himself naïvely with the hope that animals feel no fear. In other words, he hoped that there are certain aspects of human experience which are lacking in animals. The question whether animals may have their own particular and "non-human" way to feel and fear does not occur to him. Romanes explored the spiritual life of animals from the standpoint of psychology, as if apes and dogs can be nothing else than undeveloped human beings that have not yet acquired the latter's finest qualities. Indeed, man not only seeks himself in everything that breathes, he assumes that even the processes of the elements are as humane as his own deeds—that is, he presumes that nature should be imbued with European civilization. The world is evil because it does not correspond to his ethics. If the good and evil of the European were not eternally valid and a law for all of nature, it would be madness to pass judgment on an earthquake as good or evil, right or wrong. To be pained by the meaninglessness of a natural catastrophe is only possible when one assumes that it ought to be ethical.

The evolutionist speaks about nature as if it were a great human being; it is dreadful, or it is merciful when it shortens suffering. It is indeed a human being when he disguises it as an animal with bloody claws and teeth; the picture is meaningless if one does not presume that an animal ought not to wallow in blood until it stinks so that the human being must hold his nose. Of course these words are symbolic in the mouth of the evolutionist, but the moment one takes the metaphor away there remains nothing but the fact that animals frequently die a violent death, although sometimes after only a brief struggle. And this sentence cannot be taken into the argument without destroying it, for the reasoning depends entirely upon the metaphor. Darwin and Huxley are culturally related to the Israelites who demanded a god who was just with the justice of Israel, only more unsparing and clearer of vision; and of course this spiritual relationship is no accident. Indeed, the ideal of justice and goodness is so awe-inspiring that man believes the worst of his fellow creatures, and does not observe how much animals really work and suffer together; or in any case he does not permit this observation to have equal importance with the statement of nature's guilt.

It is the fixed quality of ideals which makes man doubt the validity of the idea. Despair overcomes the clearest of consciences. Superficial people can always find a way out by simplifying actuality and consoling themselves with the notion that suffering is the result of hidden stupidity or secret sin—or in any case, that the suffering will lead to good, though we may fail to see it. But those who see clearly cannot take the name of justice in vain. They set life before the judgment seat of their ideals and condemn it mercilessly if it does not correspond to their own requirements. They renounce God, because He does not fulfill His own commandments.

Chapter X

Salvation Through Evolution

WHEN THE NEED was greatest, science provided the solution, and it turned out that the lover of truth who dares look actuality in the face will find an answer to the painful question and can draw strength from despair. Justice does exist; goodness and happiness exist and thrive and grow. Unity does exist; but it must be sought in history.

Herbert Spencer pronounced the redeeming word. By his theories, all the bewildering phenomena are linked together like pearls on a strong thread. Within all life's revelations there is a force which causes the homogeneous to exfoliate in multiple varying forms. From the lowest animal, yes, from the inorganic world itself a chain stretches up to man in which link is joined to link by virtue of a simple, inflexible law. The existence of energy and the effect of conditions which diversify the consequence of each change into complex results, these two things explain the origin of the manifold from the simple. The law is demonstrated by the effect of the sun shining upon a sphere; as the rays strike directly or obliquely, they create different degrees of warmth and cause a distortion of the perfect orb.

The blow of a hammer on a piece of iron generates at the same instant sound and heat and sparks. The law is recognizable in the animal kingdom, where the various effects of the environment force the simple cell to develop the versatile organism of the body. In the lower species arms and legs are approximately the same length; by virtue of the multifarious activities of man the balance is destroyed, so that there results a creature with long walking instruments and short practical grasping instruments; the same law functioned at an earlier stage when the complex demands of the environment brought forth limbs from the homogeneous form exemplified by the body of the fish. The law retains its effectiveness undiminished in man's spiritual life, as that develops under the pressure of surrounding nature and through association with other men. At the lowest stage of development history reveals to us man as a homogenous creature; every member of primitive society performs every handicraft and thinks all the thoughts of the people; culture consists of the differentiation into guilds, corporations, estates, and so forth, up to the individual man's specialization as a thinker or poet. We sing in a concert hall, give comedies in the theater, and dance in the ball-room, but these several aesthetic activities had their origin in games similar to the war dances of primitive peoples, whose art consists of mimic dances accompanied by songs.

Nature functions in an unknown play of conflicting forces which educe variety from the homogeneous, but at the same time require coöperation from the several elements of the resultant manifold; for only by collaboration can the individual limb develop its possibilities. Cultural history is the doctrine that society advances from an uncivilized horde in which there exists neither freedom nor law to a ramified organization that bestows freedom of thought and of interest upon the individual, makes him a useful member of the whole, and by means of a society assures him security in his life. Thus the terror of chaos is overcome, both in nature and in human life. Behind all life we find a strong tendency to individuation, and another tendency which, with the force of a law, creates a new entity by compelling individuals to coöperate. If we search deeper we see that both tendencies make up one great tendency; through development nature forms the indefinite into the definite and educes form from chaos. Through development there arises a fixed order, or in other words, harmony. One life, one law.

Behind the apparent confusion we now perceive the functioning of law toward the perfect goal of history: the ethical, the just, man. We see how, step by step, law forces life upward through self-negation and self-education until goodness and truth assume form as a living ideal. Even in the animal world nature begins to be based upon what is ethical by teaching the individuals concord through need and death and thus restraining their crude selfishness. History contains man's own testimony of the laborious path on which he has had to make his way by trial and error in order to perfect himself; to this very day wild, primitive peoples remain as fossilized relics of a lower stage of culture. In the Australian aborigines we can see what we necessarily had to be before we could become ourselves; and by comparing ourselves with them we may learn to value the splendor of culture and to appreciate how the blessing of life rests upon him who is loyal to the law and subjects himself to its molding force.

In evolution, then, the culture of harmony proceeds from pain to a new and truer self-assertion. All the traditional ideas slip unscathed through the ordeal and rise with renewed strength. The demand for a simple world order is fulfilled in the concept of development. The world is confusing and incomprehensible as long as one looks only at individuals; it seems to consist of waste and planless groping; only he who views nature in its entirety can see that beneath all the waste there is an economy and order. One can now fearlessly observe that the world is becoming greater and richer, for this discovery does not necessarily lead to the destruction of the old actuality and to the search for a new.

Unity drives out rebellious multiplicity and reintroduces the norm to its place of domination. Once again the world has something fixed, an ideal type about which the variants can be grouped. Previously the human being was considered the crown of creation according to the order of nature. He now gains his dignity by virtue of developing, and his secure feeling of being the final goal remains unimpaired; evolution modifies the old idea so that it becomes new wisdom.

No philosopher from the age of harmony could wish to use stronger words than those with which the evolutionist expressed his conviction that chance has no place in the world. In the picture which science paints of the universe, energy and matter are like web and woof, ingeniously woven together without the breakage of a single thread, and woven into the world we know, the world of harmony which eternally directs the current of progress. Huxley formulates his credo thus: "If the doctrine of a Providence is to be taken as the expression . . . of the total exclusion of chance from a place even in the most insignificant corner of Nature; if it means the strong conviction that the cosmic process is rational; and the faith that, throughout all duration, unbroken order has reigned in the universe, I not only accept it, but I am disposed to think it the most important of all truths."[34]

The ethics of harmony are reborn in the concept of evolution. Science demonstrates that egoism necessarily must overcome itself, for the welfare of the self demands sacrifice. Only through coöperation with my environment can I achieve the complete development of my powers and fulfill my desire for happiness. The fear that my fellow man will repay me in the same coin which I offer him forces me to obey laws which maintain justice. Coöperation gradually generates sym-

138

pathy in me; egoism makes me almost philanthropic, precisely as in the Renaissance. "The just is always the expedient, as well as the right," states Wallace, with conviction.[44] Moreover, history bears witness that egoism and coöperation have become more and more harmonious in their relation to one another. From the very first, man must force himself to create laws that will maintain a balance between men; but in the course of time the balance becomes a harmony in the mind; and ultimately, duty will become an instinct which it will be a pleasure to satisfy.

Apparently man seeks in vain his noblest desires in nature; for there he finds no love and no gentleness, and so far he is justified in saying that nature is amoral and in complaining of its egoism. But its lack of morals is pregnant with ethics, and its egoism must give birth to love and gentleness. And the pillar of all ethics, the virtue which characterizes the Renaissance, justice, extends to the very roots of existence.

Evolution proclaims the victory of the spirit over the flesh with gravity and with an enthusiasm which surpasses all ecclesiastical eloquence. History demonstrates that the beginning of culture is the surmounting of the "lower" instincts. It reveals human desires to be a relic of the animal in man, and consecrates the duty of resignation by transforming it from a command into a law. In the great book of nature the scholar reads that desires have a servile spirit, and that true life begins when the lower desires are forced downwards into the humble position of slaves and are governed with an iron hand. He who achieves this insight will overcome his fear of the fact that desires and morals are indivisible, since he will know that the slaves serve to elevate the master higher and higher, indeed that they must work themselves to death when they finally have become superfluous. History teaches that the desires die when the higher life of the soul has become strong enough to exist by itself.

History lays bare the roots of virtue and allows man to see that they are immediately intelligible. The ethical has achieved lasting form because it is based upon necessity; this is nothing less than a revelation of the fundamental law of existence. That nature is just, strikes the researcher with almost frightening force. Violation automatically incurs punishment, so that the artificial punishment of sin is unnecessary. Huxley has seen nature as few have seen it; undaunted he has looked himself in the face, he has observed life about him, and his testimony is as follows: "The gravitation of sin to sorrow is as certain as that of the earth to the sun, and more so—for experimental proof of the fact is within reach of us all—nay, is before us all in our own lives, if we had but the eyes to see it."[45] Nature is even more just than man-made religion, because it apportions punishment according to the sinner's qualifications, Huxley wrote. Christianity demands that the outlaw must both hang and repent when he has used a knife; nature spares him that part of the punishment which has no justification within his experience. Thus for the incisive observer nature reveals that ethical conduct alone leads to true and general happiness.

The desire of the Renaissance for happiness found its confirmation within nature. Science lifts man up to true nobility by revealing the principle which carries the world forward and upward to the negation of the self. Evil has been conquered, fear has been banished; the confidence in victory with which the Renaissance examined evil has been revived, for now one sees confirmed by the light of history the old conviction, namely, that sin is a weakness which can be overcome. To be sure, evil is a reality, like something deformed or sick; it is horrible, as the deformed always is for a healthy soul; but it is powerless when it is confronted with true goodness; unlike virtue, it possesses no eternal life. If it were permitted to spread, it could destroy the world; but now we see that nature itself holds it in check. Existence is so harmonious that evil must serve to strengthen and restrain. In history we can understand how suffering has had as a function the ennobling of the worthy. Through life's relentless selection the half-good is rejected, so that whatever possesses the promise of perfection can arise and be disciplined to develop all its force. Death itself is transfigured in history. Without death there could be no progress. The lesser dies so that the greater shall live: this is the solution for him who observes nature in its entirety; the lesser dies so that the fittest will have elbow room for itself and its healthy offspring: this is the wisdom gained by the observation of particulars.

Thus the old ideals gained stability and power by becoming independent of human commands and divine threats, and by being based solely on the law of nature. For the eighteenth century the laws had been contained in a single commandment which nature herself impressed upon the world: do unto others as you would have others do unto you. The evolutionists repeated this creed but with more conviction, since they did not need to appeal to "the voice of nature"; they could demonstrate that the commandment arose as a result of the law of evolution. "The social instincts—the prime principles of man's moral constitution—with the aid of active intellectual powers and the effects of habit, naturally lead to the golden rule . . . and this lies at the foundation of morality," says Darwin.[46] Evolution ends in a confirmation of experience; the best world is that which grants a happy life at the expense of a minimum of suffering and pain; and that definition, correctly viewed, fits the world in which we and our fellow creatures exist. In the light of evolution, despair and the struggle for existence are transformed into a vigorous encouragement to man to cry a continuous *excelsior*! And the scientist sings a hymn to man, the glory of creation, which drowns out all the church's praise of God's creation, Adam: When thinking men have disentangled themselves from the delusion of an earlier tradition they will find in the modest origins of man the best testimony to the splendor of his natural capacity, and by observing his tenacious progress in the past they will find a firm basis for their belief in the nobility of his future.[47]

Chapter XI

The Renaissance and the Concept of Evolution

IN THE HISTORY of the universe the student sees a development, a steady approach to the goal of creation—that is, to man. And in truth the Infusoria heralded not man in general, but the European: for it is his ideal, his justice, his aesthetic sense which are decisive in the judgment of phenomena either progressing, stagnant or (occasionally) regressing. And if one looks more closely, it turns out that the European really occurs in only one place, in England. From the time of the very first sign of life, English ethics and English ideals have inspired nature and put in its cells the unrest of a million years. Of course, the Englishman is not perfect; he is perhaps only an indication of the perfect man; but the way forward, beyond him, is quite clear in terms of evolution.

In the nineteenth century, the belief of the evolutionists that they stood at the focus of a million years of history directed their observations and generated their systems; and if the lines of the systems were sometimes threatened by confusion, it was because the strength of experience had grown greater than the attraction of clarity. All ethical history points toward the individual who demands the right of free development, with the single limitation that his development shall not hinder a fellow-creature from enjoying the same right. The human desire to make demands and establish laws represents the awkward striving of nature towards a conscience by which a feeling of social responsibility will be transformed into immediate altruism. The upward struggle of the universe has ended in the ideals of the European vassal and their happy sublimation in England into the bourgeois obligations of loyalty, justice, chastity, and charity—an ethical system which excludes all the unproductive virtues, all the vague enthusiastic yearnings that lead to no useful goal. The development of culture through its innumerable stages has aimed at the English constitution, in which order and freedom, if they have not already merged, approximate an harmonious unity. Darwin was surprised to learn that some Germans had identified socialism with evolution by natural selection.

That socialism, or any other ism, should be produced by the development of nature was to him so incomprehensible that only fools could suggest it. Finally, the course of the spirit throughout history has been determined by the yearning of the universe to experience the victory of English Puritanism—that is, of religion purified of all illusions about the supernatural—over the lower desires of man. The variegated religions of the earth have prepared the way for England's ethical atheism.

Like Carlyle, evolution passed through the eternal No of doubt to the eternal Yes of affirmation; but its assent was more penetrating, and made life richer and more real. And its affirmation was vigorous precisely because doubt had been allowed to run its course until there appeared a problem that must be solved and that could not be assigned by the *quand même* of faith. The new men were not satisfied until they had gained sufficient courage to rid culture of all the formulae which were no longer true expressions of experience. Carlyle and his kindred spirits had inherited nature and history from their fathers; and they used the inheritance as their fathers had used it, as a divine picture book in which the earnest reader could find passages that taught virtue or illustrated the terrible end of the disobedient man. But actuality no longer corresponded to the picture book; only by the use of a great deal of imagination and much rhetoric could one educe from it the proper morality. Evolution let history and nature themselves reveal their contents, and instead of the earlier picture book, there was now a world for man to comprehend.

The strength of evolution lies in the fact that it recognizes actuality and forms its doctrine directly upon observation. It never needs to evoke an authority or even an exceptional experience; it is self-sufficient because it lets actuality explain itself. With tireless patience science synthesizes the conclusions to which a truth-loving and penetrating observer must come, and we see that when a man honestly looks life in the face and honestly reports what he sees, there is generated within him a philosophy comparable to the proudest philosophical systems.

Evolution gives the old culture new substance; it increases the substance of the soul, and for this reason it exudes power. So in his later years John Stuart Mill felt a fresh breeze pass over his parched spirit. Even at mid-century he had looked with dismay on the flabby convictions, the paralyzed thoughts, and the loose principles of his generation; but ten years later hope rose within him when he observed new thoughts which presaged a spiritual emancipation. The new men did not have to close their eyes out of fear of the evil and the stupidity in the world. They did not need to believe in administration by God, for with their own eyes they saw the ideal progressing through the centuries with ever firmer step, and in their mind's eye they could follow its course into the future. They felt God to be the Law within them, and they concluded that they could see Him in history.

But the concept of development does not mean a revolution, still less a break with the Renaissance. Its nature and its history are those of harmony, a harmony enriched, extended and deepened; it is not a completely different world. Each strand of nineteenth-century research depends upon the experiences of older culture, which it continues along the old lines and to which it subordinates new material.

The concept of evolution was not discovered by a single man of genius; it emerged as a natural expression for the experience of coherence in the universe. The Renaissance always saw the general before the single example, so that the individual disappeared into the species. When man glanced about him he first saw nature as an entity, the background for his own life. Under closer observation classes appeared in the whole, and finally the individual became distinguished from the class. But the individual never achieved his own independent life; at most he only stood in relief before a background of the typical. The Renaissance had taken pleasure in observing the variations in human life and in defining categories; it could enjoy peculiarities and eccentricities because it knew that below the more or less superficial differences there was a basis which assured common ethics and common ideals. But as the world grew in size and the peoples outside Europe poked forth their irregular physiognomies, individuality became so striking that it threatened to destroy the type. Experience created the problem: Why does man assume such unlike forms? Experience also found an answer. In the eighteenth century various thinkers had noticed the significance of environment in the formation of the individual, and by the use of the word "adaptation" they secured a solution which united the individual and the type. Montesquieu made climate and soil responsible for the multiple variations of culture. In a colder climate the skin contracts, and a more rapid circulation of the blood causes an increase of energy. As the taut skin has a smaller network of nerves, stronger impressions are required in order to move the soul. Therefore the Northern peoples are characterized by courage, honesty, a deficiency in imagination, and insensitivity toward pleasure and pain. A rich soil makes happy slaves; a poor soil produces champions of freedom. In such ways there are created, by the admixture of virtues and vices, dissimilar national characters.

All observation seems to have as its driving force the conviction that true existence consists in progress from the imperfect to the perfect. Every night the individual reviews his ethical striving, and now and then a people renders its account for a century; and each instance of self-examination shows that the ideal of justice and truth has drawn nearer than before. The men of harmony do not believe in progress, they feel it; for all their energies are devoted to improving and ennobling a life which Providence has given into their care, and for this reason all their thought must partake of the power of progress. In the nineteenth century the new discovery of the interplay between the spiritual and the material is united with the certainty of progress, and generates a vision of history as the education of Providence or nature—or, in other words, as the development of man. In the new history man acquires the unity within multiplicity which he needs, and he is freed from the necessity of having to explain the ancient Egyptians as well as the modern Chinese as unprejudiced followers of God, Virtue, and Immortality so that they may be included in the society of polite peoples.

The concept of adaptation as a basic tendency was similarly applied to the animal and vegetable kingdoms, in which more careful observations had now discovered such a wealth of forms that the distinctions between classes were almost obliterated by gradations. Lamarck saw that it was hopeless to maintain the inflexibility of types, but in place of the permanence of species he found a more profound unity; the indistinguishable transitions became for him a proof of the fundamental kinship among all things that live, such a kinship as man had dreamed of earlier. In order to live on, creatures must be able to exploit their environment and to change as conditions change. They must be able to acquire useful habits and to discard habits no longer useful; but habits are not enough; the creatures must also produce organs and limbs, such as the long legs of wading birds and the webbed feet of swimming birds. Because of life's adaptability, the world is filled with a swarm of running, creeping, flying, and swimming creatures which as plastic organisms reflect changes in the earth's surface. Nature has gradually produced these creatures, beginning with the simplest and ending with the most nearly perfected.

Lamarck looked upon development and progress as a tendency in all of nature; the English scientists transformed this tendency into a law by tracing its means and paths. Darwin posed the problem with the question: how does adaptation come about? And the answer came in the famous phrases: by natural selection and the struggle for existence. This development occurs because nature favors the individual which has come into the world with characteristics that better fit it into the environment and make it especially well qualified to grasp opportunity and to avoid danger. Through its victory over less well-equipped competitors, the fortunate creature establishes the type which it founds, since the characteristics of the progenitor are inherited by the progeny (Darwin continues); and by a continual selection of the most fortunate among the fortunate in subsequent generations, the victorious abilities are shaped continuously into more perfect harmony with the surrounding world, so that the race grows superior to the dangers of nature. Darwin was not satisfied merely to conceive the idea of evolution; he tested its laws by experiments on pigeons and plants.

Both Darwin and A. R. Wallace—who was his noble competitor for the honor of having conceived the basic principles of evolution— thus felt the truth of development and made it into a driving force in research. Within surrounding actuality they saw a god who moves life along its track, saw him reveal himself as Need and Death, sort out, and stimulate, all according to his inexorable law. They saw the functioning of history in every life-and-death struggle between two creatures; the stronger conquered because he made the moment and the environment his allies.

Goethe and Herder were touched by the same current which carried Darwin and Spencer onwards, but it does not follow that the German thinkers prefigured English theories of evolution. While the Englishmen see form as everything, at the same time embracing and expressing life, the Germans' world is like the periphery of an area that is itself indestructible. For the Englishmen a form is a point along the line of development, while Goethe recognizes in the center of the world an eternally unchanging something which reveals itself only in transitory, changing shapes but is not identical with any of them. An Englishman takes part in a race in which each runner at the end of his course hands to his successor the torch of life before he falls to the ground. Should the torch fall from his hand and be trodden under foot, for his side that is the end of the race, and the end. For Herder and Goethe the race is like a great game; the runner can fall, the torch can be extinguished, but the spirit of the game lives on and can at any time inspire a new contest in which runners may again take part.

The difference between the two conceptions did not arise because the Englishman thought more accurately than the German, or vice versa: each simply described his world. Spencer and Darwin and Huxley knew no other actuality than what they could observe and feel; animals consisted of bones and hair, claws and teeth; their being could be circumscribed in the concepts of form and of the struggle for self-preservation. Plants represented nourishment transformed into stems and leaves and the struggle for the continuation of the species; the organic world came about through an interplay of form and its environment. For the scientist a stone is a mass in the landscape; it can be analyzed into its constituent parts and classified according to the way it was compounded. Everything that goes beyond this analysis falls into the category of what Huxley would call personal wishes, which the scholar must conscientiously prevent from influencing his observation of facts; or it is ascribed to another category as a mood, and becomes subject to treatment by the poet and artist, only. For Herder and Goethe and Schlegel the facts of observation are only half of actuality; the tangible becomes a world only when it is filled with the spirit's intangible actuality permeated by emotions, an actuality which for them was quite as immediately real as that which is known to the senses. In the same way, the soul is for the Englishman something tangible; it consists of psychological elements: feelings, passions, and thoughts which materialize in commandments, myths, and philosophical systems—and can be studied through these, its products. One can learn to understand the soul by breaking it down into its constituent parts. Justice can be explained as a simple social feeling which is a necessary requisite for the continuation of the species; one can see how it acquires substance by the admixture of good will, or rather of two sorts of good will: first, passive good will which puts no hindrance in the path of a fellow man who seeks his fortune, and, second, active good will which even aids a fellow man in his efforts. One seeks in vain in the evolutionist's doctrine of the soul for any of the religious and artistic experiences which have changed the world: the selfless moments of inspiration, the mystic's subjugation by the power of actuality, the ecstasy of anguish and the pain of pleasure—all the things are excluded which Wordsworth and Shelley, Goethe and Schlegel struggled hardest to express. Shakespeare's characters are alien to the psychology of Spencer and Darwin; even as simple a character as Cromwell arouses in Spencer only the question whether he should be viewed as an honest fanatic or as an ambitious man, and the question has not sufficient interest to move him to read three volumes of letters in order to find the answer. This is all quite natural: in Spencer's world, the mystics do not exist, any more than the characters of Shakespeare, and an explanation of the world cannot be constructed on the basis of something of which the existence is not acknowledged. In England the conquest of the infinity of the soul had never been carried out so completely that the universe of the Renaissance was destroyed; it had never become necessary to create a new heaven and a new earth. I have never looked into myself, said the honest Darwin,[48] and this declaration, correctly understood, is a confession valid for the entire generation; it had never looked within itself, but only at itself, and it observed the contents of the soul only as those contents appeared upon the surface.

The Englishman never *experienced* history as Herder and Schlegel had experienced it. Spencer worked out laws for everything that lives, has lived, or will live, Greeks as well as Anglo-Saxons, without even having read the *Iliad*. He once tried to work his way through the poem in order to study the superstition of the Greeks at first hand, but the tiresome catalogues of heroes and weapons, the childish repetition of adjectives, and all the other barbarisms repulsed him, and he quickly laid the book aside. Moreover, from a few pages he had gathered enough to dissipate his desire to know a poetry which appealed exclusively to the brute instincts. Fortunately he could lay down the law of history without an intimate knowledge of the Greeks; for history, like nature, was for him a mass which revealed the same law in all its parts, and since he had discovered the law elsewhere by his study of primitive peoples—the Australian aborigines, Polynesians, and Indians —he knew the truth about Homer and Plato.

Chapter XII

Evolution as the
Religious Expression of the Time

EVOLUTION REPRESENTS A REBIRTH of the religion of harmony in a purified form. The Renaissance had possessed a similar triumphant faith
in the laws of nature and their adequacy. God, the creator and main-
tainer, had served only as a symbol of the dominance of law in nature;
since the actuality never showed a trace of his intervention, his action
was limited to his original determination of the laws of movement,
which therefore functioned by themselves. This God, dragged along by
tradition, was really superfluous; or, rather, one should say that he
existed beyond reality, and therefore was necessarily felt as a *deus ex
machina* whose only function was to replace an explanation of origins.
Evolution met actuality on its own territory, sought God within experience, and found him in laws. With a ruthless love of truth it dismissed
all attempts to improve actuality by the use of the imagination; mercilessly it brushed away the withered leaves in which earlier generations
had clad their experiences, and then provided a rational costume for
experience. In evolution the nineteenth century found a religion which
simultaneously makes actuality into a cosmos and transmits the energy
from this cosmos to the individual. Its cult consists of a search for
truth for the sake of truth alone, without any consideration of preconceived wishes and with a candid desire to allow the evidence of
nature to disprove misleading illusions. Its ethics rest upon the recognition that life itself is ennobling, and advances from the search for self
to noble self-expression, from egoism to altruism and justice.

Its hope arises in the past and gives to the future the security of
systematic coherence without miracles and without gaps; faith in the
future rests upon a basis of experience, without the crutches of miracles
or revelation. Moreover, it gives a complete picture of the world constructed exclusively of actuality and needing no confirmation from
latent possibilities. It sanctifies belief in progress by giving it a deep and
firm footing in necessity. At the same time it excites to enthusiasm the
conviction that there is hope for the human race in the future, and casts

light into the darkness beyond us, so that it seems as if times yet unborn come within our ken. "Believing as I do that man in the distant future will be a far more perfect creature than he now is, it is an intolerable thought that he and all other sentient beings are doomed to complete annihilation after such long-continued slow progress,"[49] says Darwin. The concept of development makes prophets out of the directors of laboratories.

Science elevates, until it transfigures, the deep pleasure that the times take in cognition; it makes the search for truth man's greatest mark of nobility, his true divinity. Man can seek truth, and in it he can find the eternal and the fixed; or rather, by intense search the lover of truth can achieve better and better insight; for the profundity of existence assures that human cognition shall remain only an approximation of truth—at least as far as we can see in time. Intellectual pleasure has its source in admiration and respect for the majestic enigma of the universe. "Nature is a study that yields to none in grandeur and immensity. The cycles of astronomy or even the periods of geology will alone enable us to appreciate the vast depths of time we have to contemplate in the endeavors to understand the slow growth of life upon the earth. The most intricate effects of the law of gravitation, the mutual disturbances of all the bodies of the solar system, are simplicity itself compared with the intricate relations and complicated struggle which have determined which forms of life shall exist and in what proportion"[50]—such was Wallace's paean after he had read Darwin's book five or six times, each time with growing admiration. Similarly, Spencer illustrates man's joy in knowledge. With lifted index finger he says: observe, I strike the table thus: knock, knock, — and at each knock the earth has gone ten miles; and he is astounded that common folk are not moved by such examples of mystery in the grandeur of the world and its laws; there is scarcely one among thousands to whom it occurs to make similar reflections. At these moments, when he sees how high a cultured person like himself stands above the half-civilized or uncivilized, he feels most deeply what development can mean in the realm of the spirit.

But truth is not only a source of joy, it demonstrates its power by ennobling man: a clear insight into the coherence of the world and its laws strengthens the will. Knowledge of the past and its errors breaks the bonds of superstition. Ask why, and thou art saved. The prophets of evolution never missed an opportunity to spread knowledge, and to admonish their hearers that they themselves should acquire knowledge in order that the people may rise as high as possible in its development, before there arrives another of those dark eras of transition which regularly cast their shadows across history. The ordinary man is sluggish, and progress does not come about without starts and stops. Sow the seed of knowledge in hope of a better age: this is the admonition which science gives to its disciples. The recognition of the truth is thus elevated to a religion; in it God is recognized, that is, the law; from it strength can be drawn for a true and altruistic life.

Teach the child what is wisdom—and that is morality; teach him what is beautiful—and that is religion, says Huxley. Huxley was religion's warm-hearted prophet, its ever-ready apologist, its faithful and eloquent preacher, who in his *Lay Sermons* gave the doctrine of evolution its manual of devotion.

With evolution, the religion of harmony descends to the people. The philosopher no longer needs, as before, to keep the esoteric doctrine to himself and to allow the truth to filter down to the people only in weak solution, lest the mass should become lawless when it no longer feels the scourge of church and morality upon its back. The contempt of the Renaissance for the masses has faded and in its stead there is a healthy respect for a man without reference to his rank. Science can be sublime and practical at the same time. Research is the high cult of religion, and the scientist its priest. If a religious ritual is needed for the common man, appropriate forms are already extant; there is no need to tear down the churches. Think, says Wallace, "What might have been the result, if during the last hundred years, the twenty thousand sermons which are preached every Sunday in Great Britain instead of being rigidly confined to one monotonous subject, had been true lessons in civilization, morality, the laws of health, and other useful (or elevating) knowledge, and if the teachers had been the high class of men who, if unfettered, would have gladly entered this the noblest of professions?"[51] Similarly Huxley dreams of a church in which the service would be devoted "to setting before men's minds an ideal of true, just, and pure living; a place in which those who are weary of the burden of daily cares should find a moment's rest in the contemplation of the higher life which is possible for all, though attained by so few...."[52]

The new religion has no saints, but within it there are men who bear comparison with the ethical-religious personalities that created modern England, men of the same mould as Milton, Bunyan, Fox, Cromwell, Hampden, and other proud figures. The first and greatest is Huxley. As he himself said, he was kicked into the world very young, without anyone to guide him, and, he wrote, "I confess to my shame that few men have drunk deeper of all kinds of sin than I."[53] We are reminded of the old introverts who always thought of themselves as the greatest of sinners because they applied an absolute measure to their own lives without qualifying it by reference to the achievements of their relatives and friends. Fortunately Huxley changed his course, and step by step, many of them backwards, he worked his way towards the firm ground represented by the acknowledgment of responsibility and of the unique value of truth. And he gave himself completely up to truth; he served it in good days and evil, never asking how much his championship would cost him at the moment, or what it might cost in some unknown future. Without lowering his eyes he looked actuality in the face and swore that he would serve it. Whenever he closed with opponents, in speech or print, his only weapon was truth, a weapon he carried unsheathed until his death. He did not allow himself to make unjust accusations, or to employ sophistical tricks, or to use words of derision, except when they were drawn from him by indignation at dishonesty. He ruthlessly condemned all mockery in the attack on the church; he dissociated himself from anyone whom he discovered to be fighting with improper weapons for the cause which was his cause. Even more than orthodox fanatics he abhorred the "freethinkers" who ridiculed what was holy and affronted men instead of attacking their stupidity. And from the truth which he served he drew the power to lead a life without blemish; he needed neither heaven nor hell to buttress his heart's demand for purity. He admitted no saccharine illusions even at that most bitter moment when death tore his son from him. "My business is to teach my aspirations to conform themselves to facts, not to try and make the facts harmonise with my aspirations."[54] And he repeats two of Luther's greatest sentences as if he himself had invented them: "I can only say with Luther: 'Gott helfe mir, ich kann nicht anders,'[55] and 'I have searched over the grounds of my belief, and if wife and child and name and fame were all to be lost to me one after the other as the penalty, still I will not lie.' "[56] A child has judged him: having heard that Huxley did not believe in Hell, the child said, "Then he is the best person in England." But most profound and most beautiful is his monument in the confession which he wrote to Kingsley, a priest of the established church, on the occasion of his son's death. He answers his friend's letter of consolation gently and considerately; with mildness and tact he rejects all conclusions, based on analogies, which are not founded in actuality as he had experienced it. In his letter are the touching words: "As I stood behind the coffin of my little son the other day, with my mind bent on anything but disputation, the officiating clergyman read, as part of his duty, the words: 'If the dead rise not again, let us eat and drink, for tomorrow we die.' I cannot tell you how inexpressibly they shocked me. Paul had neither wife nor child, or he must have known that his alternative involved a blasphemy against all that was best and noblest in human nature. I could have laughed with scorn. What! Because I am face to face with irreparable loss, because I have given back to the source from whence it came, the cause of a great happiness, still retaining through my life the blessings which have sprung and will spring from that cause, I am to renounce my manhood, and, howling, grovel in bestiality?"[57]

It is not surprising that his language again and again suggests the stark words of the old Puritans. In him there is the spirit of those warriors who were outwardly resolute because they had fought courageously against the enemies within. "We want a regiment of Ironsides,"[58] said Huxley when he saw mockers swarming to attack the church. He rejected all irresponsible negative criticism with the same determination that he showed when rejecting fantasies about things that can be neither seen nor felt. God's existence can neither be proved nor disproved, and he who founds his life on denial is as great a fool as his opposite—or even greater. Of the unknown we can say only one thing, the simple "I know nothing." Huxley employed a new name for himself and his friends: they were *agnostics*—that is to say, people who have no opinion and decline to form an opinion about the unknown,

154

men who base their religion and their ethics on the firm ground of actuality.

Evolution itself created a new and better theology, of which the name is the history of religion. This new discipline explained experience—or a lack of experience—in the realm of religion by the evidence of the past. The human race was explained by its history. By means of English ethnology, with its view of all the religions of the world and its clear and sober glance inherited from the Renaissance, the study of religion was raised to an independent discipline. The basis for its fruitfulness and its strength was the same which underlay the studies of Jacob Grimm, the inception of modern European historical research, namely, that knowledge has its roots in the individual need of the soul. In Grimm the love of his country engendered his scholarly respect for that which exists; in the English it was world citizenship, the feeling of union with mankind in general which created zealous and diligent scholars. The German looked backward in order to create for his people a past which will give them courage. With a good Renaissance spirit, the Englishman looked ahead, to progress and to light.

No coöperation between Grimm's successors, the folklorists, and English ethnology seems to have occurred. Each country worked for itself, simply because the average Englishman had not been willing to learn German. And the split was not healed when Friedrich Max Müller was appointed to a chair at Oxford, though his enthusiasm encouraged other workers. But below the surface the activity of the Grimms had stimulated English interest in the customs of uncivilized peoples. When English ethnology finally awoke to an independent life about the year 1860, it could work upon an accumulation of descriptions of travel and collections of materials that had been made by explorers, officials, missionaries, and physicians who in their free time had written down the remarkable characteristics of the people among whom they had labored, often for decades. This material was imbued with the European's arrogant contempt for "wild peoples"; very rarely had the observer taken the trouble to penetrate to the emotional life of the red and black men. The European's love for uncivilized man took form only in a self-sacrificing zeal to better the unenlightened heathens, with no consideration of their wishes and seldom with any desire to understand their thoughts. Nevertheless, it provided an imposing spectrum of the forms of culture.

The history of religion should above all explain the dreadful fact that man has made his own religions, and that often he has made himself a religion that seems barbaric or insane. Where does man get his fantasies about a god or gods in heaven, on earth, and in the water, when he has never seen anything in the sky except birds? How can he have come to talk about the enlivening element as a soul and to give it the attributes of a Lilliputian who sits within the heavy body and directs it as a man steers a machine? And what has given him the illusion that when the body becomes cold and motionless the soul flies to Hades, or over the hills and far away to dance with the spirits of its forefathers, when he must see as clearly as we can that the man has died and is decomposing? Evolution treats the origin of religion as a fundamental concept in the same way that the earlier German historians of religion evolved their wisdom from a primeval religion or primeval revelation; but the picture they draw does not exhibit the same Golden Age that the later Romantics painted in pure colors. Evolution proves that all the meaningless myths and religious rites have come about quite naturally during man's fumbling attempts to understand himself and his environment, for man could attain nothing more than guesses and theories so long as he lacked the wisdom to examine the laws of nature. He speculated about death—how can it be that a self-respecting man, who returned every blow that was given him, now lies before me insensible? The warmth of life has become the coldness of death—has that which warmed him disappeared? These speculations suggested to man the notion of a soul which makes the body move and leaves it at the moment of death. By contemplating dreams he acquired further information about the character of the soul, such as its ability to leave the body at night and go off on its own adventures. The union of these speculations called forth an illusion of the soul's independence of matter and space—in one night it could fly to distant places and obtain information—and in consequence the illusion of its immortality. In this newly acquired belief in a soul lay the embryo of the primitive philosophy, called *animism* by Tylor, which affords a tentative explanation of the manifold phenomena of the universe. The animal and the plant have a soul as I do, says the man, and by analogy he draws a further

156

conclusion: when the stone hurts me it is because the stone has a hostile soul. No wonder that these naïve philosophers of nature began to cultivate the mighty souls which they felt about them, principally the souls of the dead, who haunt the dark, but also the impressive forces of nature who express their wills in thunder and lightning and landslides. Perhaps the two theories could be combined, so that it was the soul of a dead sorcerer who had entered a tree or a stone and now animated it?

In his great book *Primitive Culture* (1870) Tylor provided from this viewpoint a panorama of the religions of the world, based upon a tremendous mass of reports from all the corners of the earth. He traces lines of thought through changing cultures, and shows how men gradually cast off explanations which have become superfluous when they acquire more accurate ideas about nature: first men lose the belief that a stone lives; little by little they also begin to doubt the existence of immortal souls in animals; then finally in our time they draw the consistent conclusion that the soul, supposed to reside within themselves, is only a feeble explanation of psychological phenomena. Tylor shows the tendency of religion to lift old concepts, which have become sacred by virtue of their age, to a higher plane on which they continue to exist as relics. By this observation history explains why Europe continues to cling to religious customs and thoughts which no longer correspond to our understanding of the world; the belief in the soul and its immortality, ecclesiastical dogmas and forms, are relics, "survivals" from earlier epochs.

At almost the same time Herbert Spencer had erected a history of religion on his laws of evolution. What Tylor says about dreams and death, Spencer accepts, but subsequent to the invention of the soul the theories of the two scholars part. Spencer does not believe that the desire for knowledge is active enough at lower stages to start a line of thought; he himself had had the opportunity to observe how indifferent peasants could be toward his most interesting theories. In his opinion primitive people must have been moved by much stronger impulses to invent anything as weird as religion; and such an impulse he finds in fear. Moreover, it is not commensurate with the law of development that the human being make such a colossal error as to seek supernatural reasons for natural phenomena, since we do not find any trace of such a logical fallacy in animals. A dog lies quiet upon the grass and observes phlegmatically that the wind moves the bushes, but it begins to bark when a parasol is carried away by a gust, which shows that it clearly distinguishes between normal and abnormal phenomena and is not misled by the daily movement of branches to the hasty conclusion that there is a spirit in the tree. Consequently it contradicts sound scientific method to suppose that primitive man invented spirits as an explanation for the daily phenomena of heaven and earth. But if the human being by virtue of his first blunder has acquired a belief in spirits, the seed of religion is given; for in the existence of these invisible beings man now has a ready explanation which he can apply when his attention is captured by something unusual in nature like a storm, or an earthquake, or clouds. Men quite naturally conceived the dead to be much worse than the living; they had trembled before a warrior or sorcerer while he walked about in the flesh—it was much worse if he could approach them while invisible. The living naturally sought to appease the mighty spirits of the dead, and so sacrifice, fasting, and prayer came into the world. Then by a natural confusion, because of the inadequacy of language, men no longer venerated a man named Sun (people bore such names in those times) but imagined a god, that is to say, a frightful spirit, in the sun. If man has entered on the path of error, chance pushes him constantly onward until he reaches the end.

So through the history of religion the human race acquired an understanding of Christianity, and learned to see that it had had an historical function in the times of ignorance. In this way Europe was freed from the errors of superstition, which had oppressed the men of the Renaissance. That men had permitted themselves to be held in thralldom by stupidity had formerly been a puzzle which could scarcely be solved without desperate hypotheses, such as that religion had been invented by unscrupulous priests who wished an easy and profitable mode of living. In its wisdom evolution could do justice even to priests and churches, for it saw that the history of human thought affords a complete explanation of the origin and development of religion. In earlier times the church had been both natural and necessary, and no one should despise the men of those days because they proclaimed the myths of Genesis at a time when the Biblical tale of creation was then the only possible explanation of how the world was put together. On the contrary, those who respect true research know how to evaluate such cosmological speculations as a preliminary stage, necessary to science. Thus the hostility between culture and religion is dissipated. But evolution must not deny its nature as a living culture which requires honesty and dedication to truth, and therefore it must necessarily oppose a church that would press upon the present a certain understanding of the world simply because that was the best which man had achieved at some earlier time.

In all areas of historical research ethnology was a refreshing breeze. Tylor's book opened the way for the sober observation of religious life as it exists in the form of myths and cults among uncivilized peoples. By Tylor and his many disciples and followers, research was freed from the ruts in which German post-Romanticism had stuck fast. Moreover, they did not stop with uncivilized people but used the description of primitive life provided by the missionaries and discoverers to throw light on the peoples of antiquity and ancient Israel, since these also had once been uncivilized and lived under the same conditions as the nomads and hunters of today. Thus from Africa, Asia, and Australia one could fetch living illustrations for the understanding of Homer and the stories of the patriarchs, and prepare the way for more profitable studies in the fields of Greek, Scandinavian, and Hebrew religion. Everywhere they invoked the sober sense of actuality that seeks, or at least pretends to seek, facts before it loses itself in theory. Ethnology became a new and better fulfillment of Herder's prophecy than Teutonic mythology had been, although in a much narrower sense than that in which the prophecy had been given.

Chapter XIII

Evolution and the Church

IN EVOLUTION official religion had a mighty rival. Churchmen were perturbed by the intellectual support that the new idea brought to unbelief. They raised a war-cry to save the myths; and a feud began about the Book of Genesis and the apes' claim to be man's ancestor. The struggle spread; it was carried on with that bitterness which only close relationship can give to partisans. A war was fought with the spoken and written words, in books, periodicals, newspapers, and devotional literature—and it ended in an overwhelming victory for science. One of the great battles which echoed throughout the country was fought at the famous Oxford meeting in 1860, where the sharp sword of debate was swung with such vigor that listeners fainted and had to be carried out. Bishop Wilberforce attacked the champions of evolution, their good names and reputations, by speaking disparagingly about their earliest forefathers; but he succeeded only in striking himself in the face, for Huxley openly confessed his preference for a progenitor who had not discovered the art of speaking about things which he did not understand by replacing argument with rhetoric.

When we read about these bloody battles we are surprised to learn that it was a discussion of the origin of the harmonious order of the world which roused an entire country to an uproar. Where we should expect combat concerning what is usually called the fundamental problem of life, religious experience, the salvation of the soul, or some similar phrase, we find a dispute about the correct interpretation of accepted facts and speculation as to whether or not these prove that the world order was personally arranged by God.

The crux of the matter was this: the scholar and the Christian were in agreement on all significant points. The most pious churchman could not express his faith in the planned order of the universe more eloquently than the heretical evolutionist. There was no difference from sacred oratory when such unordained men as Darwin and Huxley spoke about the lofty ideals of humanity, about ethical responsibility and firmness in self-denial; indeed, the latter's adjurations to overcome the animal within us seemed more convincing, because they were reënforced by scientific explanation. The most pious of the pious could not be more inexorable than Huxley in his assertion of the traditional virtues, of purity, compassion, justice, and truth; from Huxley's essays the church could have fetched "Aphorisms to be taken to heart" for Sunday leaflets to the distinct edification of the readers. Before the two warriors could confront each other they had to make their way to the empty infinity of hypotheses, where the passing clouds of possibility and probability provide the only footholds. The bishop points to the marvelous structure of the universe and to human life and poses the question—may we not conclude that the world-order is based on the will of a God whose hand directs all things, albeit obscurely? And the scholar who sees the same splendid order in the universe says, No; to our knowledge there is no hand which intervenes—we see only the order and the natural means by which that order is consummated. Man does not spring forth fully equipped from the mind of a god; humbly he arises before our eyes within the realm of nature. Whether history once was conceived in a visionary mind; whether a being like us, though larger, once started it all, is a question which we can answer neither in the negative nor the affirmative on the basis of the facts at our disposal; and therefore it is the duty of a truth-loving man to let the matter lie, and to turn from sterile problems to fields of work where as many minds and hands as possible are needed.

The church was unable to produce an experience of reality of a different type; it had no experience of a world of higher values which could destroy the reality upon which evolution was founded. If there is a God, he must be a God of the law of development and reveal himself in visible objects. The disagreement between the bishop and the scientist arose because the prelate demanded an extension of the natural into the supernatural and postulated that there is a spirit behind the monotonous motion of the pendulum of law, while the scientist stopped at the limit of experience and would not permit probability to be included as part of the world of actuality. As far as his observations took him, he followed faithfully, but where they ceased he refused to make imaginary leaps. There is, says Huxley, an abyss between the personal Creator, propounded by theology, and the unemotional impersonality which we may perceive behind the veil of phenomena; the two do not match according to the sound logic of experience. Therefore belief and disbelief were in agreement up to the point where the problem must be formulated. For both, the religious question was founded on the dilemma; do we need a God as a consequence of experience, in order to explain its nature? Or is God superfluous and does religion rest on an illogical argument—since there is nothing in the world of fact which requires us to proceed beyond actuality into the supernatural? In all the English discussions of the time, God was identical with probability, and the religious struggle centered about the question of how far it is right to put probability in the saddle and pray that it may illuminate the laws which we see function. Does theism provide an explanation both true and worthy of our ethical principles? That was Sidgwick's deep-felt question when he was torn between his childhood faith and his need for truth. "Religion is an *a priori* theory of the universe . . . and a theory which assumes intelligent personality as the originating source of the universe,"[59] Romanes wrote; or as he defined it elsewhere, "By the term 'religion' I shall mean any theory of personal agency in the universe, belief in which is strong enough in any degree to influence conduct. . . . The above seems to be most in accordance with traditional usage."[60]

The churchmen had no counterargument: they had to be satisfied to insert a "perhaps" in the places where science, for lack of material evidence, left a question open. They could rejoice every time they succeeded in poking a hole in the reasoning of scientists by refuting some inconsequential detail; but by their polemics they were unable to shake the foundations or to dislodge the conclusions which rested on those foundations. Their greatest pleasure was a childish malicious triumph when they caught an adversary in an error, or saw two disbelievers disagree about a subsidiary issue. Yet to all intents and purposes the churchmen were better armed for the strife. They met arguments first with derisive laughter at the simplicity of their antagonist, then with a condemnation of the aspects of his assertions that were deleterious to the social system; and finally they decried the lack of literary talent which his style revealed. Moreover, they had a magic formula by which they could disarm their antagonist without a struggle. They could say: To be sure, there is here an important element of truth—one which the church always has proclaimed with vigor. And they could always select the weapon which best fitted the needs of the moment and the character of their antagonist, while he had only one blade which he must wield under all conditions. Nevertheless, his single weapon, the truth, proved to be more effective than the many swords that could not pierce him, easily as they might have given him a death-blow had he not been out of reach. When the battle went against the churchmen, they retreated to the possibility that there is a mystery beyond experience. By this they meant exactly the same thing as the agnostic when he said that the basis for existence cannot be comprehended; but now, satisfied with little, and rejoicing every time a scientist honestly admitted the limitations of his knowledge, the churchmen drew the conclusion: therefore, there is a God. In fact, the defense of theism consisted of an unbroken series of withdrawals. For a time the church was satisfied with the logical possibility that a God is conceivable and therefore probable, and in triumph it raised the cry: Theism can never be disproved, or in any case it will always be an alternative hypothesis as good as any other. But once again the respite was of short duration, and theism could not feel itself quite secure until it had transcended all the arguments and made the discovery that in order to conquer, the adversary must demonstrate that God does not exist.

Thus science won a clear and decisive victory, through the force of truth and reality, as Kingsley told his fellow clergymen. Huxley could be himself in every word; he had no other principle than the truth that the facts forced him to accept. He did not let himself be led astray by personal animus into any compromise with his conscience. The clerical party spoke loudly about the demands of truth but always considered beforehand whether this or that argument, this or that fact, would improve or damage its position, and modified the truth accordingly. No wonder that in the eyes of disinterested observers defenders of the truth resembled a man who sits in church and carefully feels in his pocket to make sure that he does not place too large a coin in the collection plate—while he joins the congregation in singing, "The gold of all the world were not too much to give to thee." Huxley laid the entire truth in the collection plate every time it was passed to him.

The scientists demonstrated their right to victory by creating abundance and a joy in work which only those conquerors can achieve whose ideal is in unison with the actuality which has produced it. The concept of evolution brought a new vitality to all sciences: raw material teemed in the hands of the scientist and made him consider an infinite series of possible methods of investigation. The unbelievers were able to support all their ethical ideals with a force and conviction which no churchmen would have dared to adopt if they could; man's victory over his animal inclinations they extolled in prose hymns which, better than any spiritual song, could evoke in man the child of God, and they did this with a confidence in victory which the church long since had lost. The men of disbelief did not need to preach the demands of virtue; they felt its force in the course of their life and work.

In evolution the church met itself without knowing it. Blindly eager to attack a presumed enemy, the church did not discover until later that it had wounded itself every time it struck. Everyone believed that the struggle was about the literal truth of the Bible; even Huxley was misled by the power of the word and announced that evolution could never be made compatible with the Mosaic legend of creation. Blinded by traditional phrases, men threw Biblical citations at one another without discovering their fundamental unity of thought. Modern man pronounces the word "creation" as aggressively and as unctuously as he is able; by this word he unconsciously conveys a modern interpretation of "natural" origins which would have been incomprehensible to the ancient Israelite. He speaks of days and means periods; and if a painter were not to portray God holding Adam's rib or with an auger in his hand, ready to bore a hole into Adam, modern men would either pity the artist or be angry with him.

Indeed, the modern Christian offers kindly to instruct the literal-minded believer—that is, the historian of religion—since the latter has not realized that God is a merciful God who always modifies his words in relation to the current capacity of man's reason, and therefore spoke symbolically during the childhood of the human race. In the nineteenth century the Creation was an hypothesis, well modified to correspond to other existing ideas, and for this reason scholars like Owen and Lyell were skeptical of the concept of evolution and tended to use the word *creation* — without, however, producing works in the spirit of the Pentateuch. Scientists before Darwin worked with laws just as much as any modern scientist, and when they had achieved better insight, the transition to a new standpoint was no more a revolution in their research than in Huxley's when he, after a long period of skepticism about all speculation concerning the transmutation of species, decided to work on the basis of the theory of evolution. That theory does not burn bridges behind it; there is no more difference, then, than that which every new vision evokes: it opens the way for fruitful impulses. And no more than the natural scientist does the theologian look upon God's law as something with which He toys arbitrarily. When he uses an expression like "God's thoughts" the theologian means the order to which God is bound as well as His creation.

Quite unjustly the church has been accused of being reactionary, of being an artificial antiquity. The only reason which the accusers can give for their charge is, that the church has never shared their particular illusion. No doubt, its extreme feeling of spiritual union with the figures of the New Testament kept the church unaware to what degree the words of Jesus and the speeches of the apostles changed character when spoken by a bishop. Equally unjust were the slanderers of the church who called it arid or worldly, as the argument demanded. Only an impudent hatred can misunderstand a religion which exists and functions in the spirit of Renaissance optimism. For the church as for the man of the world there was one central principle: do unto others as you would that others do unto you. Both expressed this principle with the vigorous conviction that the wisdom of nature forces true egoism to function for the good of his fellow men at the very moment when a man is most intent on his own spiritual and physical welfare. The theologian as well as the philosopher based his ethics on the eternal laws of nature, a harmony which carries man toward happiness along the path of virtue. To be sure, the churchgoer was of the opinion that it was Jesus who had expressed the great rule that for him summarized the laws and the prophets; he naïvely confused the concept with the sovereign requirement of self-devotion which was the spirit in the rule as spoken by the prophet of Nazareth. In reality he was no closer to and just as far removed from the thought of Jesus as were Darwin and Huxley. The common man is struck by the superficial similarity between his ideas and the words of Jesus about goodness and purity, and he does not know that he could find the same and in fact more and greater correspondences if he compared his own ideal with the maxims of Judaism. He overlooks the fact that the unity of the Gospels is quite different from the cohesive principle in his own life, because the

165

thoughts of Jesus are the nucleus of an ideal which is not applicable to our times—as one can see most clearly from the fact that the church never has been able to assimilate the Sermon on the Mount organically into the catechism.

There is a fusion of words and meanings that leads astray both friends and enemies. The church calls itself Christianity and quotes Paul without seeing the chasm that yawns between modern culture's high ethical evaluation of happiness in the world and Paul's own hatred for life, which made eschatological dreams a necessity for him. The Protestant reads in Paul of the struggle of the flesh with the spirit; he reads the passages loudly and clearly and nods in agreement; but by doing so he does not mean that the world is evil; he thinks instead of the struggle between the noble and the ignoble; he believes in the happiness and progress that must be achieved by overcoming our animal instincts. As soon as he attempts to explain his agreement with Paul, it turns out that his view has only a superficial relationship to the Epistle to the Romans. He cannot deduce his own world directly from an organic reading of the Holy Scriptures; he must reconstruct it by bringing various Biblical passages together artfully—and he must modify them slightly in order to achieve a truly modern unity. He must interpret, and during his exegesis he must constantly ask, as Newman did when he read Dr. Arnold's mildly liberal attempt to interpret the Old Testament: is this a Christian reading? In other words, is it congruous with my culture? Were this not the case, churchmen would not be so deathly afraid of the history of religion, for its interpretation of Judaism and of primitive Christianity should, better than any theology, provide firm bases for ecclesiastical thought. Nor can the Protestant of today employ words like *Heaven* and *Hell* without an admixture of modern ideas concerning the nature of immortality; he must translate the music of harps and eternal peace into pleasures which more nearly correspond to his own ideas of what is festive. He is quite as much repelled as Huxley by the thought of several billion years spent singing to the accompaniment of a harp, and in his Hell there is noticeably little left of the powerful aroma exuded by the brimstone of Judaism and the Middle Ages.

As soon as the orthodox reader begins to interpret the word of God, the gap between church dogma and the New Testament becomes apparent. And—naturally enough—the churchman exposes himself quite naïvely by confessing his genuine faith in the literal truth of the Scriptures. The pious cleric F. D. Maurice attempted to construct a defense against rising unbelief by maintaining the Bible's complete credibility. The departure of Israel from Egypt, the passage through the Red Sea—everything, he maintained, is realistically described. Is there any difficulty about miracles? "I do not confess so many miracles —not a hundredth part so many—in the flight of the Israelites from Egypt as in the flight of the French from Moscow," he said.[61] That in Egypt the sea stood as a wall, while in Russia nothing more occurred than the fall of snow, made no difference to him. As further evidence of his belief he even added that he saw miracles—that is to say, the direct interference of God—in all the military retreats he read about in the *Times*. On his principles, it is difficult to understand why one cannot find the same edification in reading the *Times* as in reading the Old Testament, and why the day's lessons from the Gospels might not be varied with selected passages of foreign correspondence. When, as a corroboration of his faith in the Bible, he quoted the resolute theologian Pusey's description of Genesis as the "divine Hymn of creation," he showed that his respect for the literal truth of the Old Testament meant no more than the right to read into it what one thinks should be there. The four words are so skillfully joined that they have become mere baubles, and the reader is at a loss to know what and how much meaning he should give to any one of them. To his own harm Maurice could not see that the weapons with which he wished to smite the assailants of retreating faith were only words, and that the only thing which differentiated him from unbelievers was that they spoke the truth directly while he expressed it by circumlocution.

The churchman fully recognizes the world of evolution and orders his life according to its laws and limitations. He establishes his business on the law of supply and demand and his life upon justice and goodness, just as all ethical human beings do. He discovers the hand of God in the daily course of life, where the zealous and the capable and the virtuous reap their reward in the form of worldly success. Even if there are to be found in the Book of Revelation signs indicating how far God has progressed in His preparation for the Day of Judgment, the course of the world is nevertheless first and foremost determined by physical laws. One can therefore, like one zealous clergyman of London, prophesy the coming of the Lord for the year 1867 and instruct a congregation to prepare to meet the Lord in the sky at that time—but simultaneously secure housing on earth by renewing one's lease for twenty-one years, until the end of 1888.

The church found solace in the immutability of nature, its perfect order, and its ethical harmony. Quite as much as the philosophers, the theologians professed a natural religion which saw the Bible of Creation in the revelation of Nature. The church's system was still that *Analogy of Religion* by which Bishop Butler in 1736 had given final form to Christian theism. What separated the theologian and the philosopher was only a disagreement about the use of the bible of Nature: does it require interpretation, or can the common man understand it by means of the light which God Himself has given him? The theologian held that the Old and New Testament contain a divine commentary on the bible of Nature which is valuable in many respects, and indeed which many feel is indispensable; the philosopher maintained that Nature explains itself. The pious of heart agreed with the confident philosopher. Thus one pious natural scientist wrote to Darwin, concerning the *Origin of Species,* "I can prove that God always acts for the good of His creatures."[62] Evolution seems superfluous to such a man, since it contains only what the church always had maintained: "God acts according to laws which we can investigate and understand." If one seeks conclusive evidence one need but turn to the ever-orthodox Gladstone. Gladstone possessed that happy simplicity which is unmoved by anything in the world; he assumed that what he did not know did not exist, and therefore he always had counsel to offer when wise and reasonable men were ready to give up. He had not noticed that the world had changed in the nineteenth century from what it had been in the eighteenth, and he laid down the law: a rational philosophical method will create proper barriers against the thoughtless attack of unbelief. Whatsoever unbelief brings forth is nothing but a little oppositional rubbish which may be brushed aside by the proper use of Butler. And he devoted his old age, when he had won a respite from politics, to demonstrating the correspondence between the Hebrew and Olympian revelations.

Chapter XIV

Orthodoxy and Culture

THE CHURCH lagged behind—a single step: it defended the religion of the Renaissance which no longer conformed to actuality. Yet it was the minimal tardiness that created for culture the greatest danger, since it evoked great tension between the orthodox and the skeptics. A struggle between fathers and sons is the bitterest struggle in the world. On the one side a son fights for the soul within him, which is stronger than his conscious will; on the other hand, a father fights to fulfill the responsibility he has assumed, to give his son his own soul. The clash appears to be a comic wrangle over opinions. Unfortunately, as the history of culture shows, disagreements over fundamental values held in common make men into mortal enemies.

When the young discovered ethos to be the immediate and sacred demand of the soul, they necessarily hated those of their fellow men who sought the basis for the duty of man beyond actuality. The young hated the orthodox man, not only because he displayed such a feeble conviction of the authority of the ideal, but also—and more basically —because he endangered the sovereignty of the soul by making virtue and truth dependent upon something which would crumble, either tomorrow or later, and involve the nobility of man in its fall.

Because the church felt itself to be identical with culture, and to be the embodiment of responsible nobility in man, it could envisage only one alternative to its dominance: there must be either culture, or anarchy, materialism, and bestiality: there must be Christianity or nothing. To his bitter regret, Carlyle found that when he had demolished dogmatism, the church remained so closely identified with culture in his mind that he could see beyond it nothing except a bestial materialism, lacking ideals and devoid of ethos. His salvation came through his discovery that, though the moral components of culture were present in ecclesiastical thought and were indeed its essence, culture was by no means identical with the dogmas that the church had imposed. And precisely because the church was centrally in accord with culture, it was unable to thwart the development of "free thought." It could not frustrate the course of logic by fiat. Therefore Cardinal Newman was quite right when he hurled his accusation in the face of his age: Protestantism necessarily leads to atheism. Confronted by the genuine development of their culture in the new claims of science, the theologians stood helpless. They produced no reply to their critics except the hopeless advice to "Wait, wait, make no move, wait to see whether some solution may not be found." In his view that procrastination was the wisest policy, the Catholic Newman agreed with Liddon, the cultured dean of St. Paul's, the apostle of the High Church.

At the same time, since the Protestant theologians neither would nor could acknowledge the validity of the dilemma that Newman posed, and since there was no natural barrier to stem the torrent of actuality, they had to use all their energies to construct a dike against it. They labored not only for the church, but for culture; they strove to preserve justice and truth, beauty and nobility. Though they may not fully have recognized the fact, this was the motivation of the princes of the church —Pusey, Liddon, and their peers; and it imbued them with an intense energy in the struggle, and forced them to pursue devious paths when no straight road led to the goal. For them there existed but one culture, that of the Renaissance; they saw it falling to pieces about them, carrying all ideals down to destruction with it; in revulsion, they threw themselves ardently into a struggle to maintain justice and truth. They fought night and day, in the hope that they could save the fabric of culture for some happier time. They saw thrown down, neglected, trampled into dust all things beautiful and good that they had inherited from their ancestors, and the sight aroused in them the conviction that they had been chosen by God to oppose complete ethical dissolution. Within the walls of the church dwelt the ancient virtues, now ridiculed by worldlings; within the church were maintained the ancient methods for strengthening the soul: the daily perusal of the articles of faith, unflagging prayer, and the preservation of the Sabbath. The Renaissance had created and upheld a society by the virtues of loyalty, industry, beneficence, purity and chastity; and that society had thrived, in felicity and fortune. One could already see the consequences of apostasy: social problems on every side, the revolt of servants against their benevolent masters, and among those who sat in high places a frequent neglect of the secular and spiritual welfare of the working class. And all these so-called social questions men imagined they could ameliorate without correcting the fundamental, underlying defect! On the contrary, Liddon and Pusey had the same vision as the wise man of Chelsea, Thomas Carlyle; like him, they were too keenly aware of the rootless condition of the current ethos to take any interest in mere social reform. The old and proven morality being moribund, it was futile to work for petty improvements. They had more than enough to do to bring the old ideals, the ancient ethos, to the attention of their contemporaries. The social reformers, the preachers who spoke of the material shortcomings of the age and the needs of the workers, these, they knew, wished only to destroy: what was required was constructive effort, was resuscitation.

In the crucial hour it was not enough to function as an example, still less merely to proffer an example; one must actively resist the new forms which were the vehicles of "unbelief" and hastened the dissolution of ethical harmony. First and foremost, there were the new literature and the new sciences. Having realized their destructive character, a man could not be too conscientious in his vigilance against them. And so unequal was the struggle that the church must use every means at its disposal; and as the legitimate heir of traditional culture and its institutions, it could do so with full right. For example, the chair of Greek at Oxford enjoyed the income of investments which were controlled by Christ Church; and when in 1855 the chair was given to Jowett, a man who served the forces of destruction by teaching liberal theology, the leaders of the church, at the particular inspiration of Pusey and Liddon, obstructed the payment of his salary, and continued to do so for years. But with the ruthless weapons which the times put in their hands, the iconoclasts drove the leaders of the church from their positions, step by step. This particular matter they brought up again and again in the University Senate; they forced one vote after another, and even attempted to involve Government in the academic struggle. Pusey tried to cut the ground from under his opponents by an offer which he must have known could not be accepted, and when they naturally rejected it he turned to the public and sighed in despair—these people! After ten years of strenuous and loyal opposition the men of Christ Church had to yield; but they upheld their principles and salved their consciences by surrendering in these words: Though we yield to legal authority, we acknowledge no moral obligation.

This feud aroused tremendous interest throughout England. Many

171

people were puzzled by the conduct of the clergy. They saw that men who combined superlative piety and humility with good breeding were freely using methods to which no man of the world would condescend, even one who broke the first, second, third, and sixth commandments without a qualm. Some people became indignant and called the clergy hypocritical; other people remained mute in their amazement. They failed to comprehend this mixture of evil and good in a prelate who was as self-sacrificing and charming as the Dean of St. Paul's. Yet the conduct of Liddon and Pusey was a simple conscience of their piety— that is to say, of their culture. Their ethics were sound, for all ethics enjoin that the lower should give way to the higher; it is better to amputate a leg than to waste a life; it is better to starve an unbelieving professor than to allow the heathen to pervert the thoughts of God.

But if the culture of the Renaissance, as it is embodied in the church, is the only culture, its adversaries must be impelled by nothing else than a revolt against the ideal, a yielding to carnal temptation. When therefore a right-thinking young lecturer was chosen to deliver an official university sermon, the spirit moved him to speak this necessary truth, even though it would grate upon the ears of unbelievers. The origin of modern skepticism must be shown to lie in sin, in intellectual indolence, and in the sweet secret vices which one dreads to have dragged forth into the sight of the omniscient God. Such was the truth that must fall from the lips of the young judge. How could he be silent when the very stones about him cried out? — We have here to do not with stupidity or malice, but with the great tragicomedy of history as it is played again and again where two cultures meet, whether those of Dr. Johnson and the Graveyard School or those of the European and the Indian. The lecturer was honestly unable to comprehend the agonized and moving struggles of a Sidgwick or a Leslie Stephen in any terms except those of the revolt of the carnal heart against truth; and the reason was not that the young man believed in Paul, but that he believed in Locke.

And surely it is false to say that the church sides with the rich against the poor. The church loves with equal fervor a rich patron and a poor man who is imbued with the ideals of goodness and purity in their ancient strength. The church should not be blamed because the ideal has more adherents in the classes that in the past created culture and now enjoy the fruits of their fidelity and zeal. By this train of

172

thought the good churchman became the protagonist of the old optimism when he considered that stratum of society which still represented the ancient virtues. Those men that still feel throbbing within them the culture that the church embodies will rejoice in the prosperity of the land, in an exuberance of piety that flowers in altar candles and chasubles, in widespread almsgiving, in the network of railroads, in the piety of the court, in the dividends of corporations, and in the increase of the domestic affections. And in dark times they may draw consolation from the very impotence of the church. A true church can never perish, for it has an independent principle of life; nay, in the times when it seems nearest to disintegration it will provide the strongest evidence of its vitality. For the fabrics of the churches may decay, the clergymen may play whist instead of preaching, the populace may swig brandy instead of partaking of Holy Communion: despite these things, the church will live on. It may wither but it will not die—men who think in these ways do not realize that it is the culture which elevates the church, rather than the reverse.

The Protestant dignitaries did not acknowledge the deduction of the perspicacious Newman. They were convinced that the church should and could halt halfway in its development; that in the best interest of culture the deism of the eighteenth century should become perennial. If there were no natural terminus in the development of culture, one must be built, possibly at the very spot where in the previous age had stood the ramparts through which life had burst. The Renaissance had specified a fixed harmonious universe with an immovable central point; it was now necessary to find a spike by which culture could be held fast. To the degree that inner necessity disappeared, the more necessary did some outward guarantee become. An ethic, to be effective, must be made secure by threats of punishment and promises of reward; so Heaven and Hell, which for earlier times had been actualities of the same kind as the sea, become vital necessities, to be invented if they did not exist. The harmony of the universe could not be relied upon unless there was a God who accepted the responsibility of seeing that no theorists should ever replace the old order by a new one. And furthermore, God Himself, who had formerly been assumed an obvious fact, now became a necessary probability. (The church declared that for people in general He could never become more than a probability; on

173

the other hand, it would not allow that the assertion of probability implies the notion of improbability.) In order to hold fast to this probable God it is necessary to live as if He were ever-present. Religious experience consists of the repeated audition—in the divine service and the sermon—of the truth that God is a fixed point, so that the soul is daily impressed with a confident assurance, and so that the truth is enveloped in the awareness, that it is He who moves men to transmute His commandments into life. —This process was called experience: how far the nineteenth century had receded from true religion!

Thus there was created a new faith which in its dependence upon authority can scarcely be matched in history, a faith distinguished from what we call blind faith by being conscious, deliberate, and meticulous. One could never be too careful. Bishop Stubbs once happened to travel in the same railway compartment as the historian J. R. Green, early in his career as a man of the cloth, who sat with a volume of Renan in his hands. The bishop asked if he might borrow it—and despite repeated requests Green never saw his book again. He did not know that the bishop, for the sake of his young friend's purity of soul, had burned it, uncut, on his hearth.

When inner life has disappeared and experience has ceased, system becomes everything. No most minute, insignificant detail may be altered, for if the smallest stone is dislodged, the entire edifice may collapse on the heads of the inhabitants. In the golden age of English Puritanism, despite their deference to the Word of God, when men wrestled with the Bible and tradition they had been conscious of a bourgeoning vitality. Now the doctrines of the inspiration of the Bible —and above all of the symbolic books—of the power of the sacraments, of the authority of the church, became merged into one indivisible matter of faith; and he who did not believe that Jonah was swallowed by the whale could never see the Kingdom of God. — This was the new gospel of Jesus that the church discovered in the Scriptures.

The last convulsive effort to find a fixed point other than the Bible was Tractarianism, which got its name from a series of polemic pamphlets called *Tracts for the Times* that Newman and some of his friends published in the 'thirties. In this movement which under Newman and Liddon ventured to the border of Catholicism, world-weary and aesthetically cultivated youth sought to satisfy their yearnings. The

174

leaders attempted to affirm a continuity with the past by returning to an earlier liturgy, as it was still possible to do within the regulations of the Church of England. They stressed the similarities which in fact existed between the ritual of Catholicism and the ritual of the Anglican Church, for during the seventeenth century the alterations in the English church had never been as radical and thorough as in the Continental reformation. They pleaded—correctly—that the Church of England never had given up the sovereign concept of the Middle Ages: namely, that the liturgy is a sacrament, a temporal rite by which man partakes of eternity. In this way they believed they had saved from extinction a feeling of relationship with the past, and they proclaimed that the continuity of the church was just such a fixed point as all Renaissance men in Northern Europe had desired. Long before Newman felt any need to transfer his loyalty to Rome, he taught that the church must stand as a mighty fortress outside the world, free from all secular interference. The church is God's guarantee of the truths which man finds in nature independently of revelation, and for that very reason it is privileged to curb speculative thought which seeks to venture out beyond its depth. A center of scholarship like Oxford must submit to the discipline of the church in order to preserve its ecclesiastical character; and from it spiritual nourishment must seep downwards to the people.

But actuality could not be outwitted. The continuity with the past remained quite superficial. The movement ended in a farcical dispute about the instants when one should face east or west, about altar candles and the symbolism of the clergyman's costume, about whether it is God's will that water be mixed with wine, about whether, when a congregation requests evening communion, it is a sign that God's spirit has touched human hearts or the work of the Devil who wishes to change the established order. This religious movement agitated not only clergymen and bishops but Parliament, ministers of state, and the law-courts; it aroused thousands of men to sign petitions and documents of protests. Appealing to the aesthetic sensibility of the age, it created a divine service with lights and incense and music. But the waters remained untroubled; the spirit had departed forever. So the boldest men sought harbor at Rome, for the Anglican reaction led to

Thomas Aquinas, and Thomas to the Fathers of the Church—not to the New Testament.

Anyone who wishes to see how firmly the actuality of the Renaissance has taken root in the English soul—and in that of the North European—should study Newman and remark the spiritual needs which forced him into Catholicism. It is not the difficulty of faith or comprehension which makes him throw himself into the arms of the authoritative church and still less is it the longing for a new meaning in life which makes him kneel before the Host. The motive for his conversion is the hope of maintaining the stability proclaimed by the Renaissance. He must preserve the certainty that the universe is harmonious, that the virtues are eternal, that the reward of faith is perpetual bliss, that sin brings perpetual damnation, and that a God is the guarantor of harmony. Yet for him God is nothing but a probability; and to live by religion, he teaches, means to live with probabilities as if they were actualities. He sees clearly enough to realize that Protestantism is drifting farther and farther away from the ideals of harmony, and therefore he seeks a church where he believes they will be firmly secured. His distress leads him into a Catholicism which he believes is genuinely catholic, though in actuality it was only the Renaissance in ecclesiastical disguise.

The church had tradition on its side; the past echoed its words. Factory owners gladly bore witness to its truth, citing as evidence the success of their enterprises. As long as the new actuality was not acknowledged, as long as the divine power of law had not replaced the time-honored personal deity, it was a treachery to culture to cast out the ancient faith where it could be trodden upon by unclean feet. The church was battling for the dignity of man; for the highest ethic is to be unfree, to be united to a potent actuality which sternly overrules all mandates, high or low. But the condition for applying the supreme imperatives is that what one is bound to must be verily actual, and unfortunately the actuality of the church was now obsolete; it had thinned to a shadow. This was the reason that the ethical judgments of Pusey and Liddon were in such contrast with those of the world about them, and indeed that clergymen of all kinds in England had an illusory appearance of being clever and scheming, subtle as serpents and unscrupulous. It was the church's misfortune that its ethos had

176

become different from the world's, that its territory was not a realm in which a man of normal conscience would care to remain. More and more bitter grew the complaint: The best, nay the good among the young, those with fine minds and calm consciences, will not serve at the altar, but flee. Even the churchmen saw that there was developing a peculiar clerical conscience; clergymen, as it was remarked, had grown accustomed to use words in senses other than the usual, without calling attention to the discrepancies, in order to avoid serious problems; they often had recourse to empty phrases in place of explanations. This vice tainted the souls of the clergy, and even those of the so-called liberal friends of progress whom the attitudes of the church constantly perturbed. Honest and upright men like Stanley, the Dean of Westminster, and fearless warriors like Jowett, who never flinched from a fight when it was a matter of freedom of conscience as opposed to Scripture, time and again found themselves confronted with the question: Is it useful, is it expedient to speak the whole truth now? The difference between them was only that Jowett almost always answered yes, while Stanley preferred to answer no. It must be placed to Stanley's credit that when his friends were attacked by the orthodox he moved without hesitation instinctively to their side; but before such a crucial moment he urged his friends to wait, not to goad their adversaries unnecessarily, and above all not to put weak souls in greater danger than the minimum demands of truth required. When he was not forced to express his own doubts about the Pentateuch and the Creed, he preferred to stress unity rather than divergence.

Though the struggle was about God, He had long been dead. The evidence of His death was clearly visible in the life of the people. Men forgot Him; they did not fight against Him, they no longer ridiculed Him, they simply no longer noticed Him. If God had not been dead in England, Spencer could have never explained Him as an old myth, or sought his origin in a confusion of names with a man called Sun. With such incredible simplicity one can explain only phenomena completely unknown and devoid of any embarrassing reality. Darwin once wrote, in answer to a question: "I have never observed God's existence, but I am disinclined to discuss the question, since I have never given it any particular or lasting thought."[63] As one might expect, during the century the common people unconsciously drifted away from all religion, in the old-fashioned sense of that word. Many times well-meaning demagogues arose to proclaim a Gospel of sin and punishment, and grace—but mostly of sin and punishment, since powerful methods were necessary to arouse the conscience; by religious instruction miners should be "led to a sincere recognition of revealed religion and of a future state of rewards and punishments."[64] Judgments were proclaimed, but no one paid attention to them, since they had no actuality. Indeed the reformers had to rouse themselves, as well as others; they had to preach about defiance of the hatred and contempt of the world, persecution, and suffering for the sake of Jesus—but there was no one who persecuted them, no one who ridiculed them for anything more than their uncouth conduct and meaningless talk. The illusion that one was persecuted was supposed to replace an inner experience of something worthy of being persecuted. The same slow tide which carried the masses away from the church bore the best men of the age out into agnosticism.

In the memoirs of his youth John Morley masterfully described the unreal quality which religious problems had for his generation: "It was idle to demand from us, as some did, what pains we had taken seriously, accurately, definitely to master controversies about the authorship of the Fourth Gospel, or the Epistle to the Ephesians. . . . Such questions, to be sure, had their own importance and they were left unsettled, but they found the rationaliser uninterested and indifferent. The wind has risen and questions such as these were dissipated. The rationalist . . . withdrew into the spirit of a poet's line, 'To the eternal silence of the divinities above, cold silence must be the only meet reply.' This was to be agnostic. There was no mental indolence in the rationaliser; more of that might be charged against the other side."[65]

History has rightly elevated the debate at Oxford to the status of a turning point, a modern Diet of Worms. There Huxley proclaimed that God is dead; that actuality is hand-to-mouth—the way leading to a brighter day and a more beautiful world, but not to eternity. He demanded that truth be made paramount, and through his zealous efforts truth won the victory. Soon the law-courts affirmed the dawn of a new time by quashing an accusation of heresy against liberal clergymen; the Lord Chancellor, who acted as judge in the matter, was widely considered to have rejected a complaint made by the Devil against all attack on his time-honored rights, and thus to have robbed orthodox members of the Anglican Church of their last hope of eternal damnation.[66]

Uncounted multitudes were relieved to be rid of an inert God who only preyed on the mind. For many others the awakening of the new day was painful; they felt that they had suddenly become poorer. Though they were mistaken in their belief that science had stolen their treasure, their loss was no illusion; while they had slumbered, reality itself had shrunk. The culture of the Renaissance had been upborne by an historical feeling for the past. The Old Testament and classical antiquity were the spiritual roots of man; one could recognize oneself in them, their concepts were heirlooms, precious, to be revived and remembered. Socrates and Moses, the champions of Hellenic freedom, and the castigators of the kings of Israel were not figures in a distant age but fighters in my fight. Every idea was the richer for being apprehended through the ancients. It was my fate which was described when the Bible was read or Greek verse was scanned—then the past revived and became the present. Now this feeling of unity had been destroyed, and man stood, restless, looking about him. It was not science which destroyed the relationship; science only proved that culture had destroyed the world-fellowship which had permitted a ready transmission of ideas from one generation to another. Man now stood and stared into a naked, dun-colored, gross reality which had not encompassed the peoples of the past, a reality where no beauty, no spirit, shone through the grey mass of facts. From every land there was heard the same moving complaint: Whence? Whither? — for together with the security of the past all hope for the future had disappeared. The particular instrument by which man had revived the pleasures and sorrows of the past had been the church. When the New and Old Testament had found resonance within the church, a feeling of kinship touched men's hearts and the narrow walls opened up; a distant horizon lay on all sides of the pews, and the church became a world of time and space. Therefore one might believe that in the formulae of the Creed the thoughts of the past were preserved in their pristine purity. And the collective feeling which made a little world of individuals into a society was also bound to a common experience through the divine service. Now such cohesion had disappeared and the individual stood alone, not only without God but alone without a brother in the world. The experience drove many to Catholicism; it came over Morley when he attended mass in an impoverished country parish in Ireland. Many who felt themselves forced to leave the church were haunted throughout their lives with a strange sadness; to their dying day they bore the scars of their profound spiritual battles, the wounds which they had suffered when they detached themselves from orthodoxy. In fact, the wounds never healed in the men of the first generation after the awakening.

Chapter XV

Evolution Outside England

THE THEORY OF EVOLUTION did not stop at the shores of England; throughout Europe it was greeted with a sympathy born of experience, for everywhere it met a spiritual need in a world become both too extensive and too narrow.

In Germany Schopenhauer meditated upon happiness and morality, and delineated the ineluctable clash between the demands of the soul and the brutal reality that rules the world. From Italy came Leopardi's complaint and curse of a world in which all men cry that fortune is their right, but every felicity drowns in a sea of blood and tears. Leopardi condemned God to the hell of contempt in much stronger words than any Englishman allowed himself to use, for he saw God as a hypocrite who breaks his own laws, a despicable weakling who cannot fulfill his own commandments. Like Feuerbach in Germany, Leopardi came to the conclusion that religion is a form of self-deception, a child's cosseting of its illusions. The child demands the toys called goodness and beauty; it refuses to see that the toys are in the moon; it pretends that it has changed the earth into a moon like that which it desires.

From all sides there resounded echoes—from France, in Vigny's cold disciplined verse, which disguises the fears of a passionate soul. Thus speaks the earth: "I am the scene which the foot of the player cannot move; my emerald steps, my alabaster courts, and my marble pillars have gods as their architects. I hear neither your cries nor your signs and I scarcely notice the human drama which passes over me and in vain looks to heaven for its mute spectators.

"In contempt I force people ahead like ants, I bear up peoples and do not even know their names—one calls me mother; I am a grave. My winter swallows your dead like a sacrifice and my spring is not aware of your worship."[67]

As a consequence the theory of evolution was celebrated everywhere with gratitude, after brief opposition from the older men of science. One might expect that the experience which Herder, Goethe, and the Romantics had formulated would give the theory greater power in Germany or at least would there contribute its own peculiar life; but

181

quite to the contrary, the dogma of development was included rather than reborn in the souls of those who there accepted it. It almost seemed that Germany had again broken with its own past and dedicated itself to the service of foreign thought. Even the evaluation of the country's own spiritual champions and their significance was controlled by the English *Weltanschauung,* so that Goethe—for example—was celebrated in his homeland as a Darwinian prior to Darwin.

If the theory of evolution did not cause any schism, the reason was that in Germany culture had followed the same direction as in England, heedless of the experience of great minds. It was impossible that German thinkers should introduce Goethe's thoughts into the theory of evolution, because his world was as alien to them as to the English. The theory set intellectual forces to work but brought about no renewal of spiritual life; in German hands it acquired no new characteristics which would have enabled it to return across the North Sea in greater fruitfulness. The Germany whose scientists were the world masters of research produced few poets and seers who put the past behind them because they saw a new world worthy of conquest. The world of evolution enclosed German intellectual life like a rocky vault, at the bottom of which science was hammered to purity night and day. Every kind of force was harnessed, both vigor and sloth were pressed into service. Pedantry became the art of detailed research, and a man without talent was particularly prized, since he was in no danger of engendering independent ideas that might destroy his objectivity.

Evolution conquered because of its truth; that is, because it denoted what Europeans had experienced both within and without themselves. In evolution the actuality of the nineteenth century finally found a statement which truthfully and consistently concentrated the experience that men had hitherto struggled to couch in the terms of Renaissance myths and dogmas. The substance of the European world was so closely approximate to the English historical vision that the dream of development did not kindle minds like a thought which suggests more than it enunciates; instead, it satisfied souls and gave them the strength to work. It was this correspondence between vision and actuality which made the idea of evolution such a source of inspiration, not only for science and thought but also for practical life. It aided men to cope with contemporary problems, even such problems as social legislation and revolutionary utopias. Natural selection and the struggle for existence became slogans, which could be used to justify the most brutal as well as the most humane social principles. If these slogans encompassed all the thought of the time, it was because they corresponded to what the heart had experienced in its depths and had gained the courage to proclaim.

In the realm of religion, evolution led in Germany only to a renewal of the Romantic restoration of the church's dogmas; what Schleiermacher had tried to do by means of symbols, men now attempted with the help of historical delusion. One gave unto Caesar—that is to say, history—that which was Caesar's, and slipped God his share afterwards. The church was saved as it was in England, but upon a more solid, scientific basis; one gave history its due by dismissing the reasons for the dogmas, but nevertheless preserved them, so that faith suffered no loss. This restoration won fame under the name of Liberal Theology. Christianity was a link in history, Jesus was an historical man endowed with humane ideas, a rational hygiene, and divine wisdom—though prejudiced, as one might expect, by the *Weltanschauung* of his day. No one need believe that conception by the Holy Ghost and the Virgin Birth set him apart; such a miraculous and special position was enjoyed by many men who lived before the carpenter of Nazareth. For myths are attributes which attach themselves to any hero who has been enveloped by admiration. In ancient Greece the miraculous was a normal rather than an exceptional aspect of the equipment of great personalities. True, for religion the carpenter of Nazareth is something else; He is Christus, Who lives in the church, that is, in the human heart—a God-man. Without a relation to Jesus of a quite special kind, Christianity is powerless. His divinity is not external, but is found in His living words and His rich spiritual life. Liberal Theology sought to disentangle the historical Jesus from the myths spun by his followers. It envisaged an ideal human being, nourished by historical conditions, in thoughts and images a child of His time, but eternal in the profundity of His spirit. By introducing something mystical about Christus, a tincture of God-man was smuggled into science, and it became possible to attain a belief in Jesus as the central point of history and the Lord of the church. He revealed *the* Religion—not *a* religion —and through the society He created, human beings can to this very

183

day be reborn and become branches of the Vine. The layman has difficulty in understanding where all the lovely fog has come from to obscure the clear daylight of history, and he never will find out without theological instruction. Actually, this is one of the few points, perhaps the only point, where there exists a relationship between Liberal Theology and genuine German thought. The context of the Christus-theology was nothing else than the Romantics' experience of genius, conveyed by Schleiermacher to a region in which it had no associations and where it could not put down roots. For the Romantics the God-man was a personal experience of the world and the soul; every man can if he will become a Christus, for there are no limits to the expansion of that eternal life which is the essence of mankind. For the orthodox rationalist, Jesus is the only Christus in the world and therefore His coming is quite as miraculous as His conception through the Holy Ghost, or even more so. The orthodox were quite right when they said: we think that it is easier and in reality more probable the old way. The theory hung in mid-air, for behind the theology there was no experience of either the world or the soul—except that which is expressed clearly and truthfully in the doctrine of evolution. Suffering and passion, those experiences which rise to the zenith of heaven and descend into the depths of death and sin, the awful horror which is more indispensable than abundance or security—these do not exist in the world of harmony, and without them neither Jesus nor the other great figures of the spiritual world can be understood. For this reason the ideal human being of Liberal Theology had to assume traits which rather remind one of Goethe, or of an astute professor. Liberal Theology did not point the way to undiscovered worlds nor to a new and more profound Renaissance; it was only the creed of a culture which lived at peace with itself in its own little world. And it proves that those who wished to undermine theology had found skillful allies within the ranks of theologians.

Herder had demanded of the historian that he should understand each epoch on the basis of its particular historical conditions before he judged its significance for the life of the world as a whole. Though the master's delicate sense of human individuality, and above all his great respect for everything that lived, did not descend to any of his successors, his demand for historical research in every cultural epoch prodded the conscience of German historians. Motivated by the concept of evolution there arose a cultural history which in many ways has altered our comprehension of the significant eras of classical antiquity and has deeply affected the religious life of our time. By such historical research modern theology has done work for which the future will be continuously grateful.

First, there was developed an historical understanding of the Old Testament, which was torn from its privileged position and assigned a normal place in the history of the spirit. Israel had been "primitive" in the days of the judges and the first kings, when the people had worshipped Jahweh, their national God, who lived in a holy place and inhaled the sweet odors of the sacrifice. The belief in Jahweh as a merciful and just god, the creator of heaven and the judge of the world, developed in the painful times that followed Israel's brief era of prosperity. It rose out of the people's struggle to hold to their god and his promises after history had destroyed their earlier confidence in a tribal deity who would smite all neighboring aliens to the ground by the spears of his people. The belief was nourished by prophets who, trusting in the god of their fathers, had the courage to seek him in their hour of need and who by their inner struggles achieved a new ideal: that which God desires is not the worldly prosperity of the people but purity and truth in the human heart. Whereas the ancient Israelites had believed that God's omnipotence would be revealed within their little world, and therefore lost heart when Jahweh was not in the spears of his chosen people, the prophets achieved a new hope by bursting national boundaries and viewing God's thoughts as minted for mankind. Jahweh's goal is the salvation of his chosen people, for he intends that his people shall become the light of the entire world, whatever it may cost in agony. While an older generation when speaking of the people had always meant the nation, in the hearts of the prophets the chosen were transformed into the spiritual Israel, the only true Israelites.

The old obstacle to a rational consideration of the development of Israel had been the nature of the Scriptures. How could one speak of a development when the prophets' fear of God is expressed as clearly in the first books of the Old Testament as in the last? And what was even more noticeable, a primitive cult of Jahweh, which assumed that god lived on a hill outside the city, occurs in the books of Samuel, though the Pentateuch already had proclaimed that local shrines were idolatrous. Fortunately, consistent application of the doctrine of evolution solved the literary problem: The Old Testament is not a series of documents arranged in their pristine order; it unites documents of various ages in a sequence determined by the intellectual standpoint of an editor. Happily, the editor did not harmonize the older sources which he used; he merely established a sequence by the help of transitional paragraphs. And thus it happens that memories from the Hebrew religion of the time of their judges, with its absolute trust in the power of sacrifice, are preserved in a religion which can be explained only as an historical experience subsequent to even the earliest prophets. One learned to look upon faith in Jahweh not as an almost supernatural doctrine but as a conviction acquired by experience, which drew its character and warmth from every soul through which it passed; it could be followed from prophet to prophet and from the seer's prophecy to the Jewish dream of the Judgment Day, which based all hope on a day of reckoning when the righteous Jahweh would destroy evil in the world and smite all the heathen for the sake of his true son, Israel.

From the Old Testament, research hurried to the New, and discovered that there too religion was caught in a mesh of outmoded thoughts. The historical study of the New Testament had not ceased since the time of Herder, though it had had to live in the shadow of orthodoxy, within the church. Herder's principle that the ideas of a time must proceed from the conditions of that time was maintained by the Tübingen school, and what men like Baur had attempted to do with old-fashioned techniques was continued by means of more intense historical study. Those thoughts and images were tracked down which connect the recorded words of Jesus with the teaching of the Rabbis and with the phantasies about the Judgment Day that occur in late Judaism. An attempt was made to understand the world of Jewish thought that lay about Jesus and his disciples, for not until one fully comprehends the fears and hopes which affected Jesus' own times can one understand the power that the man of Nazareth possessed to stir men and to arouse indignation. One traced the growth of faith through the struggle of the individual personality within Israel and its interplay with the surrounding spiritual world. Above all, the variegated realm of Hellenism must be mastered by the historian; without its enthusiasm for mysteries Paul is unthinkable, and without clear insight into the religious confusion of the Greek world his letters are incomprehensible. It became clear that the heathen apostle throughout his theology, and more particularly in his diction, was dependent upon contemporary thoughts and dreams.

From Paul the problems lead one to the earliest history of the church, and there doctrine fades into external events. Neither the thoughts of the church nor its forms can be explained by the Gospels, nor can they be explained solely by the epistles of Paul. Once again scholarship must proceed era by era and follow the play of interrelated forces in order to see how Mosaic and Alexandrian religiosity, the ritual of the Jewish synagogue and of the Hellenic mystery cults, met and were united in the new cult and religion of the Sacraments. Step by step German research attempted to delineate the peculiar character of each epoch and to demonstrate the indebtedness of each to earlier and contemporary conditions. The earliest history of Christianity lost its privileged theological position as it took its proper place in the sequence of historical events. The aura of absolutism which the church had upheld for so long faded, together with the belief that the church had a history which, although a part of the history of mankind, did not depend upon it.

In Scandinavia the religious struggle was a feeble reflection of larger events. Grundtvig presents an interesting parallel to English ritualism. His attempt to change the Danish community, defined by dogma, into a cultic church proves that the church's need was the same throughout Northern Europe. He wanted to short-circuit Danish culture by reëstablishing its connection with the early Christian church, in order to give a sacramental basis to the religious life. But as he was a Protestant he sought security in words rather than in ritual, and he was happy to find in the Creed the uninterrupted connection — *successio* — which Newman found in the cult and the see. As a Protestant, Grundtvig tried to ascribe the Creed to Jesus, for he suffered from the Lutheran naïveté which, disregarding history, identifies the early church with the Master. In his opinion all roads led to Jerusalem; he did not know —he did not wish to know—that within the church all roads lead either to Rome or to Carthage. Being a faithful disciple of Romanticism, he associated the early church with Scandinavian antiquity, and in his mind the double origin of Scandinavia fused into one culture.

187

The Romantic concept of life and the world as media between the eternal and the finite helped him to surmount his difficulties by equating Gimli and the New Jerusalem. In a way, God revealed himself to heathen Scandinavia through the sublime doctrine of Valhalla. Thus Grundtvig succeeded in seating Thor of Asgard and the pope of Rome side by side in a Danish temple, a cathedral resonant with congregational chorales. From this union a new religion could have arisen if the times had not been so evil that their actuality opposed the development. In his hymns Grundtvig really revived the faith of the common people, and provided a sketch for a myth of Thor as Our Saviour. By his poetry he transformed the sacred stories of the church into genuine Scandinavian mythology. On the day of creation Denmark rises from the sea like a lovely garden . . . in the garden there grow cedars and beeches; many birds fly about, but one hears first the trill of the lark, singing overhead. The river-banks teem with white sheep, the pastures with red cows, the woods with stags and brown does; in the fields they meet and dance. Just before the great flood, when the sons of God take wives from among the daughters of men, there is born a litter of giants who adorn the halls with red gold, just like Gimli; but as God did not create his earth for the sake of trolls, he lets it sink into the sea again for a moment, in order to purify it. The marriage in Cana becomes not only in form but in reality an event in the medieval ballads. The apostles become a St. Peter's guild of human fishermen, a ferrymen's company, such as we all know to have existed in Aarhus and similar towns down into the nineteenth century, where the members drank a toast to the Savior just as Lazarus did when Jesus visited Bethania. And the ferrymen's company was really established on the day that Peter sat thoughtfully in his boat and heard Jesus speak words more alluring than the songs of the mermaids. The apostles were good Danish fellows in their love of their master and their contemptuous hatred of His enemies, the heathen dogs, that pack of knaves. They go out into the world and fight for his honor, and He follows them in an invisible garment, just like his predecessor Odin. That the Danes are God's chosen people is a natural result of this rebirth of religion. In true folk fashion the new religion is really planted in the soil, not introduced from without and superimposed by conversion; its great events take place in Denmark. Earlier generations live in us; we arm now for the decisive battle with the dragon; all the trolls still grin and the serpents hiss in their lairs, for the Lord is still clothed in his invisible garment; but when he casts aside the magic cloak and rouses his champions in Valhalla against the god of the wind, and the giants of untruth and death, then God will draw the white and red cruciform flag on the sky, and Ragnarok and Gimli will arrive. Until that time we must be satisfied with visits from the god during holy days and nights; on Christmas night the elves, dressed as angels, come down to earth and predict a good year for the birds and the sleeping seeds—fertility in the field and fertility in the barn, and cradles rocking in every corner.

But this religion did not advance beyond the mighty poetry of the hymns, and Grundtvig's immeasurable significance for Danish spiritual life lies, curiously enough, in his magical creation of popular enlightenment as a medium between science and the layman. It is an ideal of rationalism transformed into practical reality. Unfortunately he sowed tares among the wheat by his contempt for scholarship, for never-ending research. Only what had been formulated in his youth was true wisdom; everything later was the bookish learning of the Black School. He really was without a peer, if one except Kierkegaard.

The theology prevalent in Denmark derived in all its forms from Germany, and one can safely say that German brilliance was not improved in translation.

Because of the aesthetic bent of the Danes, when the showdown between past and present came in the 'seventies there was no brutal battle between belief and disbelief concerning God and immortality, but an elegant if vehement jousting, upon horses descended from Pegasus. After the revolution better novels and better poems were written in better Danish than before; but one can scarcely speak of any upheaval in the intellectual life.

189

Chapter XVI

After Evolution

THOUGH THE VICTORY of evolution had far-reaching consequences, its triumph was brief. When it became an accepted scientific method it lost its hold on the human spirit. At the very moment when spiritual problems had been solved they sprang up again with renewed vigor. Even within the circle of biologists there was a feeling that the quiet time was no more than a pause. Though Spencer and Darwin were soothed by the consistency of their own thought, such a profound and individual soul as Huxley was torn between triumph and resignation. In masterful speeches he had pointed to nature as the great teacher of true virtue and true happiness; he had proclaimed that the laws of ethics can be found only by observation and experiment, like the other so-called laws of nature. He had pictured nature as a strong quiet angel who plays chess with men and inexorably smites his opponent if he makes a mistake, who plays a hard game but plays to teach his son how to win. Fortified by the strength of his experience he had sung the proudest and purest hymns of the time about the victory of the spirit over the flesh, about the triumph of man over the animal within him, about the pure hero of the future who will arise through pain as the fulfillment of the prophecy of history.

But when he descended to the plane of hard reality, he sighed in despair. Would human nobility ever have arisen if the human will had not set itself up in opposition to the brutality of nature? It is culture that has created us, and culture is a break with—indeed a revolt against —the egoism of nature. There are no virtues in the world of animals; they appear suddenly at the point where organized society supersedes the mere struggle for existence. Better than anyone else, Huxley made eminently clear the basic law of justice, and the effects were felt to the very basis of existence; but after his triumph he suffered from a re-signed recognition that in the just realm of nature man feels himself to be exiled and alone. Was development the same as progress? To be sure, Darwin and Spencer had put the question and answered it with a cautious "No, not exactly." But the question served only to quiet criticism by honoring doubt; when one had bowed in acknowledgment

190

to the possibility that retrogression plays a role similar to that of progress, one continued to act as before, with one's faith in the course of development quite unaffected. The expectation of the best possible result was so nearly absolute that Darwin and his disciple Romanes speculated why the Greeks had ceased to develop when they were in their prime; they found historical reasons why virtue could not operate without a respite. Huxley put the question in a more aggressive way, however: the fittest conquer—yes, the strongest, the most brutal; but do we mean the strongest in the ethical sense when we speak of progress?[68]

When Huxley had said that, he added: I nevertheless believe it justifiable to maintain that progress is the meaning of history.[69] There were in a sense two Huxleys—though not in the sense that a younger man was succeeded by an older one, for the two walked side by side into old age; furthermore, the powers of the second Huxley increased with the years. The longer he lived, the more life overwhelmed him; it seemed more expansive, more heavy-handed, more remarkable, and more irregular than harmony could permit. Not only in the embattled world of the brutes does life scoff at harmony; within human society as well it is both more evil and more beautiful than any optimist would suffer it to be. When Huxley is overcome by his observations, he finally confesses: The doctrines of hereditary sin, of the rule of Satan, and of an evil demiurge functioning beneath a benevolent omnipotence, seem nearer to the truth than all the liberal illusions about the goodness of human nature. At other times he is overwhelmed by the ethical and artistic stature of man; who is it, Huxley asks, that creates history if not these men who seek their own ideal with a complete disregard of advancement, happiness, expedience, the judgment of society, and all the other temptations and threats which natural development employs in order to elevate man above the brute? Must we not say that certain men have within them an innate sense of beauty and goodness?

But when Huxley lets life speak for itself, he is brought to a sudden halt; he must require that life in addition to being powerful and beautiful shall be well-balanced, restrained, considerate, and beneficial to society. It should lead to quiet peaceful happiness rather than to continual affliction; it should first of all engender those virtues which an Englishman considers to be the essence of morality: justice, kindness, and chastity. He cannot relinquish his assumption that these virtues exist in nature; if not fully elaborated there, at least they are clearly indicated. He is bound within the depths of his soul, rather than by any external theory; and since he can neither reconcile his culture with his reality nor give up either of them, he stands confronted by a paradox: the goal of nature is to condition man to combat nature; nature's rough treatment of its ward will teach him contempt for his guardian. The world is one deafening cry of pain; nevertheless there exists in it such a wealth of "superfluous loveliness" that the pessimist is struck dumb. "A hopeless riddle"—with these fading words harmony takes its departure.[70]

Beyond the circle of the devout stood the many thousands who had no more faith than Huxley but who—consciously, semiconsciously, subconsciously, anxiously, obstinately—demanded that the world should contain something more than hard realities. Within us we hear a demand for beauty, passion, a selfless abandonment to love, and the fullness of eternity. But when we follow this voice, we soon find ourselves beyond actuality; we grope confusedly in the infinity of poetry and mood. Why should that which is most valuable and most exuberant lie beyond the world instead of constituting its center? Why must the most valuable and exuberant, "the source of undivided pleasure," as Huxley puts it, only be an "elevated solace for the tired human soul," instead of being the vitality of the world?

And they revolted, all these individuals, against science, against what they called "materialism." And they were right, except on one count: It was not science that was at fault; the error lay in actuality, the little grey narrow world which culture had constructed from the infinite possibilities of the universe. For this evil men found no cure in beautiful figures of speech, even those they inherited from the times when the world was larger and richer. Men who despaired were not interested in the outstretched hand of the church; men who clung to the church as a sanctuary could never feel that their longing had been satisfied, for they realized that the church had no more to give them than did culture. The church met them with beautiful words, sincere and well-meant words; but the words signified no more than Huxley's puzzled second-thoughts; the church could do no more than admonish questing souls to recognize conditions as they were—afterwards, religion would try to smuggle a little solace into actuality. For the time being the insurgents were homeless and unhappy; beside the triumphal procession of science walked a column of wailing men.

Complaints do not satisfy, however, and men began to bestir themselves. The old cry was sounded anew; let us find a new reality, let us recreate the world—and the last decades of the century swarmed with restless warriors who took up the task from those who had conquered the eighteenth century. But to recreate the world, words are not enough, nor poetry nor dreams; therefore, the artists rise in revolt against the degradation of culture, against the ugliness of the common life and the brutalization of labor—and now an echo is heard from the masses. If words are not enough, then neither reform nor revolution is enough; man must find reality within himself before he can create it about him. The time teems with men of a new Storm and Stress, who go out to find themselves anew. They desire again to discover the majesty of passion and suffering, the endless urge of the soul to assert itself and to lose itself. They wish to give authority to beauty again, not as a "force" to which men pay lip service but as a reality, and they will investigate ugliness though to do so they must descend into mire and filth.

In a fashion typical of the nineteenth century, Spencer and Huxley were full brothers of the Methodists; they sought to control themselves by diminishing themselves. In order to construct a little heaven on earth they excluded everything that might bring discord; not only did they call it devilish, they made it into an evil power, and constructed for it a vast hell. For when a man dismisses part of himself—whether it is the so-called "bestial" desires or "enthusiasm"—it is slowly brutalized in its exile and becomes truly daemonic. The sense of actuality on which Europe prides itself is based upon a false confidence in the sovereignty of the spirit. Goethe is admired because he is thought to have been an apostle of the gospel of limitation; but Goethe lived too profoundly to think of curtailing himself; instead, he repressed his ardor and recommended obedience to given conditions, to Fate—as a necessary condition for healthy development.

Now men again called upon the devil, upon the flesh; they examined the strongest urges, the most indescribable experiences, in order to discover the inscrutable ego; and once again the adherents of the golden mean stood wringing their hands as they saw how indecently, and at

193

the same time how ridiculously, youth was acting. Nor did the church understand the times; it readily took its place among the stabilizing forces of society; it was indignant at the paganism of poets and thinkers; in season and out it admonished men to strive, and to strive for that which is worthy, that which is acknowledged by everyone. Strangely enough, the church's own men sometimes complained that the church lacked pronounced personalities. And meanwhile the undaunted pagans explored the unmeasured horror of man and his equally inexhaustible splendor; they continued to look for something behind or, more accurately, within what was splendid and dreadful, sometimes they called the object of their search God. One after the other they discovered the man of Nazareth as a new figure, whom they had never seen before, and to Him, the friend of publicans and sinners, to Him who taught that the prodigal son had gained a wisdom hidden from his more respectable brother—to Him their thoughts were led without reference to any rational Christology.

After fermentation, clarification; a new harmony must be found and it will be found. But whether the new times will make use of the old forms, religious and social, or whether they will weave a new garment for experience, no one knows; and the question is idle, since everyone who seeks life is at the same time helping to create form.

Notes

1. *Boswell's Life of Johnson*, ed. George Birkbeck Hill, rev. L. F. Powell (Oxford, 1934), IV, 22.

2. Chateaubriand, *Atala*, in "Les Funerailles," "C'est une de nos grandes misères: nous ne sommes pas meme capables d'être long-temps malheureux." Cf. *Atala*, Édition critique par Armand Weil . . . (Paris, 1950), p. 118.

3. Schiller, "Die Grösse der Welt":

> "Segle hin, wo kein Hauch mehr weht
> Und der Markstein der Schöpfung steht!
> 'Steh! du segelst umsonst — vor dir Unendlichkeit!'
> Steh! du segelst umsonst — Pilger, auch hinter mir!"

Schiller, *Sämtliche Werke*, Säkular-Ausgabe, I, 247.

4. *Iliad*, XXII, 345-48.

5. Johann Peter Eckermann, *Gespräche mit Goethe* . . ., March 28, 1827.

6. Unlocated quotation.

7. From "The Progress of Poesy. A Pindaric Ode." (*The Poems of Gray and Collins*, ed. Austin Lane Poole [London, n.d.], pp. 49 ff.)

8. Herder, "Von Ähnlichkeit der mittlern englischen und deutschen Dichtkunst . . .," " . . . wo man träumt, weil man nicht weiss, glaubt, weil man nicht siehet und mit der ganzen, unzertheilten und ungebildeten Seele würket. . . ." Cf. *Herders Sämmtliche Werke*, ed. B. Suphan (Berlin, 1893), IX, 525.

9. From the end of the fifth "Memorable Fancy" in "Marriage of Heaven and Hell." Cf. *Poetry and Prose of William Blake*, ed. Geoffrey Keynes (London, n.d.), p. 203.

10. From "Proverbs of Hell," in "Marriage of Heaven and Hell." Blake, *ibid.*, p. 194.

11. From "Visions of the Daughters of Albion," Blake, *ibid.*, pp. 214 f.

12. From the first sentence of "Europe. A Prophecy," Blake, *ibid.*, p. 232: "For stolen joys are sweet & bread eaten in secret pleasant."

13. Wordsworth, *The Prelude*, Book II, lines 397-99.

14. Wordsworth, *The Prelude*, Book II, lines 170-74, which in the original reads:

> "Oh! then the calm
> And dead still water lay upon my mind
> Even with a weight of pleasure, and the sky
> Never before so beautiful, sank down
> Into my heart, and held me like a dream!"

15. "Lines Composed a Few Miles above Tintern Abbey . . .," lines 41-49 (*The Poetical Works of William Wordsworth*, ed. E. de Selincourt [Oxford, 1944], II, 260).

16. "Lines composed a few miles above Tintern Abbey . . .," lines 93-102 (Wordsworth, *ibid.*, pp. 261 f.).

17. Herder expresses this idea in the *Briefe zur Beförderung der Humanität* (Riga, 1793). Cf., especially, Book IV, letter 73.

18. Herder, "Auszug aus einem Briefwechsel über Ossian und die Lieder alter Völker," "Wehe dem Menschen, dem die Scene missfällt, in der er auftreten, handeln und sich verleben soll! Wehe aber auch dem Philosophen über Menschheit und Sitten, dem Seine Scene die Einzige ist, und der die Erste immer, auch als die Schlechteste, verkennet!" Cf. *Herders Sämmtliche Werke*, ed. Suphan (Berlin, 1891), V, 168.

19. Goethe to Herder, from Rome, Dec. 2, 1786, "Ich zähle einen zweyten Geburtstag, eine wahre Wiedergeburt von dem Tage da ich Rom betrat." There is mention of a rebirth in several other letters, without the use of the word "Geburtstag," however. Cf. *Goethes Werke*, Weimar ed., Series IV, Vol. 8, p. 77.

20. "Erste Bekanntschaft mit Schiller," 1817, ". . . das ist keine Erfahrung, das ist eine Idee." Cf. *Goethes Werke*, Weimar ed., Series I, Vol. 36, p. 251; Series II, Vol. 11, pp. 17 ff.

21. "Aus einem Brief an Gräfin Auguste zu Stolberg":
   "Alles geben die Götter, die unendlichen,
   Ihren Lieblingen ganz
   Alle Freuden, die unendlichen,
   Alle Schmerzen, die unendlichen, ganz."

22. *Hymnen an die Nacht,* 4, "Wahrlich der kehrt nicht in das Treiben der Welt zurück, in das Land, wo das Licht in ewiger Unruh hauset." Cf. *Novalis Schriften,* ed. Paul Kluckhohn (Leipzig, n.d.), I, 57.

23. Fr. Schlegel, "Fragmente" (from the *Athenäum*), Nr. 297, "Es muss durch alle drey oder vier Welttheile der Menschheit gewandert seyn, nicht um die Ecken seiner Individualität abzuschleifen, sondern um seinen Blick zu erweitern und seinem Geist mehr Freyheit und innre Vielseitigkeit und dadurch mehr Selbständigkeit und Selbstgenugsamkeit zu geben." Cf. *Friedrich Schlegel (1794-1802), Seine prosaischen Jugendschriften,* ed. J. Minor (Wien, 1882), II, 252.

24. Spoken four times by Edgar, not by the fool, in Shakespeare's *King Lear,* Acts III and IV.

25. Fr. Schlegel, "Ideen," aphorism nr. 6, "Das ewige Leben und die unsichtbare Welt ist nur in Gott zu suchen. In ihm leben alle Geister, er ist ein Abyssus von Individualität, das einzige unendlich Volle." *Jugendschriften,* ed. J. Minor, II, 289.

26. Novalis, *Hymnen an die Nacht,* 1, "Himmlischer, als jene blitzenden Sterne, dünken uns die unendlichen Augen, die die Nacht in uns geöffnet." *Schriften,* ed. Kluckhohn, I, 56.

27. Novalis, *Hymnen an die Nacht,* 2, "Zugemessen ward dem Lichte seine Zeit; aber zeitlos und raumlos ist der Nacht Herrschaft." *Schriften,* ed. Kluckhohn, I, 56.

28. Novalis, "Tagebücher," for May 13, 1797, contains the entry, ". . . das Grab blies ich wie Staub vor mir hin — Jahrhunderte waren wie Momente — ihre Nähe war fühlbar — ich glaubte, sie solle immer vortreten." Grønbech has misunderstood the passage, for "ihre" and "sie" refer to Sophie (Novalis' deceased fiancée) and not to "Jahrhunderte." *Schriften,* ed. Kluckhohn, IV, 385.

29. Novalis, *Hymnen an die Nacht,* 4, "Gern will ich die fleissigen Hände rühren, überall umschaun, wo du mich brauchst — rühmen deines Glanzes volle Pracht — unverdrossen verfolgen deines künstlichen Werks schönen Zusammenhang — gern betrachten deiner gewaltigen, leuchtenden Uhr sinnvollen Gang — ergründen der Kräfte Ebenmass und die Regeln des Wunderspiels unzähliger Räume und ihrer Zeiten." *Schriften,* ed. Kluckhohn, I, 58.

30. Goethe, "Vermächtnis," "Das Ewige regt sich fort in allem."

31. Fr. Schlegel, "Ideen," nr. 18, ". . . dieses lichte Chaos von göttlichen Gedanken. . . ." *Jugendschriften,* ed. J. Minor, II, 291.

32. Herder, *An Prediger. Fünfzehn Provinzialblätter,* 1774, Nr. X, p. 73, Cf. *Herders Sämmtliche Werke,* ed. Suphan (Berlin, 1884), VII, 276.

33. First stanza of Chamisso's poem, "Nachtwächterlied."

34. Novalis, *Die Christenheit oder Europa,* final paragraph: "Wann und wann eher? danach ist nicht zu fragen. Nur Geduld, sie wird, sie muss kommen die heilige Zeit des ewigen Friedens, wo das neue Jerusalem die Hauptstadt der Welt sein wird; und bis dahin seid heiter und mutig in den Gefahren der Zeit, Genossen meines Glaubens, verkündigt mit Wort und Tat das göttliche Evangelium, und bleibt dem wahrhaften, unendlichen Glauben treu bis in den Tod." *Schriften,* ed. Kluckhohn, II, 84.

35. *Friedrich Heinrich Jacobis auserlesener Briefwechsel* (Leipzig, 1827), II, 478, Jacobi to Reinhold, October 8, 1817: "Du siehst, lieber Reinhold, dass ich noch immer derselbe bin, durchaus ein Heide mit dem Verstande, mit dem ganzen Gemüthe ein Christ, schwimme ich zwischen zwei Wassern, die sich mir nicht vereinigen wollen so, dass sie gemeinschaftlich mich trügen; sondern wie das eine mich unaufhörlich hebt, so versenkt zugleich auch unaufhörlich mich das andere."

36. Cf. Eusebius Pamphili, *Praeparatio evangelica*, ed. E. H. Gifford (Oxford, 1903), I, 112 (Book II, ch. 1, text p. 84).

37. Cf. Hallam Tennyson, *Alfred Lord Tennyson: A Memoir* (London, 1897), I, 319 f.

38. This exact definition has not been located in Shaftesbury.

39. Paraphrase of H. S. Vodskov, *Sjæledyrkelse og Naturdyrkelse* . . . (Copenhagen, 1897), I, cxlviii, "Skal vi saa virkelig blive ved at drømme om et nyt Kulturfolk, hver Gang vi træffer et nyt Mønster paa et Potteskaar, blive ved at tro paa en anden Menneskehed, saa ofte vi se Redskaber, som ikke have været paa Slibesten? . . . . Var det saa ikke bedre at sige et langt Farvel til disse vandrede Kulturfolk, der lægge saa mange Tons Nefrit og Bronce, Visdom og Kraft i deres Kufferter og saa drage Jorden rundt for at se paa Lejlighed?"

40. *In Memoriam*, LVI.

41. In a letter to Asa Gray, May 22, 1860, Darwin wrote: "There seems to me too much misery in the world. I cannot persuade myself that a beneficent and omnipotent God would have designedly created the Ichneumonidae with the express intention of their feeding within the living bodies of Caterpillars, or that a cat should play with mice." *Life and Letters of Charles Darwin*, ed. Francis Darwin (New York, 1887), II, 105.

42. Cf. *Life and Letters of Thomas Henry Huxley*, ed. Leonard Huxley (New York, 1901), II, 143.

43. From "An Apologetic Irenicon," 1892, cited in *Life and Letters of Thomas Henry Huxley* (New York, 1901), II, 320-21.

44. Cf. Alfred Russell Wallace, *My Life* (London, 1905), II, 120.

45. Cf. *Life and Letters of Thomas Henry Huxley* (New York, 1901), I, 236.

46. Darwin, *The Descent of Man* (New York, 1896), p. 126.

47. Paraphrase of Darwin's concluding paragraph in *The Descent of Man*.

48. Unlocated quotation.

49. Cf. *Life and Letters of Charles Darwin* (New York, 1887), I, 282.

50. Alfred Russel Wallace, *My Life* (London, 1905), I, 372.

51. *Ibid.*, p. 432.

52. From "Administrative Nihilism." Cited in *Life and Letters of Thomas Henry Huxley* (New York, 1901), I, 386.

53. Huxley, I, 237.

54. *Ibid.*, p. 235.

55. *Ibid.*, p. 238.

56. *Ibid.*, p. 233.

57. *Ibid.*, p. 237.

58. Huxley, II, 342.

59. George John Romanes, *Thoughts on Religion* (London, 1895), p. 43. The first clause is a quotation from Herbert Spencer.

60. Romanes, p. 107.

61. *The Life of Frederick Denison Maurice Chiefly Told in His Own Letters, ed.* Frederick Maurice, Third Edition (London, 1884), II, 453, in a letter dated June 3, 1863.

62. The Rev. Adam Sedgwick to Darwin. Cf. *Life and Letters of Charles Darwin* (New York, 1887), II, 43.

63. On September 6, 1871, Darwin wrote to F. E. Abbot, "I feel in some degree unwilling to express myself publicly on religious subjects, as I do not feel that I have thought deeply enough to justify any publicity" (*Life and Letters of Charles Darwin*, ed. Francis Darwin, I, New York, 1887, 275).

64. Unlocated quotation.

65. John Viscount Morley, *Recollections* (New York, 1917), I, 17 f.

66. Paraphrase of the humorous epitaph on Lord Westbury, who, as Lord Chancellor, pronounced the judgment reversing the sentence imposed by the Ecclesiastical Court upon two contributors to the controversial *Essays and Reviews* (1860): "Towards the close of his earthly career he dismissed Hell with costs and took away from Orthodox members of

the Church of England their last hope of everlasting damnation." Cf. J. B. Bury, *A History of Freedom of Thought* (London, 1957), p. 165.

67. From "La Maison du Berger":

> ". . . Je suis l'impassible théâtre
> Que ne peut remuer le pied de ses acteurs;
> Mes marches d'émeraude et mes parvis d'albâtre,
> Mes colonnes de marbre ont les dieux pour sculpteurs.
> Je n'entends ni vos cri ni vos soupirs; à peine
> Je sens passer sur moi la comédie humaine
> Qui cherche en vain au ciel ses muets spectateurs,
> Je roule avec dédain sans voir et sans entendre,
> A côté des fourmis les populations;
> Je ne distingue pas leur terrier de leur cendre,
> J'ignore en les portant les noms des nations.
> On me dit une mère et je suis une tombe.
> Mon hiver prend vos morts commes son hécatombe,
> Mon printemps ne sent pas vos adorations.

Cf. *Œuvres complètes de Alfred de Vigny,* ed. F. Baldensperger, *Poèmes* (Paris, 1934), pp. 189 f.

68. *Life and Letters of Thomas Henry Huxley* (New York, 1901), II, 322. Paraphrase of a passage in "An Apologetic Irenicon," 1892.

69. Cf. "Controverted Questions," 1882, reprinted in (*Collected Essays,* Volume V) *Science and Christian Tradition* (London, 1894), p. 7, ". . . the historical evolution of humanity, which is generally, and I venture to think not unreasonably, regarded as progress. . . ."

70. *Life and Letters of Thomas Henry Huxley* (New York, 1901), II, 143.

Index

Abbot, F. E., 197n63
Abraham, 130
Achilles, 35, 39, 130
Alcibiades, 86
Apollo, 98, 117
Aquinas, Thomas, 176
Ares and Aphrodite, 116
Arnold, Matthew, 166

Baur, F. C., 186
Bible: and Carlyle, 125 f.; Genesis, 160, 167; and myth, 98; New Testament, 166 f.; Old Testament, 35, 38 f., 130, 179, 185 f.; Pentateuch, 98, 164, 186; Revelation, 167; Samuel, 185 f.
Bismarck, Fürst, 110
Blake, William, 46 ff.; and Gnosticism, 49; and the soul, 122; 19n9-12
Boswell, James, 195
Brentano, Clemens, 100
Browning, Robert, 23
Bunyan, John, 153
Butler, Joseph, 168
Byron, Lord: Cain, 27 f., 33; and the old order, 122; and the soul, 32 f.; and vanity, 36 f.

Carlyle, Thomas, 124 ff.; and Christianity, 169; and history, 143; and reform, 171; Sartor Resartus, 125; and society, 128
Chamisso, Adalbert von, 101, 196
Chateaubriand, F. R., Viscount de: and the Church, 46; René and Atala, 29, 36, 45; and revolution, 50; and sensationalism, 29; and the soul, 32 f.; and vanity, 36; 195n2
Cromwell, Oliver, 148, 153

Dante, 86
Darwin, Charles, 132 ff.; and Christianity, 165; and dogma, 160 f.; and evolution, 142 f.; and God, 132, 177; and Goethe, 182; and morality, 141; and progress, 190 f.; and Sedgwick, 168; and Wallace, 151; 197n41,46,62-63
David, 35
Dickens, Charles, 126 f.
Dostoyevsky, F., 23

Eckermann, J. P., 195n5
Edda, the, 116
Eusebius Pamphili, 197n36

Feuerbach, Ludwig, 111 f., 181
Fox, C. J., 153

Gimli, 188
Gladstone, W. E., 168
Goethe, J. W., 64 ff.; and art, 107 f.; and the eternal, 96; and evolution, 146 f., 181; and fate, 193; Faust, 75 f., 108; and folk songs, 42; and German culture, 119, 121; and God, 23, 93; and Hellas, 40 f., 99; and immortality, 95; and inspiration, 84; Italienische Reise, 67; and Liberal Theology, 184; and limitation, 193; Metamorphose der Pflanzen, 72; and myth, 76; and nature, 71 f.; and Palermo, 68; and the past, 50; Protestant, 97; and the Renaissance, 71, 108; and revolution, 106 f.; and Romantics, 81 f., 90; and Schelling, 117; and Schopenhauer, 112; and F. Schlegel, 86; and Sophocles, 39 f.; and Sterne, 28; "Über allen Gipfeln," 34; and Urphenomenon, 69, 71, 73, 74 f.; Werther, 45, 49, 65, 67, 106; Wilhelm Meisters Wanderjahre, 107; and Wordsworth, 54; 195n19-20, 196n30
Gray, Asa, 197n41
Gray, Thomas, 29, 33, 41 f.; 195n7
Green, J. R., 174
Grimm, Jacob, 118 ff., 155
Grundtvig, N. F. S., 116, 187 ff.

Hampden, John, 153
Heimdal, 116
Heine, Heinrich, 34
Heinse, Wilhelm, 27
Herder, J. G. von, 56 ff.; and ethnology, 159; and evolution, 146 f.; and folklore, 118 f., 121; and folk songs, 37, 114; and German culture, 119; and God, 23, 93; and Goethe, 64, 70; and historiography, 114; and history, 43 f., 61, 104 f., 184 f.; and humanity, 62; and the past, 50, 121; and the Renaissance, 59 f.; and Romantics, 81 f., 97 ff.; and world spirit, 73; 195n17-18, 196n32
Hermes, 116
Hoffmann, E. T. A., 32, 100
Homer, 35, 38 f., 130, 148 f., 159
Huxley, T. H., 190 ff.; agnostics, definition of, 154 f.; and dogma, 160 f.; and God, 132, 134, 161, 178; and justice, 190 f.; Lay Sermons, 152 ff.; Oxford debate, 178; and progress, 191; and Providence, 138 f.; 197n42-43,45,53-58, 198n68-70

199

Jacobi, F. H., 109, 196n35
Jahweh, 185 f.
Jesus, 24, 97, 165 f., 183 f.; and Blake, 49; and myth, 88; and Schleiermacher, 113
Johnson, Samuel, 30, 35, 40, 172
Jowett, Benjamin, 171, 177

Kierkegaard, S., 189
Kingsley, Charles, 154, 163
Klinger, F. M., 27

Lamarck, J. B. P. A. de Monnet, Chevalier de, 145 f.
Lavater, J. K., 64
Lazarus, 188
Lenz, J. M. R., 27
Leopardi, G., 181
Lessing, G. E., 119, 121
Liddon, H. P., 170 ff., 176
Locke, John, 172
Loki, 116
Lucifer, 28
Luther, Martin, 114, 153 f.
Lyell, Charles, 164

Macpherson, James, 36, 40
Maurice, F. D., 167, 197n61
Methodism, 23, 193
Mill, J. S., 128, 143
Milton, John, 153
Mörike, Eduard, 34
Montesquieu, C. L. de Secondat, Baron de, 144 f.
Moravian Brethren, 25
Morley, John, 178, 197n65
Moses, 98, 179
Müller, F. Max, 116 f., 155
Müller, Wilhelm, 34

Newman, John H., 166, 169 f., 173
Novalis (Friedrich von Hardenburg), 77 ff.; and brotherhood of artisans, 103; *Die Christenheit oder Europa*, 102; and the Church, 100; and God, 93; *Hymnen an die Nacht*, 84 f., 93 f., 96; 196n22,-26-29

Odin, 107n., 119, 188
Oehlenschläger, Adam, 85
Ossian, 36
Owen, Richard, 164
Oxford University, 171 f., 178

Patroclus, 39
Paul, St., 154, 166, 172, 186 f.
Percy, Thomas, 29
Peter, St., 188
Phyllis and Amaryllis, 127
Pindar, 41 f.
Plato, 86, 149

Pope, Alexander, 35
Pusey, E. B., 167, 170 ff., 176

Rig-Veda, the, 116
Romanes, G. J., 134, 162, 191, 197n60
Rousseau, J. J., 33
Rubens, P. P., 41

Schelling, F. W. J., 114 ff., 117
Schiller, Friedrich: iconoclast, 28; and death, 29 f.; "Die Grösse der Welt," 31; and Goethe, 73; 195n20
Schlegel, Friedrich von, 77 ff.; and actuality, 147 f.; *Bildung,* Schlegel's concept of, 82 ff., 86 ff.; brotherhood of artisans, 103; and the Church, 100; and ecstasy, 95; and eternity, 95; and God, 93; and Goethe, 108; and Herder, 105; and history, 148; and laziness, 30; *Lucinde,* 84, 92; *Witz,* Schlegel's concept of, 84 ff.; and Wordsworth, 54; 196n23,25,31
Schleiermacher, F. E. D.: *Reden über die Religion,* 87, 113; and Schelling, 117; and dogmas, 183 f.
Schopenhauer, A., 112 f., 181
Schubert, F., 34
Sedgwick, Adam, 197n62
Shaftesbury, Earl of, 127
Shakespeare, 78, 84, 86, 148, 196n24
Shelley, P. B.: *Alastor,* 33, 50; and evolution, 148; and God, 23; "Ode to Intellectual Beauty," 50; and the past, 50 f.; *Prometheus Unbound,* 50 f.; and the soul, 122; and Wordsworth, 55
Sidgwick, Henry, 162, 172
Socrates, 47, 86, 179
Sophocles, 39
Spencer, Herbert, 136 f.; and actuality, 147, 151; and God, 177; and Methodists, 193; and progress, 190; and psychology, 148; and religion, 157; 197n59
Stanley, A. P., 177
Stephen, Leslie, 172
Sterne, Laurence, 28
Strauss, D. F., 110 f.
Stubbs, William, 174
Sturm und Drang, 26, 64
Sulamith, 35
Swedenborg, E., 49

Tennyson, Alfred, 123 f., 126, 132, 197n-37,40
Thomas Aquinas, 176
Thor, 119, 188
Tractarianism, 174
Tylor, E. B., 156 ff.

Uhland, L., 116

Vigny, Alfred de, 181, 198n67

200